T0349305

DEONTIC LOGIC AND LEGAL SYSTEMS

A considerable number of books and papers have analyzed normative concepts using new techniques developed by logicians; however, few have bridged the gap between the Continental (i.e., European) and Latin American traditions in legal philosophy. This book addresses this issue by offering an introductory study on the many possibilities that logical analysis offers the study of legal systems.

The volume is divided into two sections. The first section covers the basic aspects of classical logic and deontic logic and their connections, advancing an explanation of the most important topics of the discipline by comparing different systems of deontic logic and exploring some of the most important paradoxes in its domain. The second section deals with the role of logic in the analysis of legal systems by discussing in what sense deontic logic and the logic of norm-propositions are useful tools for a proper understanding of the systematic structure of law. Arguments are provided to stress the relevance of a systematic reconstruction of law as a necessary step in the identification of the truth conditions of legal statements and the reasons for accepting or rejecting the validity of logical consequences of enacted legal norms.

Pablo E. Navarro is a professor of philosophy of law at the National University of the South and Blaise Pascal University. He is also a researcher for the National Council for Research in Science and Technology (CONICET) in Argentina. Navarro has published several books and has written papers on legal theory and deontic logic for journals such as *Law and Philosophy, Ratio Juris, Rechtstheorie,* and *Theoria.* He has been a visiting professor in many European and Latin American universities. He obtained a Guggenheim Fellowship (2001–2002) and was recognized by the Konex Foundation (2006) in the discipline of legal philosophy and was awarded with the Bernardo Houssay Prize (2003).

Jorge L. Rodríguez is a professor of legal theory at the National University of Mar del Plata School of Law and a visiting researcher in the department of law at the University of Girona. He has published several books and articles in Argentina, Brazil, Canada, Colombia, Germany, Italy, Mexico, and the United Kingdom on legal theory and deontic logic. Rodríguez was awarded the Young Scholar Prize by the International Association for Philosophy of Law and Social Philosophy (1999) and was recognized by the Konex Foundation (2006) in the discipline of legal philosophy. He has served as a criminal judge in Mar del Plata since 2009.

CAMBRIDGE INTRODUCTIONS TO PHILOSOPHY AND LAW

Series Editors

Brian H. Bix
University of Minnesota

William A. Edmundson
Georgia State University

This introductory series of books provides concise studies of the philosophical foundations of law, of perennial topics in the philosophy of law, and of important and opposing schools of thought. The series is aimed principally at students in philosophy, law, and political science.

Matthew Kramer, *Objectivity and the Rule of Law* (2007)

Larry Alexander and Emily Sherwin, *Demystifying Legal Reasoning* (2008)

Larry Alexander, Kimberly Kessler Ferzan, and Stephen J. Morse, *Crime and Culpability* (2009)

Robin West, *Normative Jurisprudence* (2011)

William A. Edmundson, *An Introduction to Rights, 2nd edition* (2012)

Gregory S. Alexander and Eduardo S. Peñalver, *An Introduction to Property Theory* (2012)

Brian H. Bix, *Contract Law* (2013)

Liam Murphy, *What Makes Law* (2014)

Pablo E. Navarro and Jorge L. Rodríguez, *Deontic Logic and Legal Systems* (2014)

Deontic Logic and Legal Systems

PABLO E. NAVARRO

Blaise Pascal University, Argentina
National University of the South, Argentina

JORGE L. RODRÍGUEZ

National University of Mar del Plata, Argentina

With a Prologue by
Eugenio Bulygin

CAMBRIDGE
UNIVERSITY PRESS

. . . things are never odd *in logic, only* different.

P. T. Geach

. . . there is a good deal of unfinished business for analytical jurisprudence still to tackle, and this unfinished business includes a still much needed clarification of the meaning of the common assertion that laws belong to or constitute a system of laws . . .

H. L. A. Hart

CAMBRIDGE
UNIVERSITY PRESS

32 Avenue of the Americas, New York, NY 10013-2473, USA

Cambridge University Press is part of the University of Cambridge.

It furthers the University's mission by disseminating knowledge in the pursuit of education, learning, and research at the highest international levels of excellence.

www.cambridge.org
Information on this title: www.cambridge.org/9780521139908

© Pablo E. Navarro and Jorge L. Rodríguez 2014

This publication is in copyright. Subject to statutory exception and to the provisions of relevant collective licensing agreements, no reproduction of any part may take place without the written permission of Cambridge University Press.

First published 2014

Printed in the United States of America

A catalog record for this publication is available from the British Library.

Library of Congress Cataloging in Publication Data
Navarro, Pablo E., 1963–
Deontic logic and legal systems / Pablo E. Navarro, Jorge L. Rodriguez.
    pages cm – (Cambridge introductions to philosophy and law)
ISBN 978-0-521-76739-2 (hardback) – ISBN 978-0-521-13990-8 (paperback)
1. Law – Methodology.   2. Deontic logic.   3. Law – Philosophy.   4. Semantics (Philosophy)
I. Rodriguez, Jorge L., 1964–   II. Title.
K213.N38   2014
340′.1511314 – dc23   2014011555

ISBN 978-0-521-76739-2 Hardback
ISBN 978-0-521-13990-8 Paperback

Cambridge University Press has no responsibility for the persistence or accuracy of URLs for external or third-party Internet Web sites referred to in this publication and does not guarantee that any content on such Web sites is, or will remain, accurate or appropriate.

Contents

Prologue

by Eugenio Bulygin

Logic and law have a long history in common, but the influence has been mostly one-sided, except perhaps in the fifth and sixth centuries BC, when disputes at the marketplace or in tribunals in Greece seem to have stimulated a lot of reflection among sophistic philosophers on such topics as language and truth. Most of the time it was logic that influenced legal thinking, but in the past fifty years, logicians began to be interested in normative concepts, and hence in law.

From the fourth century BC until the nineteenth century AD, logic was basically Aristotelian logic. Aristotle was not only the founder of logic but also the first to formulate a theory of systems.[1] An important result of this influence was the theory of judicial syllogism. The justification of a judicial decision was regarded as a typical case of syllogistic reasoning, where from a normative and a factual premise the decision of the case was inferred by the judge. It was with the Enlightenment that the theory of judicial syllogism became dominant, based on two important ideas: the doctrine of the separation of powers (above all, the separation between the legislative and the judicial power) and a sharp distinction between the creation and the application of the law. The law is conceived of as a set of all general legal norms created by the legislative power (Parliament); the task of judges is limited to the application of the law to particular disputes. But to be able to fulfill this role assigned to judges, the law must provide solutions to all legal issues; it must contain one and only one solution for each legal problem, which entails that the law must be complete and consistent. If the law does not contain a norm solving the problem (i.e., if there is what traditionally is called a legal gap) or if the law contains two or more incompatible norms applying to the same

---

[1] E. W. Beth, *The Foundations of Mathematics*, Amsterdam, 1959, 31–39; C. E. Alchourrón and E. Bulygin, *Normative Systems*, Springer, 1971, Vienna–New York, 44–53.

case (conflict of laws), then the judge will not be able to solve the problem by mere application of the law. The codification of law by Napoleon was the first serious attempt to create a legal system that would allow judges to apply the law without modifying it. In the nineteenth and twentieth centuries, therefore, the logical ideas of completeness and consistency occupied a very important place in legal practice. But the treatment of these issues by legal thinkers was rather unsatisfactory; it was incomplete and sometimes even inconsistent. It was incomplete because they never defined satisfactorily the concept of incompleteness distinguishing between different kinds of "gaps," and it was inconsistent because some legal philosophers insisted that there were no gaps or inconsistencies because such situations always can be eliminated by interpretation.[2] Instead of asking such questions as what does it mean that a legal system is incomplete or inconsistent, it was proclaimed dogmatically that all legal systems are necessarily complete and consistent. Even such an outstanding and sharp legal philosopher as Hans Kelsen maintained during his whole (and rather long) life that all legal systems are necessarily (for conceptual reasons) complete, and he recognized the possibility of conflicts in the law only in 1962,[3] when he was already over eighty.

The second half of the nineteenth century began with, as is well known, an enormous development of logic, which was not followed by jurists. Symbolic logic remained for a long period practically unknown by legal writers and philosophers. This led to an almost complete isolation of law from logic. This regrettable situation lasted for about 100 years and began to change only in the second half of the twentieth century. The publication of Georg Henrik von Wright's famous paper "Deontic Logic" (1951) is generally regarded as the birth of a new branch of logic, deontic logic, and it constitutes the beginning of a new era in the relation of these two disciplines.

In the past sixty years, a considerable number of books and papers have analyzed normative concepts – such as norm, obligation, prohibition, and permission – using the new techniques developed by logicians. The very notion of a legal system became the center of concern for many legal philosophers. Books by G. H. von Wright (*Norm and Action*, 1963), Joseph Raz (*The Concept of a Legal System*, 1970), C. E. Alchourrón and E. Bulygin

---

[2] See Giorgio Del Vecchio, *Filosofía del Derecho*, Barcelona, 1947, 399; Luis Recaséns Siches, *Tratado General de Filosofía del Derecho*, México, 1959, 323–325; Carlos Cossio, *La Plenitud del Ordenamiento Jurídico*, Buenos Aires, 1947, 42.

[3] "[T]he science of law is just as incompetent to solve by interpretation existing conflicts between norms, or better, to repeal the validity of positive norms, as it is incompetent to issue legal norms": "Derogation," in R. Newman (ed.), *Essays in Jurisprudence in Honor of Roscoe Pound*, Indianapolis, New York, 1962, at 355.

(*Normative Systems*, 1971), and Lars Lindahl (*Position and Change*, 1977) exer-
cised a considerable influence and were soon followed by a great number
of publications dealing with logical aspects of the law. It is significant that
this trend is almost exclusively limited to the Continental (i.e., European)
and Latin American traditions in legal philosophy. The influence of symbolic
logic on Anglo-American jurisprudence is still rather scant. In this sense, this
book by Pablo E. Navarro and Jorge L. Rodríguez may be regarded as a new
bridge between these two legal traditions. It is an updated introduction to
deontic logic (Part I), and it shows the importance of the logical analysis of
legal concepts, especially for the concept of a legal system (Part II).

Part I contains a survey of several systems of deontic logic, especially the
Minimal, the Classical, and the Standard systems, and analyzes their main
problems. The authors discuss some objections to the very possibility of deontic
logic (i.e., the so-called Frege-Geach problem and Jørgensen's dilemma). They
also analyze the main paradoxes of deontic logic (among others, Ross's paradox,
the paradox of derived obligation, and several "contrary-to-duty" paradoxes).

Paradoxes are rather common in logic; they appear in different domains
(propositional logic, modal logic), but it would be a mistake to think that they
might pose a danger for logic. As von Wright puts it:

> The paradoxes traditionally belong to the most lively debated matters in logic.
> Attempts to "solve" them have contributed decisively to the development of
> logic after Frege. To me the fascination of the antinomies has been that they
> challenge reflection about the most basic ideas of logical thinking: property
> and proposition, truth and demonstration, the meaning of "contradiction."
> These ideas are intertwined in their roots. The antinomies make us aware of
> this. There is no unique way of untwisting the connections – and therefore
> no *one* way of "solving" the paradoxes either.[4]

This dictum fully applies to the paradoxes of deontic logic.

In Chapter 2 the authors face what David Makinson has called the "fundamental problem of deontic logic,"[5] which is raised by the rather obvious
feature of norms: their lack of truth values. This problem was clearly stated
by the Danish philosopher and logician Jørg Jørgensen and is known as
Jørgensen's dilemma, but it was regrettably ignored by many logicians. Navarro
and Rodríguez analyze the different attempts to overcome this dilemma, from
the "skeptical solution" (as norms lack truth values, there is no logic of norms;
Kelsen), to the different substitutes for truth – satisfaction (Hofstadter and

---

[4] G. H. von Wright, *Philosophical Logic*, Basil Blackwell, Oxford, 1983, VII.
[5] D. Makinson, "On a Fundamental Problem of Deontic Logic," in P. McNamara and H.
Prakken (eds.), *Norms, Logics and Information Systems*, IOS Press, Amsterdam et al., 1999.

McKinsey), validity as binding force, and validity as membership (Weinberger); and they accept the proposal of Carlos Alchourrón and A. A. Martino –
a logical system independent of the notions of truth and falsity, based on the
idea of an abstract notion of consequence.[6] Navarro and Rodríguez reach the
conclusion that "the only open alternatives to deal with Jørgensen's dilemma
would be the two radical views ... either accepting that, after all, norms are
proposition-like entities, and thus susceptible of truth values, or abandoning
the idea that logic is restricted to the realm of truth ... and each of these views
corresponds to two fundamentally different conceptions of norms." These two
conceptions are the semantic and the pragmatic, which roughly correspond to
the distinction between hyletic and expressive conceptions of norms.[7] But the
authors hold that the semantic conception of norms as proposition-like entities requires that norms have truth values, and in this case norm-propositions
are not distinguishable from norms. In any case, they regard the pragmatic
conception as the only one that offers a possibility of developing a genuine
logic of norms.

Especially important seems to me Chapter 3, which deals with three much
discussed problems of the logic of norms: (1) the distinction – crucial to my
mind – between norms and norm-propositions (i.e., propositions about norms);
(2) conditional norms; and (3) the problem of defeasibility.

Although norms and norm-propositions can be expressed by similar or even
the same words, they are very different in nature, and so the logical structure
of norms differs significantly from that of norm-propositions. This is shown by
the role played by negation. When applied to norms, negation is analogous
to ordinary negation as it is used in descriptive language; the negation of a
norm is also a norm; for any norm there is only one negation-norm; they are
reciprocal, mutually exclusive, and jointly exhaustive. But the negation of a
norm-proposition is more complex. There are two ways to negate a norm-
proposition. The negation can operate over the membership, or it may affect
the norm itself. The negation of the norm-proposition "p is prohibited in S"
can mean: (1) there is no norm in S prohibiting p, or (2) there is in S a norm
that does not prohibit (i.e., permits) p. The distinction between the external and the internal negation of a norm-proposition allows one to detect the

---

6   C. E. Alchourrón and A. A. Martino, "Logic without Truth," *Ratio Juris* 3 (1990), 46–67, and
    C. E. Alchourrón, "Concepciones de la lógica," in Alchourrón et al. (eds.), *Lógica. Enciclo-
    pedia Iberoamericana de Filosofía*, vol. 7, Trotta, Madrid 1995, 11–48.
7   C. E. Alchourrón and E. Bulygin, "The Expressive Conception of Norms," in R. Hilpinen (ed.)
    New Studies in Deontic Logic, Reidel, Dordrecht-Boston-London, 1981, 95–124. Reprinted in
    S. L. Paulson and B. Litschewski Paulson (eds.) *Normativity and Norms: Critical Perspectives
    on Kelsenian Themes*, 383–410, Oxford University Press, Oxford, 1998.

ambiguity of "permission" in norm-propositions: *negative permission* as the mere absence of a norm prohibiting the action in question and *positive permission* as the presence of a norm permitting *p*. Therefore, we have three concepts of permission: one prescriptive, occurring in norms, and two descriptive, occurring in norm-propositions. This gives rise to two different logics: the logic of norms aiming to reconstruct the rationality of the activity of the legislator (i.e., the activity of enacting norms), whereas the logic of norm-propositions is concerned with the reconstruction of the logical consequences of a given set of norms, a normative system. The two logics are isomorphic only under the assumption of completeness and consistency.

These conceptual distinctions show that the principle "What is not legally prohibited is legally permitted" (which is often used to maintain that all legal systems are necessarily complete) is also ambiguous; if "permitted" means negative permission, then the principle is trivially true, for it only states that what is not prohibited is not prohibited. And if "permitted" means positive permission, then the principle is clearly contingent, for from the absence of a prohibition we cannot infer the existence of a permissive norm. In neither case can this principle be used as an argument that all legal systems are necessarily complete.

Once we clearly distinguish between norms and norm-propositions, we must face the problem of the nature of the logic of norms. If norms are conceived of as acts of command or permission, as is postulated by the pragmatic conception shared by Navarro and Rodríguez, then it seems that there can be no logic of norms, for there are no logical relations between acts of prescribing. Navarro and Rodríguez try to base the logic of norms on the idea that there are incompatibilities between certain acts of commanding or permitting. Von Wright was the first to elaborate on this idea.[8] Certain acts such as issuing such commands as *!p* and *!~p* (to command *p* and its negation, that is, e.g., commanding one to open the window and not to open it) or *!p* and *¡p* (i.e., to command *p* and to reject *p*) are in normal circumstances regarded as irrational. Such relations are logical in a different sense, for they are based not on the idea of truth, but on the rationality of the activity of norm-giving. Therefore, the logic of norms may be regarded as a logic of rational legislation.

A very important part of the book is dedicated to the analysis of conditional norms. The authors discuss the two main conceptions of conditional norms, the so-called *bridge conception*, in which the deontic operator affects only the

---

[8] G. H. von Wright, "Norms, Truth, and Logic" (1982) reprinted in *Practical Reason*, Basil Blackwell, Oxford, 1983, 130–209; cfr. also C. E. Alchourrón and E. Bulygin, "Pragmatic Foundations for a Logic of Norms," *Rechtstheorie* 15 (1984), 453–464.

consequent of the conditional ($p{\rightarrow}Oq$), and the *insular conception*, in which both the antecedent and the consequent of the conditional are within the scope of the deontic operator (e.g., $O(p{\rightarrow}q)$). C. Alchourrón has proposed both terms.[9] A thorough discussion of this issue leads the authors to the conclusion that each conception has its raison d'être, for there are two different concepts of conditional norms: the one admits the factual detachment (($p{\rightarrow}Oq{\wedge}p$) ${\rightarrow}Oq$) but not the deontic detachment (($O(p{\rightarrow}q) \wedge Op) \rightarrow Oq$), and the other admits the deontic but not the factual detachment. In natural languages, there are conditional norms that are better represented by one or another of these two different conceptions (the bridge and the insular conception). This, I think, is a very valuable insight.

Finally, Navarro and Rodríguez analyze the problem of defeasibility of legal norms. This is a much debated topic and a rather popular field of research in recent times, especially in legal philosophy.[10] The outcome of their discussion is that if rules are regarded as defeasible in the strong sense that they are subject to an open list of exceptions (which cannot be exhaustively listed), then this implies that general rules (and especially legal rules) are incapable of justifying any deontic qualification in a particular case and so lack inferential force and become useless for practical reasoning.

Part II is dedicated to the analysis of logical problems that are basically related to the systematic nature of law and so are of utmost importance for jurisprudence. Legal norms never appear in isolation, but form part of what jurists call a legal order or legal system. The term "system" is frequently used in legal contexts, but it is seldom clear what is meant by it. A legal system is often described as a set of all valid legal norms, where the term "valid" is even more ambiguous. By "validity" different authors understand different things: membership in a system, existence, or binding force of a norm. Even great legal philosophers do not always distinguish clearly between these concepts. Therefore, a conceptual distinction between these items is a necessary prolegomenon. This is what the authors do in the first chapters of the second part of the book. Their discussion of the lack of terminological and conceptual distinctions related to the notion of validity brings to light several difficulties, especially in the works of Kelsen, such as his theory of the alternative clause that proves to be incompatible with some of the main tenets of his Pure Theory of Law.

---

9   C. E. Alchourrón, "Detachment and Defeasibility in Deontic Logic," *Studia Logica*, 57 (1996), 5–18.
10   A good survey of publications on defeasibility can be found in J. Ferrer Beltrán and G. B. Ratti (eds.), *The Logic of Legal Requirements*, Oxford University Press, Oxford, 2012.

The distinction between generic and individual cases leads to the problem of the connection between general norms and the solution of individual cases. This relation is internal or conceptual; general norms regulate all individual cases belonging to the generic case. So the solution of an individual case can be determined by analyzing the logical consequences of general norms. But there is a grain of truth in Kelsen's contention that a judicial decision cannot be regarded as a "normative syllogism," because the connection between a general norm and an individual legal norm that regulates the individual case requires a normative act – that is, the decision of a judge. However, this does not mean that individual cases are not regulated by general norms. Navarro and Rodríguez distinguish between an individual case and a *judicial case* – that is, a particular controversy litigated in the courts, a practical problem that calls for an institutional solution. As both individual cases and judicial cases are particular cases, the question about the relation between general norms and particular cases becomes ambiguous. The answer to this question depends on the kind of case; the relation between general norms and individual cases is internal or conceptual, but the connection between a general norm and a judicial case is external or institutional. This leads to the distinction between the *internal* and the *external applicability* of a norm.

The introduction of the notion of applicability, which should not be confused with validity in the sense of membership, is of the utmost importance. Invalid norms can be applicable, and inapplicable norms can be valid. A derogated norm is no longer valid and does not belong to the system, but it can be applicable to certain cases.

The structure of a legal system is determined by internal relations between its norms. An important distinction must be made between *independent* and *dependent* norms.[11] Dependent norms are those that satisfy a relation of validity with other norms, but as the chain of validity cannot be infinite, it follows that for logical reasons there must be some independent norms in every system. Independent norms belong to the system not because they are created according to other norms, but by definition. They are the point of departure of a system of norms.

Two criteria for the validity of dependent norms have been analyzed by legal scholars: deducibility and legality. According to the first, a norm belongs to a legal system if it is a logical consequence of other norms of this system, and according to the second, a norm belongs to a legal system if it has been

---

[11] This terminology is from R. Caracciolo, *El sistema jurídico. Problemas actuales*, 31–33, Centro de Estudios Constitucionales, Madrid, 1988; von Wright uses the expression "sovereign norms" instead of independent norms.

created by a competent authority (i.e., if there is a valid norm that authorizes its creation). But Navarro and Rodríguez maintain that these two criteria cannot determine the membership of norms to the same entity; whereas deducibility determines the membership of norms to static sets of norms, legality determines the membership of sets of norms to a dynamic sequence of such sets. Therefore, we have two concepts of a legal system, a static and a dynamic one, although the two are deeply intertwined, and logic is essential not only for explaining the relation among norms but also for a reconstruction of legal dynamics.

The next step is the analysis of formal properties of static legal systems, completeness and consistency, or, rather, of their formal defects: gaps and conflicts. There is, in the book, an exhaustive discussion of the concepts of normative and axiological gaps. Even if the authors follow the steps of previous analyses, they manage to introduce many new developments, especially in discussing the idea that there are no gaps in the case of the silence of law (Raz) and such notions as (descriptive and prescriptive, positive and negative) normative relevance and irrelevance, leading to considerable refinement of the concept of axiological gaps.

One of the main problems of deontic logic is the notion of inconsistency. Are the norms Op and $\sim Op$ (commanding p and not commanding p) inconsistent (contradictory)? If $\sim Op$ means $P\sim p$, then it seems reasonable to assume that these two norms are incompatible, for the obligation of p and the permission of its omission are indeed incompatible in the sense that the fulfillment of the obligation makes it impossible to use the permission, and vice versa. Similarly, the norms Op and $O\sim p$ (obligation and prohibition of the same action) cannot both be obeyed. But this only shows that the norm contents p and $\sim p$ are inconsistent, not that the norms Op and $O\sim p$ (or $\sim Op$) are inconsistent, for the norms Pp and $P\sim p$ are perfectly consistent. This shows that the problem lies in the normative operator and not in the norm-contents. So the inconsistency of norm-contents proves to be a necessary but not a sufficient condition for the inconsistency of norms. The authors adopt the characterization of inconsistency proposed by Carlos Alchourrón,[12] who gives separate criteria for sets of O-norms, for sets of P-norms, and for mixed sets of O- and P-norms. These criteria are based on two ideas: inconsistency of norm-contents and the logical impossibility of complying with all such norms. The authors also discuss several problems not identical to logical contradiction but related to it, such as inconsistency via certain facts and conflicts of instantiation,

---

[12]   C. E. Alchourrón, "Conflicts of Norms and Revision of Normative Systems," *Law and Philosophy*, 10, 413–425.

in which the impossibility of complying stems not from logical incompatibility, but from factual circumstances.

The sixth and last chapter of the book is particularly fascinating. It deals with legal dynamics, a very difficult and complicated topic of legal theory. Legal dynamics means change: the changing of norms (as a consequence of incorporating new norms and eliminating existing norms) and the changing of systems of norms as a consequence of the change of norms. These are the two main problems of legal dynamics.

These problems have not escaped the attention of legal philosophers and theoreticians, but they have not been successfully analyzed until very recent times, and even today there is no complete agreement on several topics.

Legislation as the deliberate incorporation and elimination of legal norms is certainly the main source of change in the law; consequently, the authors concentrate on acts of legislation (promulgation, amendment, and derogation) and the consequences that such acts produce in a legal system. They express their hope that other kinds of change stemming from custom or precedent can be analyzed in a similar way. Moreover, as amendment is nothing more than the combination of derogation and promulgation, we can dispense with it.

Navarro and Rodríguez analyze the acts of promulgation and derogation of norms and the consequent indeterminacy of the resulting system that is produced under certain conditions, following the lines of the analysis of C. Alchourrón and E. Bulygin. But they simplify considerably the whole issue by rejecting the idea that the logical consequences of promulgated norms are also valid norms of the system. In short, in their view, derived legal norms are not necessarily valid, but they must necessarily be taken into account in the application of legal norms and for the explanation of legal dynamics; they belong to the set of applicable norms and play an important part in the dynamics of law. I do not quite agree with this tenet, but the arguments they produce in its support certainly deserve close attention.

Perhaps the main problem of legal dynamics is the characterization of the concept of a legal order that, in spite of change in its contents, preserves its identity over the course of time. Whereas the notion of a legal system understood as a set of legal norms correlated to a given temporal point (momentary system in the terminology of Joseph Raz) is a static concept, the notion of a legal order is dynamic. It is a temporal sequence of legal systems (a family – that is, a set of sets of norms). Its identity is given by the identity of the criteria for the identification of norms belonging to the systems of this sequence. Therefore, to give an account of the structure of law, the interplay of three different concepts is necessary: the momentary legal system (a set of legal norms valid at a certain temporal moment), the applicable system (a set of legal norms relative to the solution of a certain individual case), and the legal order (a sequence of momentary systems).

A few words about the authors of this book are in order. They belong to a relatively young generation of Argentinean legal philosophers, but they are already well known internationally. Pablo Navarro has been teaching in Córdoba (Argentina), in Barcelona (Spain), and in México. He is now a full professor in Bahía Blanca, Argentina and a member of the Research Council of Argentina (CONICET), and he also teaches at Blaise Pascal University (Cordoba). Jorge Rodríguez is a professor at the University of Mar del Plata, Argentina, and was awarded the Young Scholar Prize of the IVR (International Association for Legal and Social Philosophy) in 1999. Both of them have published several books[13] and a considerable number of papers in well-known philosophical journals, and they have participated in many international conferences in Europe and in America.

They have not been, technically speaking, my students, but in an extended sense they can be regarded as such. At least I regard them as my former students, who have the disagreeable property of having surpassed their teacher.

An interesting feature of legal philosophy in countries with Latin tradition, especially in Argentina, Spain, and Italy, is the relatively large number of joint publications, not found as frequently in other disciplines. This highlights friendship, frequent dialogue, and intense discussions and is (at least partly) responsible for the high level of philosophical production of the younger generation of legal philosophers.

---

[13] The following books deserve special mention: José Juan Moreso and Pablo E. Navarro, *Orden jurídico y sistema jurídico*, Centro de Estudios Constitucionales, Madrid, 1993; Jorge L. Rodríguez, *Lógica de los sistemas jurídicos*, Centro de Estudios Constitucionales, Madrid, 2002; Jordi Ferrer Beltrán and Jorge Rodríguez, *Jerarquías normativas y dinámica de los sistemas jurídicos*, Marcial Pons, Madrid-Barcelona-Buenos Aires, 2011.

Preface

In *The Critique of Pure Reason,* Kant claims that from the time of Aristotle until his time, logic had been "unable to take a single step forward, and therefore seems to all appearance to be finished and complete."[1] Moreover, he adds that some alleged improvements were only minor changes or, even worse, confusing and full of misunderstandings. But contrary to this vision, the last two centuries have witnessed an extraordinary rebirth of logic. New approaches to classical problems, as well as new horizons opened to logical exploration (e.g., modal logic, the logic of relevance, the logic of action), have gained a legitimate reputation in contemporary philosophy.

One of these new logical domains is *deontic logic,* the branch of logic that offers a formal analysis of normative discourse. Law is one of the most important normative fields, and deontic logic constitutes an invaluable aid for legal scholars and philosophers in the analysis of fundamental legal concepts. More specifically – as we try to show – deontic logic can be regarded as an essential tool to understand both the systematic structure of law and its dynamic nature. Undoubtedly, deontic logic is also useful for the evaluation of moral discourse, but in this book we limit our attention to the legal domain, with very few and merely incidental remarks on morality.

Are legal norms prescriptions or propositions? Is it possible to develop a logical system referred to objects that are not proposition-like entities? What does it mean to claim that norm N_1 is a logical consequence of another norm N_2? Can legal arguments be grounded on the fact that a certain solution is implicit in the content of explicitly enacted legal norms? Is logic relevant for understanding the dynamic nature of law? These are the kind of questions that are central in our analysis, and their answers reveal part of the relevance of deontic logic in law and legal theory. Two related aspects are particularly

---

[1] Kant 1781: 106.

important here. On the one hand, deontic logic is a necessary conceptual device used to make clear the *implicit* content of law. In a certain sense, law is not exhausted by the explicit material provided by legal sources, but also includes the consequences that follow from explicitly enacted norms. On the other hand, the *structure* of legal systems is determined by relations that connect their elements, and to the extent that logical consequences are regarded as legally binding, deontic logic seems unavoidable in the explanation of the systematic nature of law.

In *The Concept of Law*, H. L. A. Hart mentions some recurrent issues that are responsible for the persistence of the debate about the concept of law. One issue concerns the relations between law and morality.[2] He points out three things that relate law and morality: a shared vocabulary, coincident contents, and practical normative force. These connections explain to a certain extent our bewilderments when we try to determine the (conclusive) solutions that a particular legal system offers to certain recalcitrant cases. Law and logic exhibit at least two of these three coincidences that relate law and morality: a shared vocabulary and practical normative force. First, law and logic have a rich vocabulary in common. Expressions such as "rules," "reasoning," "justification," "interpretation," "validity," "systems," "coherence," "syllogism," "proof," and "decision" are basic concepts of both disciplines; of course, one can wonder whether this fact is actually something more than a "linguistic accident."

Although the origin of logic was connected to the control of legal arguments,[3] it is somewhat ironic that in modern times both law and legal reasoning have been often regarded as not being governed by logical structures and forms.[4] By contrast with this skeptical view, in this book we claim that a better understanding of deontic logic and logical analysis is of the utmost importance in the study of law and legal theory. The relations between logic and legal theory have followed two different perspectives that can be sketched as follows:

(1) *The logical study of norms and normative systems.* The central issues from this perspective are the existence of norms, the distinctive features of normative actions, the systematic structure of normative sets, the formal properties of normative systems, and so on. This approach has been developed by

---

[2] See Hart 1961: 7. Other recurrent issues are the relations between law and force and the relations between law and rules (see Hart 1961: 6–13).

[3] See von Wright 1993: 10–11.

[4] This view is reflected in the famous words of O. W. Holmes in the opening paragraph of *The Common Law*: "the life of the law has not been logic; it has been experience" (Holmes 1881: 5).

philosophers von Wright, Weinberger, Alchourrón and Bulygin, and Soeteman, among others. In this view, the fundamental challenges derive from questions like: Is a logic of norms possible? What is the logical structure of conditional norms? What are the logical properties of normative systems?

(2) *The logical study of normative reasoning.* The central issues from this perspective are the logical analysis of normative reasoning and the formal reconstruction of normative positions (rights, responsibility, competence, etc.). The main contributions to this field have been made by Hohfeld, Kanger, Lindahl, Hintikka, Prakken, Makinson, A. Jones, Sartor, and others. In this view, the fundamental challenges derive from questions such as: What are the relations between the different normative positions (e.g., rights and duties)? What is the most adequate formal structure to account for the set of normative relations involved in the notion of legal power or right? What are the differences between conclusive and *prima facie* obligations? What logical rules must follow a sound defeasible legal argument?

Both approaches are related through many common problems, but despite those connections, it seems wise to deal with each of these perspectives in a relatively independent way. In this book we favor the first approach, and the main reason for choosing it is that it seems to offer a more natural perspective for some basic philosophical problems of deontic logic, such as the nature of norms and the kind of fact that makes the statement that a certain norm exists true.[5] The answers to those questions seem more philosophical than logical and, consequently, it seems more convenient to introduce deontic logic by means of a conceptual analysis of the basic concepts of law and legal theory. As we try to show, no genuine progress on the ontology of norms can be achieved without a careful reconstruction of other more general concepts. Accordingly, the problem of the fruitful application of deontic logic to a theory of norms cannot be entirely detached from other classical problems of legal philosophy.

Over the past decades, the nature of law has been explained in terms of normative systems, and two ideas have been widely accepted. First, municipal laws, like Argentinean law or U.S. law, are mainly legal *systems*. Second, although legal norms are the most important elements of a municipal law, they also contain other elements. In other words, legal systems are *normative* systems, but their structure is more complex than the one presented by classical legal theories (e.g., Bentham, Austin, Kelsen).[6]

[5] Von Wright 1969: 89. See also von Wright 1980: 404.
[6] See Gardner 2004.

In contemporary legal theory the analysis of legal systems as a methodological device for understanding law was decisively influenced by two important works: Joseph Raz's *The Concept of a Legal System* and Alchourrón and Bulygin's *Normative Systems*.[7] From different perspectives, both books explicitly defend the priority of a systematic reconstruction of law over other traditional approaches, and both also insist on the role played by laws that are not norms (e.g., definitions, derogatory clauses). However, there are also important differences between them, which arise from the fact that the systematic nature of law is explained differently by two traditions in legal theory. Those traditions may be called the *logical model* and the *institutional model*. Whereas Alchourrón and Bulygin emphatically subscribe to the first, Joseph Raz is the most important defender of the second.

These different traditions sharply disagree on the role that logic plays in law and legal systems. Following the logical model, authors like Weinberger, Alchourrón and Bulygin, Kanger, and Lindahl understand the law as a *deductive system* (i.e., legal systems include all the logical consequences of enacted norms). According to this conception – widely accepted by deontic logicians[8] – law is much more than a set of explicitly enacted norms, as it also encompasses *implicit* norms that can be logically derived from a specific normative base. The conceptual content of such a base cannot be fully grasped without deriving its logical consequences.

According to the institutional model, legal norms are internally related by different criteria, the most important of them being the *genetic* criterion (i.e., that a certain norm belongs to a legal system if it has been created by a competent authority). This criterion helps explain the dynamic character of legal systems, the hierarchical structure of law, and its institutional nature. However, Raz stresses that genetic relations are not the only relevant internal connection between legal norms. In his opinion, genetic relations only identify raw legal materials but are unable to show the legal positions that law attributes to individuals at a particular time, which are determined by specific principles of individuation of laws reconstructed by legal philosophers. These principles of individuation show the internal connections between laws that define the *operative structure* of a legal system at a certain time.[9]

---

7 Raz 1970; Alchourrón and Bulygin 1971.

8 For example, see Gärdenfors 1992b: 195.

9 One of the most important insights of Raz is that legal systems are *momentary* systems, and that their structure (i.e., *operative* structure) mainly depends on punitive and regulative relations that we can identify at a particular moment. On the contrary, genetic relations show the development of the legal history of a certain community; they determine the structure of

Both models are deeply entrenched in our legal culture. Their main function seems to be connected to our understanding of the truth-conditions of legal statements. The institutional model helps us explain the *legal* nature of our rights and duties, as something different from other normative qualifications (e.g., *moral* ones). On the other hand, the logical model shows the reason why some norm-propositions can be true even if no explicit decision of legal authorities justifies such a claim. Thus, these approaches seem to be in mutual tension, for the institutional model emphasizes that some norms are not legally valid because they have not been enacted by legal authorities, whereas the logical model emphasizes why some norms are legally valid even though legal authorities have not (explicitly) prescribed them.

Several arguments explaining the conceptual connection between law and genetic relations among norms (e.g., Kelsen, Hart) have been offered. However, a similar argument showing the relevance of the logical consequences of legal norms is actually missing. Defenders of the deductive model seem to have confused the problem of the possibility of logical relations among norms with the different question of the legal validity of logical consequences of enacted legal norms (i.e., they seem to believe that a positive answer to the former question is also sufficient to ground a positive answer to the latter). However, this is a fallacy; a distinct argument is needed to move from the premise that there are logical relations among norms to the conclusion that those consequences are valid in a legal system. Therefore, the role of logic in an adequate explanation of the systematic nature of law is an open question in legal theory.

Our purpose in this book is to offer an introduction to deontic logic and legal systems. We will be more interested in the philosophical aspects of deontic logic (i.e., philosophical logic) than in its technical refinements. Important achievements during the past decades have been made in the domain of deontic logic, through the application of sophisticated analytical techniques to control normative arguments, especially those advanced by judges and legal scholars in the interpretation of legal sources and the justification of legal decisions. However, these developments usually focus their attention on the formal complexities of legal reasoning that go far beyond the ordinary comprehension of lawyers, and thus have generated few applicable results (apart from the very remarkable fact that they contribute to the development of logic itself). For this reason, and in spite of the progress that deontic logic registers in the formal analysis of legal reasoning, we believe that a book

---

non-momentary legal systems (see Raz 1970). Unfortunately, as we try to show, Raz's analysis of the logical relations between momentary and non-momentary systems is defective.

devoted to the philosophical problems of deontic logic is the most natural way for introducing legal scholars into the formal aspects of norms and legal systems. Hence, this book aspires to be an analytical exercise on the logic of norms and legal systems.[10]

Although there is a rich literature on logic and law, it is not easy to find introductory texts. In general terms, an introductory philosophical text can be seen from two different perspectives: it can work as a *preliminary analysis* of a complex philosophical issue, or it can be presented as a *basic* text concerning a certain discipline. In the first case, the introductory nature means a *partial* approach to a given problem; it offers a necessary step for analyzing other, more intricate problems. Such limitation says nothing about the philosophical complexity of the work at hand, and frequently the reading of these kinds of texts requires a great deal of information and philosophical skill. In the second case, an introductory philosophical text makes almost no assumptions regarding a certain discipline; it offers to the nonspecialized reader a conceptual map for exploring some problems. In general, the virtues of this type of text relate to the clarity and simplicity of the analysis, the organization of a complex agenda of problems, and the emphasis on central questions rather than the examination of details. This is precisely one of the aims of our project: to provide a general and basic introduction to the logic of norms to demonstrate its relevance and utility for a rational reconstruction of some fundamental legal concepts. Its introductory character will be seen in the abundance of quotations and bibliographical notes, the preference for arguments that do not require formalization, and the avoidance of technicalities.

The book is divided in two parts, each part is composed of three chapters, and each chapter is divided in five sections. In the first part we offer a brief reminder of the basic ideas on classical logic (i.e., propositional and predicate calculus). Only after this basis has been presented do we move on to deontic logic. We provide a brief reference to the origins of deontic logic, the discussion of the problem of its foundations (i.e., its contested possibility), and advance an explanation of the most important topics of the discipline, comparing different systems of deontic logic (e.g., *minimal*, *classic*, and *standard* systems), exploring some of the most important paradoxes of deontic logic, and so on. Special attention is given to the distinction between a genuine logic of norms

---

[10] Following von Wright, we understand by philosophical logic "the analysis of concepts which are peculiar to logic proper – such as, for example, consistency and entailment – and the application of the formal apparatus of logic for clarifying clusters of concepts" (von Wright 1993: 42). For a more general approach to philosophical logic, see Grayling 1997.

and a logic of propositions *about* norms, and to the problematic character of conditional norms.

In the second part, we analyze legal systems. Our concern is focused on three objectives: (1) to underline the relevance of a systematic reconstruction of law as a necessary step in the identification of the truth-conditions of legal statements; (2) to revise the role that logic plays in the analysis of legal systems; and (3) to discuss the reasons for accepting or rejecting the validity of logical consequences of enacted legal norms.

We are aware that writing an introductory text is a risky effort. It is always a simplification of problems that deserve a refined treatment and, even worse, in some cases it conceals the philosophical relevance of details that are essential for understanding a certain discipline. Even being conscious of those perils, we are firmly convinced that a philosophical analysis of both the logic of norms and the systematic structure of law can be presented without unnecessary logical technicalities. Thus, although many problems that need a careful analysis in an advanced book have been put aside, we expect that this introductory text promotes the curiosity necessary for dealing with deeper levels of both deontic logic and legal theory.

Many colleagues and friends have read different parts of this book and their criticisms and suggestions have been essential for improving both the content and style of our work. We would especially like to thank Eugenio Bulygin, Luís Duarte d'Almeida, Riccardo Guastini, Bonnie Litschewski Paulson, Juliano Maranhão, Leticia Morales, José Juan Moreso, Claudina Orunesu, Stanley L. Paulson, Pablo Perot, Giovanni Ratti, Cristina Redondo, and Hugo Zuleta. We are also highly indebted to Shailan Patel and Stanley L. Paulson, who have revised the English-language manuscript, for their invaluable services. Last but not least, we are greatly indebted to Professors Brian Bix and William A. Edmundson, editors of *Cambridge Introductions to Philosophy and Law*, for having encouraged the publication of this book and their careful reading, comments, and criticism on an earlier version of the manuscript.

PART I

Introduction to Deontic Logic

1

The Language of Logic and the Possibility of Deontic Logic

1.1. VALIDITY, TRUTH, AND LOGICAL FORM

An argument can be defined as a set of statements of a given language in which the truth of one of them (the conclusion) is assured by the truth of the others (the premises). Logic has to do with the study of arguments, but it is not a discipline oriented to describe our actual practices of argumentation and reasoning. It does not purport to examine the actual psychological processes or states of mind of people. In particular, it is not an empirical task whose outcome varies with different universes of analysis (i.e., different human groups and times). Instead, logic is concerned with a critical evaluation of argumentation; with patterns of *correct* reasoning.

However, this is still inaccurate as a proper characterization of logic, because any critical assessment of argumentation depends on the implicit goals ascribed to it, and there is not one but a plurality of goals we may seek to accomplish in our argumentative practices. For example, if we intend to persuade an audience, arguments will be evaluated as good or bad according to their merits to the extent that the audience is actually persuaded by our words. That would be an example of a *rhetorical* assessment of argumentation.

No doubt, the control of quality that logic exerts over argumentation is related to such rhetorical assessment, but this relation is not one of identity. Were an audience purely rational, it would only be persuaded by arguments whose premises warranted the conclusion, and this is what seems to be involved in the logical assessment of arguments. In other words, the aim that logic assigns to argumentation, and that is taken as a parameter to judge the quality and correction of arguments, is to preserve truth in the passage from the premises to the conclusion. From this point of view, it may be said that logic seeks to codify argumentative schemas that warrant the conclusion to be true if the

3

premises are true. When an argument satisfies that condition, we say it is logically *valid*.

Logical validity, although connected with truth, does not truly depend on either the premises or the conclusion to be true. The connection between validity and truth is not so straightforward; to say that an argument is valid is to say that, *were* the premises true, the conclusion *could not* be false. Therefore, as the link between validity and truth is merely *conditional*, a valid argument may have true premises and a true conclusion, false premises and a false conclusion, or false premises and a true conclusion. The only combination validity excludes is the case in which an argument has true premises and a false conclusion. When an argument is not only valid but its premises (and, thus, its conclusion) are in fact true, we say that it is a *sound* argument.

Logic aims to isolate argumentative schemas in which the truth of the premises warrants the truth of its conclusion. That is why it focuses on the structure or *logical form* that links premises and conclusion. Consider the following argument:

(1) Some logicians are not boring; Lewis Carroll was a logician. Therefore, Lewis Carroll was not boring.

Although both premises and the conclusion are true, this is not a valid argument. This becomes obvious if we change the content of the statements, but preserving the same structure. Thus, replacing "logician" by "number," "not boring" by "prime" and "Lewis Carroll" by "8," we obtain:

(2) Some numbers are prime; 8 is a number. Therefore, 8 is prime.

Here, although the structure is exactly the same as in (1), the conclusion is obviously false. Thus, validity is not determined by the content of the premises but by the formal structure of statements. Let us see now examples of valid arguments:

(3) All Parisians are French; all French people are European. Therefore, all Parisians are European.
(4) Either Spain is the FIFA World Cup winner or Germany is; but Germany is not the FIFA World Cup winner. Therefore, Spain is the FIFA World Cup winner.

In these examples, the truth of the premises leaves no room for the conclusion to be false. The meaning of "to be a Parisian," "to be French" and "to be European" in (3), as well as the meaning of "Spain," "Germany" and "to be the FIFA World Cup winner" in (4), are irrelevant for their validity, in the sense that if we replaced those expressions by any other, but preserving the structure of the statements, we would equally obtain conclusive arguments.[1] In other words, any argument that exemplifies the schema:

(3') All P's are Q; all Q's are R. Therefore, all P's *are* R.

or the schema:

(4') Either p or q; but not q. Therefore, p.[2]

will be valid. And they will be valid even if the premises are not true, because validity depends on the satisfaction of one condition: *The conclusion cannot be false if the premises are true.* Thus,

(5) All the fans of John Lennon marry Japanese women. All those who marry Japanese women are Japanese. Therefore, all the fans of John Lennon are Japanese.

and

(6) Either Al Pacino or Robert De Niro had the leading role in *The Shining*; but Robert De Niro did not have the leading role in *The Shining*. Therefore, Al Pacino had the leading role in *The Shining*.

are both valid arguments, even though their conclusions are false.

As the examples show, the meaning of certain expressions, such as "all," "some," "no," "and," "or," "not," "if... then," and so on, is of the utmost importance for linking the truth-values of the premises with the truth-value of the conclusion. By contrast, there are other aspects of the meaning of the premises and the conclusion of an argument that can be set aside to assess its validity. That is the reason why, since Aristotle, it has been said that the logical validity of an argument depends on its *form*. However, this claim requires a more thorough explanation, because it seems to suggest that each and every argument has a unique logical form, and this is not the case. For instance, the structure of (3) may be equally represented by (3') or, more simply, by:

(3") p, q. Therefore, r

where p represents "all Parisians are French," q represents "all French are European," and r represents "all Parisian are European." Now, although all

---

[1] For the different ways to define validity and logical truth, see Quine 1970: chapter 4.
[2] Later, we explain the reason for using capital letters in (3') and lowercase letters in (4') to stand for the variable contents.

arguments represented by (3') are valid arguments, that is not necessarily so with arguments that can be represented by (3").

Therefore, we might hold, on the one hand, that if an argument is an instance of more than one structure or form, and is valid according to one of them, then the argument is valid; and, on the other hand, if an argument is an instance of more than one structure or form, the richest of them should be preferred for its representation. However, although the first claim holds, the second is not justified; all arguments are capable of a diverse degree of complexity in their representation, but in many cases more complexity adds nothing relevant for the assessment of validity.[3]

In the formal languages developed by logicians, correctness in the patterns of inference may be evaluated either from a semantic or from a syntactic point of view. From a semantic point of view, a statement S (conclusion) in some language L is called a *semantic consequence* of a set α of statements of L (premises) ($\alpha \models S$), if and only if S is true for every interpretation of L in which all the statements in α are also true. In such case, we say that the sequence $\alpha \models S$ is *semantically valid* or that it is a *logical truth*.

From a syntactic point of view, a statement S in language L is called a *syntactic consequence* of the set of statements α in L ($\alpha \vdash S$), if and only if there is a finite sequence of statements $A_1 \ldots A_n$, where $A_n = S$, and each of the statements in the sequence is either an axiom of L, or an element of α, or it follows from previous statements in the sequence using a set of primitive rules of inference of L. The sequence $A_1 \ldots A_n$ is said to be *syntactically valid*, or that A_n is *demonstrable*.

The semantic approach, expressed in terms of interpretations and truth, has in a certain sense a *universal character*, because in order to prove that a statement *is not* a semantic consequence of a set of premises, it is sufficient to show the existence of an interpretation in which the premises turn out to be true and the conclusion false. By contrast, the syntactic approach, expressed in terms of axioms and primitive rules of inference, has in a certain sense an *existential character*, because to prove that a statement *is* a consequence of a set of premises, it is sufficient to show the existence of a finite sequence of statements allowing the derivation of the conclusion.

The ideal would be for these two notions of validity to correspond to one another – that is, that all logical truths (semantic consequences) were demonstrable (syntactic consequences), and all demonstrable formulas (syntactic consequences) were logical truths (semantic consequences). In the first case,

[3] See Haack 1978: 24.

the system would be *complete*; in the second case, the system would be *sound*. Unfortunately, both are contingent properties of formal systems, in the sense that they have to be proven for each formal system.

The intuitive and ordinary notion of validity that we presented at the beginning of this section corresponds to the semantic approach of formal validity, the one that has been dominant in contemporary logic. From a syntactic approach, logic seems at least at first sight to be the product of purely conventional and arbitrary choices. Being so, the creation of a logical system would be as free as the invention of a game. This seems to give conceptual priority to the semantic approach over the syntactic one. Under this view, what would guide the choice among different syntactical axiomatic calculi to identify a logical system would be that the axioms and theorems of the system are logical truths, and that the rules of inference guarantee that the truth of the premises is preserved in the conclusion.

Nevertheless, this remark should be refined in two respects. First, the intuitive notion of validity that is used to assess informal arguments of ordinary language does not have a perfect correspondence with the formal concepts of validity. Although logical systems have been developed for a rigorous representation of informal patterns of inference, precisely on account of this reason they cannot reproduce all their complexities, subtleties, inaccuracies, and vagueness. Therefore, the relation between the informal notion and the formal concepts of validity might be explained as follows: We take the intuitive and informal judgments of validity as a basis for the development of formal logical systems (i.e., rigorous theoretical systems that offer general principles for the assessment of validity). Now, in case of discrepancy between our intuitive judgments and the evaluation provided by those formal systems, we sometimes sacrifice our intuitive judgments, and sometimes sacrifice the general principles,[4] in a process analogous to the Rawlsian *reflective equilibrium*.[5] The selection of logical principles is not "fixed once and for all"; it requires adjustments between our normative standards and our intuitions.[6]

Second, the priority of the semantic over the syntactic approach of formal validity has not only been a controversial issue in the history of logic, but is also affected by a highly complex difficulty that we try to examine in the coming pages. Once again, it has to do with the connection between validity and truth. In spite of all the explanations and qualifications offered here, a strong

---

[4] See Haack 1978: 25.
[5] See Rawls 1971: 42–43.
[6] See Engel 1989: 320.

connection still remains between validity and truth in the semantic approach; if validity of an argument is ultimately characterized as the preservation in the conclusion of the truth of the premises, the domain of logic would be restricted to the realm of truth. In other words, logical relations could not hold among entities that are incapable of truth-values, which seems to be a very deep and problematical limitation.

1.2. THE LANGUAGE OF LOGIC

Propositional calculus (PC) is the most simple and basic logical system.[7] The variables of PC are *propositional letters*. They represent sentences describing states of affairs that may or may not be the case. Each variable expresses a proposition (i.e., the meaning of sentences capable of independent truth-values). The constants of PC are *sentential connectives*, which may affect a whole formula (monadic connectives) or relate two or more formulas (dyadic connectives). Those formulas composed only by a single propositional variable will be called *atomic formulas*; the rest will be called *molecular formulas*.

Language of PC:

Propositional letters or variables: p, q, r, and so on. They range over propositions, and it is assumed that there is an unlimited number of them.

Propositional connectives:
- Monadic connective: $\sim$ (negation).
- Dyadic connectives: $\wedge$ (conjunction); $\vee$ (disjunction); $\rightarrow$ (conditional); $\leftrightarrow$ (biconditional).

Auxiliary signs: ( ) (brackets). They indicate a certain order within combinations of formulas. The rules for their use will not be stated, as they should be obvious from the context.

The rules to combine all these signs to produce admissible or *well-formed formulas* (*wffs* in the sequel) of PC are the following:

Formation rules of wffs for PC (recursive definition of wff of PC):[8]

- A propositional variable is a wff of PC;
- if α is a wff of PC, then $\sim\alpha$ is a wff of PC;

---

[7] For a more detailed presentation of the basic notions of propositional calculus and predicate logic, any introductory text dedicated to elementary logic may be consulted. Our suggestions: Gamut 1991 and Makinson 2008: 189 ff.

[8] Greek letters are used here to represent any arbitrary formula. They are not symbols of the language of PC itself, but (metalinguistic) signs to refer to the expressions of our language.

- if α and β are wffs of PC, then $(\alpha \wedge \beta)$, $(\alpha \vee \beta)$, $(\alpha \rightarrow \beta)$ y $(\alpha \leftrightarrow \beta)$ are wffs of PC;
- only those formulas constructed according to the previous clauses in a finite number of steps are wffs of PC.

A basic assumption of PC is that every proposition is either true or false, but not both. We will say that the truth-value of p is T if p is true, and F if it is false:

p
T
F

This representation is called a *truth table*; it shows the truth-values of a formula for all possible values of its constituent parts. The meaning of a molecular formula is built systematically from the meaning of its component parts. Thus, the truth-value of a molecular formula is determined by the truth-values of its atomic components. In this sense, the truth-values of compound formulas may be seen as a *function*, the domain being the set of all propositions of the language, and the range being the set {T,F}.

For any molecular formula α, with n being the number of different propositional letters in α, and there being two possible truth-values of each propositional letter, the number of cases to be analyzed in a truth table is 2^n. PC only deals with truth-functional connectives (i.e., those where the truth-values of the formulas over which they operate depend exclusively on the truth-values of their components). Therefore, logical connectives in PC only capture a certain aspect of their natural language counterparts,[9] and their meaning can be defined in terms of the truth-values of the formulas connected by them:

p	q	$\sim p$	$p \wedge q$	$p \vee q$	$p \rightarrow q$	$p \leftrightarrow q$
T	T	F	T	T	T	T
F	T	T	F	T	T	F
T	F	F	F	T	F	F
F	F	T	F	F	T	T

According to this, negation ($\sim$) switches the truth-value of the subsequent formula, so that the negation of a formula is true if the formula over which

---

9 See Suppes 1957: 5.

it operates is false, otherwise the negation is false, and thus it approximately corresponds to the meaning of the English word "no," and similar expressions. The conjunction ($\wedge$) of two formulas is true if both components are true, and false otherwise, and thus it approximately corresponds to the meaning of the English word "and" and similar expressions. The disjunction ($\vee$) of two formulas is true if at least one of them is true, and false otherwise, thus approximately corresponding to the meaning of the English word "or" and similar expressions. A conditional ($\rightarrow$) formula – often called "material conditional"[10] – is true if its antecedent is false or its consequent is true, otherwise it is false, and thus approximately corresponds to the meaning of the English clause "if... then," "only if," and similar expressions. Finally, a biconditional ($\leftrightarrow$) formula is true if its constituent formulas have the same truth-value, and false otherwise, approximately corresponding thus to the meaning of the English clause "if and only if," "just in case," and similar expressions.

Using the sign v to refer to the valuation of a formula and "iff" as the abbreviation of "*if and only if*," the semantics of PC might de expressed through the following clauses:

- $v(\sim\alpha) = \mathrm{T}$ iff $v(\alpha) = \mathrm{F}$
- $v(\alpha \wedge \beta) = \mathrm{T}$ iff $v(\alpha) = \mathrm{T}$ and $v(\beta) = \mathrm{T}$
- $v(\alpha \vee \beta) = \mathrm{T}$ iff $v(\alpha) = \mathrm{T}$ or $v(\beta) = \mathrm{T}$
- $v(\alpha \rightarrow \beta) = \mathrm{T}$ iff $v(\alpha) = \mathrm{F}$ or $v(\beta) = \mathrm{T}$
- $v(\alpha \leftrightarrow \beta) = \mathrm{T}$ iff $v(\alpha) = v(\beta)$

Now, take a formula such as $(p \vee \sim p)$. Its truth table is:

p	$\sim p$	$p \vee \sim p$
T	F	T
F	T	T

This formula is true regardless of the truth-values of its constituent atomic formulas. In other words, it is true for all possible truth-values of its variables. These formulas will be called *tautologies*. Tautologies are valid formulas of PC (i.e., they are true [value T] under any assignment of value to its variables). Take now a formula such as $(p \wedge \sim p)$. Its truth table is:

---

[10] Material conditional must be distinguished from other kinds of conditional connectives, some of them stronger (like *strict* conditional) and other weaker (like *defeasible* conditional). We return to this subject when considering the formal representation of conditional norms and the alleged defeasible character of rules. For an introduction to material conditional, see Quine 1950: chapter 3.

p	$\sim p$	$p \wedge \sim p$
T	F	F
F	T	F

This is the opposite case: the formula is false regardless of the truth-values of its constituent atomic formulas. These formulas will be called *contradictions* (or *unsatisfiable*). Formulas that are neither contradictions nor tautologies will be called *contingencies*. Contingent formulas are those in which the corresponding truth tables contain at least one value T and one value F.

Truth tables can be used to analyze whether certain inference patterns are logically valid in PC. Take the following argument:

(1) If John rides his bicycle, he will arrive at his job on time; John rides his bicycle. Therefore, John will arrive at his job on time.

This argument may be represented as:

(1') $p \rightarrow q$, p. Therefore, q.

The first two formulas are the premises of the argument, and the third its conclusion. It may also be represented as a unique conditional formula in which the antecedent is formed by the conjunction of the two premises and the consequent by its conclusion:

(1") $((p \rightarrow q) \wedge p) \rightarrow q$

Under this second representation, validity can be tested through its truth-table:

p	q	$((p \rightarrow q) \wedge p) \rightarrow q$		
T	T	T	T	T
F	T	T	F	T
T	F	F	F	T
F	F	T	F	T

As this formula is a tautology, there is no logical possibility for the premises to be true and the conclusion false, so the argument is valid.

Dyadic connectives in PC are interdefinable. If we take negation and any dyadic connective, it is possible to define all the rest.[11] Using the symbol = as

---

[11] A biconditional can obviously be reduced to a conjunction of two conditionals: $(p \leftrightarrow q) = ((p \rightarrow q) \wedge (q \rightarrow p))$.

a metalinguistic sign to represent a logically valid (tautological) biconditional, we have:

$$(p \wedge q) = \sim(\sim p \vee \sim q) = \sim(p \rightarrow \sim q)$$
$$(p \vee q) = \sim(\sim p \wedge \sim q) = (\sim p \rightarrow q)$$
$$(p \rightarrow q) = \sim(p \wedge \sim q) = (\sim p \vee q)^{12}$$

We said that the meaning of logical connectives can be defined, and validity of certain inference-patterns can be tested, with the aid of truth tables. This method has the merit of simplicity, as it constitutes a mechanical procedure. But it can be very hard, and undoubtedly tedious to examine the truth-values of formulas with several variables. For this reason, formal systems for PC are often presented in an axiomatic form – that is, taking a set of formulas as basic truths that, together with a set of rules of inferences, allows demonstrating every tautology of PC.

A possible – and one of the most simple – axiomatic presentations of PC, which takes as primitive connectives only negation and conditional, is the system L, as it is known:[13]

Axioms:[14]

(A$_1$) $\alpha \rightarrow (\beta \rightarrow \alpha)$
(A$_2$) $(\alpha \rightarrow (\beta \rightarrow \gamma)) \rightarrow ((\alpha \rightarrow \beta) \rightarrow (\alpha \rightarrow \gamma))$
(A$_3$) $(\sim\alpha \rightarrow \sim\beta) \rightarrow (\beta \rightarrow \alpha)$

Rule of inference:

(MP or *modus ponens*) $\alpha \rightarrow \beta, \; \alpha \vdash \beta$

Both truth tables and axiomatic systems are closely tied to the notion of truth and, accordingly, to the semantic conception of logic, with the severe limitation such a conception implies: the impossibility of accepting logical relations

---

[12] Thus, it is possible to reduce the number of logical symbols of PC without losing expressive power. When a set of connectives is sufficient to express all possible truth functions, it is called *functionally complete* or an *adequate set of connectives*. There are sixteen two-place truth functions; the sets $\{\sim,\wedge,\vee\}$, $\{\sim,\vee\}$, $\{\sim,\wedge\}$, $\{\sim,\rightarrow\}$ are, each of them, adequate sets of connectives. Furthermore, H. M. Sheffer introduced a connective, denoted by |, usually called "incompatibility" (also known as Sheffer's stroke or as the NAND connective), which represents the negation of a conjunction. This connective is by itself an adequate set of connectives; the same occurs with Peirce's arrow, denoted by ↓ (also known as the NOR connective), that represents the negation of a disjunction. Of course, such reductions of the language of PC results in longer formulas and more difficulties for their interpretation.

[13] See Church 1956: 119–120.

[14] Properly speaking, these are axiom-schemas, because α, β, etc., are not formulas of our language but metavariables.

among linguistic expressions not capable of truth-values. This is obvious in the case of truth tables, but although axiomatic systems are paradigmatically syntactic systems, the notion of truth also extends to the idea of an axiom as an *evident* truth. There is, however, a number of alternative ways to present PC, some of which are not so tied to the notion of truth. For instance, natural deduction systems, originally developed by Gentzen,[15] do not base the calculus on a set of axioms and use only a limited number of rules of inference to demonstrate all tautologies of PC. Those rules allow defining sentential connectives, not in terms of truth, but in terms of the ways in which they may be introduced and eliminated in the course of inferences.

PC examines the structure of compound propositions through the analysis of the relations among its constituent propositions considered as whole blocks. Those propositions remain as black boxes, so to speak, as basic units of analysis. Unfortunately, there are many logically correct arguments whose validity cannot be properly evaluated with the tools of PC. Consider our previous example:

(3) All Parisians are French; all French people are European. Therefore, all Parisians are European.

Predicate Logic (PL) penetrates these basic units, decomposing them into minor units, which are not propositions themselves, but the *predicates* on which propositions are built. Testing the validity of an argument such as (3) requires an examination of these deeper structures.

Aristotelian syllogistics was located at this level of analysis. It was based on four ways to combine predicates to form propositions: "All *F*'s are *G*", "No *F* is *G*", "Some *F*'s are *G*", or "Some *F*'s are not *G*". Statements corresponding to these four structures (regardless of their formulation in singular or plural) were called *categorical*. They were labeled with letters in a code: *A*, *E*, *I*, *O*, respectively:

A (universal affirmative):	All *F*'s are *G*
E (universal negative):	No *F* is *G*
I (particular affirmative):	Some *F*'s are *G*
O (particular negative):	Some *F*'s are not *G*

The systematic introduction of formal languages generalized and improved the analysis of the relations between predicates. Paraphrasing Quine (who

---

[15] See Gentzen 1934.

does not use the terminology presented herein),[16] we may say that although propositions are true or false, predicates are *true of* one or more objects, or any object whatsoever within a certain universe, and *false of* the rest. Hence, the predicate "Italian" is true of each and every Italian and false of any people with no such nationality.

Using a different terminology, predicates "denote" the entities of which they are true. The *extension* of a predicate is the class of objects of which it is true. We may say that predicates *have* an extension just as propositions have truth-values, but there is no need to think that predicates are names of their extensions, at least no more than to think that propositions are names of their truth-values.

Those predicates for which the argument is a unique individual are called *monadic*. Predicates whose arguments consist in more than one individual – that is, those that connect two or more individuals (relations) – are called *polyadic*. In turn, polyadic predicates might be dyadic, triadic, ... *n*-adic, as they designate two, three, or *n* objects, respectively.

Language of PL:

Predicate letters: $P, Q, R, \ldots$
Individual constants: $a, b, c, \ldots$
Individual variables: $x, y, z, \ldots$
Sentential connectives of PC: $\sim, \wedge, \vee, \rightarrow, \leftrightarrow$.
Auxiliary signs: ( ) (brackets).
Quantifiers: $\forall$ (universal quantifier); $\exists$ (existential quantifier).

Formation rules of wffs of PL (recursive definition of wff of PL):

- if P is a n-ary predicate letter and each $t_1, \ldots, t_n$ is an individual constant or variable, then $Pt_1, \ldots, t_n$ is a wff of PL;
- if α is a wff of PL, then $\sim\alpha$ is a wff of PL;
- if α and β are wffs of PL, then $(\alpha \wedge \beta)$, $(\alpha \vee \beta)$, $(\alpha \rightarrow \beta)$ and $(\alpha \leftrightarrow \beta)$ are wffs of PL;
- if α is a wff of PL and x is a variable, then $\forall x\alpha$ and $\exists x\alpha$ are wffs of PL.
- Only those formulas constructed according to the previous clauses in a finite number of steps are wffs of PL.

An atomic proposition of PL is an individual constant (or *n*-tuple of individual constants) prefixed by a predicate letter (v.gr. Pa), and intuitively represents assigning a predicate to a concrete item (or a relation to an *n*-tuple of items). Predicate letters stand for ordinary language class-words (e.g., is blue, is taller

---

[16] See Quine 1950: 94.

than, and so on), whereas individual constants stand for proper names (e.g., Tom, California, and so on).

Unlike individual constants, individual variables do not designate concrete and singular individuals, but *any* individual at random in a certain *universe*. Each of the individuals of that universe is a *value* of the variable.[17] For that reason, a formula such as *Px* does not express a proposition capable of truth-values, but a *propositional function*[18] (i.e., an expression that will become a proposition when their individual variables are assigned a certain value).

There is another way for building up propositions from propositional functions; to link all the occurrences of their variables using *quantifiers*. Universal quantifiers ($\forall$) may be taken as representing the meaning of the common language expression "all," and similar ones, while existential quantifiers ($\exists$) may be taken as representing the meaning of the common language expression "some," and similar ones. To express the assertion that all individuals have the property that a certain predicate *P* designates we write:

$$\forall x Px$$

This should be read as "For all *x*'s, *Px*." Thus, a universal quantifier followed by a variable indicates that the subsequent expression holds for all values the variable may take within the universe of discourse. Similarly, to express the assertion that some individual has the property to which a certain predicate *P* refers we write:

$$\exists x Px$$

This might be read as "For some *x*, *Px*." In other words, an existential quantifier followed by a variable indicates that the subsequent expression holds for at least one of the values the variable may take within the universe of discourse.

Quantifiers are interdefinable. Using = as a metalinguistic sign to represent a logically valid biconditional, we have:

$$\forall x Px = \sim\exists x \sim Px$$

The *scope* of a quantifier is the content that immediately follows it. Thus, in the formula $\forall x \alpha$, α is the scope of the universal quantifier. In the preceding formulas, the occurrence of the variable *x* following the predicate *P* is said

---

[17] Following Quine, it could be said that "to be assumed as an entity is, purely and simply, to be reckoned as the value of a variable" (Quine 1953: 13).

[18] The concept of propositional function, an extension to the logical domain of the mathematical concept of function, is Frege's and was incorporated by Whitehead and Russell into the logical system of *Principia Mathematica*. See Russell and Whitehead 1910: 15.

to be *bound* by the corresponding quantifier. A given quantifier binds all occurrences of a variable x within a subsequent formula α, unless another quantifier occurring inside α already binds it. By contrast, the occurrence of the variable x in a given formula α is *free* (not bound) if it is out of the scope of all the quantifiers in α. All wffs of PL that lack free variables are said to be *closed*, and they express propositions.

To exemplify the language of PL, the four categorical statements of traditional syllogistics may be represented as follows:

A (All F's are G): $\forall x(Fx \rightarrow Gx)$

E (No F is G): $\forall x(Fx \rightarrow \sim Gx)$

I (Some F's are G): $\exists x(Fx \wedge Gx)$

O (Some F's are not G): $\exists x(Fx \wedge \sim Gx)$

To express PL semantics, we begin by saying that if α is a formula, a is a constant and x is a variable, then $[a/x]\alpha$ is the formula that results when all free occurrences of x in α are substituted by occurrences of a. Now, an *interpretation* within a non-empty universe U is a function I that assigns a value to each constant, variable, and predicate letter of our language, such that for each constant a, $I(a) \in U$ – that is, the interpretation of a is an element of the universe; for each variable x, $I(x) \in U$, and for each n-place predicate P, $I(P)$ is an n-place relation over U – that is, $I(P) \subseteq Un$.

We define a valuation v as another function whose domain is the set of wffs of PL and its range is the set $\{T,F\}$, so that:

- for any atomic formula $Pt_1, \ldots, t_n$, $v(Pt_1, \ldots, t_n) = T$ iff $(v(t_1), \ldots, v(t_n)) \in v(P)$;
- $v(\sim\alpha) = T$ iff $v(\alpha) = F$;
- $v(\alpha \wedge \beta) = T$ iff $v(\alpha) = T$ and $v(\beta) = T$;
- $v(\alpha \vee \beta) = T$ iff $v(\alpha) = T$ or $v(\beta) = T$;
- $v(\alpha \rightarrow \beta) = T$ iff $v(\alpha) = F$ or $v(\beta) = T$;
- $v(\alpha \leftrightarrow \beta) = T$ iff $v(\alpha) = v(\beta)$;
- $v(\forall x\alpha) = T$ iff $v([a/x]\alpha) = T$ for every constant a in PL;
- $v(\exists x\alpha) = T$ iff $v([a/x]\alpha) = T$ for at least one constant a in PL.

In traditional syllogistics, it was assumed that the following relations hold among categorical statements A, E, I, and O. First, that the pairs A and O, and E and I, are contradictory – that is, if one of them is true, the other is false and *vice versa*. Second, that A logically implies I, and E logically implies O (subalternation). Third, that A and E cannot both be true (contrariety), whereas *I* and *O* cannot both be false (subcontrariety). These relations were usually illustrated through the following square of opposition:

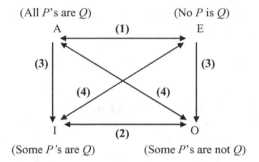

But if we use the language of PL to represent categorical statements, it is easy to see that, in fact, (1), (2), and (3) only hold under the assumption that *P* denotes a non-empty class (i.e., that ∃*xPx*).[19] Thus, using the language of PL, the former relations may be formalized as follows (with = as already defined and ⊢ as a metalinguistic sign representing a logically valid conditional):

(1) Contrariety: $\exists xPx \vdash \sim(\forall x(Px \rightarrow Qx) \land \forall x(Px \rightarrow \sim Qx))$
(2) Subcontrariety: $\exists xPx \vdash \exists x(Px \land Qx)) \lor (\exists x(Px \land \sim Qx)$
(3) Subalternation: $\exists xPx \vdash \forall x(Px \rightarrow Qx) \rightarrow \exists x(Px \land Qx)$
                          $\exists xPx \vdash \forall x(Px \rightarrow \sim Qx) \rightarrow \exists x(Px \land \sim Qx)$
(4) Contradiction: $\forall x(Px \rightarrow Qx) = \sim(\exists x(Px \land \sim Qx))$
                          $\forall x(Px \rightarrow \sim Qx) = \sim(\exists x(Px \land Qx))$

More generally, and without the need of the additional assumption under consideration, a parallel square of opposition holds for the universal and existential quantifiers:

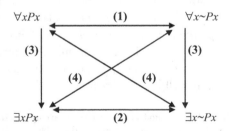

<hr />

[19] On this ontological assumption in Aristotelian syllogistics, see Church 1965: 417–424.

(1) expresses contrariety; (2) expresses subcontrariety; (3) expresses subalternation, and (4) expresses contradiction.

These relations do not limit their scope to PL, but can be recognized in other fields of logic, such as alethic modal logic and deontic logic. Let us examine this in further detail.

1.3. MODAL LOGIC AND DEONTIC LOGIC

Consider the fundamental concepts of *alethic* modal logic (i.e., the different modalities in which a given statement *p* may be true). The truth of *p* may be necessary (*Np*), merely possible (*Mp*), or impossible (*Ip*). These modalities are interdefinable in virtue of the following equivalences: $Np = {\sim}M{\sim}p = I{\sim}p$.[20] Notably, these concepts are interrelated in close analogy to quantifiers. Intuitively, the pairs *Np* and *M~p*, as well as the pairs *Ip* and *Mp*, are contradictory assertions. Moreover, *Np* implies *Mp*, and *Ip* implies *M~p* (subalternation); *Np* and *Ip* cannot both be true (contrariety), and *Mp* and *M~p* cannot both be false (subcontrariety).[21]

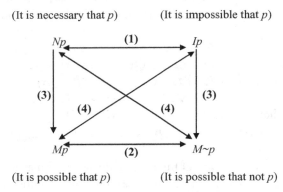

(It is necessary that *p*)   (It is impossible that *p*)

(It is possible that *p*)   (It is possible that not *p*)

For our purposes, however, the most interesting of these analogies is the one that holds between normative or *deontic* concepts. Let us first examine from an intuitive point of view the meaning of the fundamental deontic concepts, such as *obligation, prohibition,* and *permission*. It is important to stress that deontic expressions can be used both to formulate norms, and *propositions about norms*. An expression such as "you cannot park here" may be used to express a command, as well as a report of an existing command. Whereas

---

[20] Many different systems of alethic modal logic have been developed and studied. For example, system *T* was first elaborated by Feys (1937), and is equivalent to another famous modal system created by von Wright (1951b). For a classic presentation of system *T*, see Hughes and Cresswell 1996: 41–42.

[21] The numbers represent the same relations as before.

norms prescribe what should or may be done, norm-propositions describe the normative status of actions according to a certain set of existing norms. In this section, we only deal with deontic expressions used to formulate norms; later we return to the philosophical relevance of the distinction between norms and norm-propositions.[22]

A prescription imposing an obligation to perform a certain action intends to direct the conduct of the addressees in the following way. Because for any individual x in a certain time t, and regarding a certain action p, either x performs p at t or not ($\sim p$ will stand for "not to perform p"), the obligation to perform p implies directing x's conduct toward the performance of p and discouraging $\sim p$.

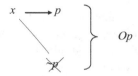

A prohibition to perform p intends to direct the agent's conduct toward $\sim p$, discouraging the option for the performance of p:

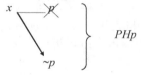

Granting what we will call a *faculty* to perform p means to authorize both the path toward p and the path toward $\sim p$,[23] and thus the choice between performing or not performing p will rest in the agent's hands:

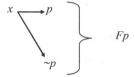

The expression "permission" is reserved here for the situation in which only the path toward p is expressly authorized. Therefore, to grant permission to perform p is compatible both with a parallel permission of $\sim p$ and with $\sim p$ being prohibited. In the former case, p is facultative; in the latter case, p is obligatory.

22 See Chapter 3, Section 3.1.
23 This terminology was introduced by Alchourrón and Bulygin 1971: 14.

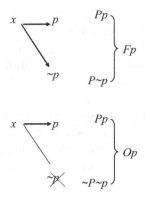

Because the facultative character of an action p might be reduced to the double permission of p and $\sim p$, in general we restrict our attention to simple permission. Along these characterizations, the deontic operators O, PH, and P can be interdefined in the following way:

$$Op = \sim P\sim p = PH\sim p$$

In other words, to say that p is obligatory is equivalent to saying that $\sim p$ is not permitted or, equivalently, that $\sim p$ is prohibited. Moreover, it seems intuitively acceptable to think that the obligation of p and the permission of $\sim p$ (Op and $P\sim p$), as well as the prohibition of p and its permission (PHp and Pp), contradict each other; that Op logically implies Pp, and PHp logically implies $P\sim p$ (subalternation); that Op and PHp cannot both be true or valid (contrariety), and Pp and $P\sim p$ cannot both be false or invalid (subcontrariety). As in the case of quantifiers and modal concepts, representing contrariety by (1), subcontrariety by (2), subalternation by (3), and contradiction by (4), we have:

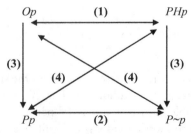

These analogies between quantified statements, alethic modal statements, and deontic statements seem, at least at first sight, so close that they cannot be the product of mere coincidence, a "philosophical accident," so to speak.

There should be some reason justifying them. Under such assumption, a possible explanatory hypothesis would be to suppose that of these three groups, two of them are reducible to the third. Thus, three possibilities should be explored; a reduction of quantified statements and alethic modal statements to deontic statements; a reduction of quantified statements and deontic statements to alethic modal statements, and a reduction of deontic statements and alethic modal statements to quantified statements.

We set aside the first of these possibilities and concentrate our attention on the remaining two, beginning with a partial consideration of the second (i.e., the attempts to reduce deontic concepts to alethic modal concepts).[24] One of the most important of such reductive attempts was provided by Stig Kanger in 1957.[25] His analysis is based on the idea that it is possible to satisfy all normative demands, represented as Md (where d stands for the satisfaction of all normative requirements), and introducing it as an additional axiom in the alethic modal calculus, generating a new modal system (Kd):

(A_1) All propositional tautologies
(A_2) $N(\alpha \to \beta) \to (N\alpha \to N\beta)$
(A_3) Md

The rules of inferences are the usual in alethic modal logic; *modus ponens* $((\alpha, (\alpha \to \beta) \vdash \beta))$ and the so-called *necessitation rule* (if $\vdash \alpha$, then $\vdash N\alpha$). Deontic concepts are now defined as:

$$Op =_{df} N(d \to p)$$
$$Pp =_{df} M(d \wedge p)$$
$$PHp =_{df} N(p \to \sim d)$$

According to this, p is obligatory if and only if it is necessary that p is a necessary condition for the satisfaction of all normative requirements; p is permitted if and only if it is possible to see to it that p jointly satisfies all normative demands; and p is prohibited if and only if it is necessary that p is a sufficient condition for the non-satisfaction of all normative requirements.

There is no doubt that the formal aspects of this reduction is a logical achievement in itself, but the immediate question this approach raises is in what sense of "necessity" is it sound to claim that an obligation to p means that the satisfaction of all obligations *necessarily* implies p. If the concept of

---

[24] In von Wright 1971, there is an attempt to reduce normative vocabulary in terms of necessary and sufficient conditions.
[25] See Kanger 1957.

necessity involved were *normative*, the purported reduction would be circular; but if *logical* or *factual* necessity were involved, then the additional axiom $(Np \to p)$ should have to be accepted and that would result in a stronger system than those usually accepted by deontic logicians, as formulas such as $O(Op \to p)$ would become valid.[26]

A similar reductive attempt was provided by Anderson, using as starting point the connection between obligations and sanctions.[27] Using S to represent a sanction, penalty, or disvalue, and assuming that it is possible not to impose a sanction $(M{\sim}S)$, deontic concepts may be defined as follows:[28]

$$Op =_{df} N({\sim}p \to S)$$
$$Pp =_{df} M(p \wedge {\sim}S)$$
$$PHp =_{df} N(p \to S)$$

According to this, an action is obligatory if and only if it is necessary that a penalty or sanction follows from its omission; an action is permitted if and only if it is possible that its performance is not followed by a sanction, and is prohibited if and only if it is necessary that its performance is followed by a sanction.

Here it seems to be beyond dispute that the violation of a norm is not *necessarily* followed by a sanction. Unlike natural laws that necessarily "govern" causal relations between events, the "necessity" of the connection between sanctions and obligations does not seem to be alethic modal necessity, but some kind of *normative* necessity. Thus, an alternative reading of S should be considered; that the wrongdoer *must* or *may* be punished (i.e., that certain officials are provided with a *right* to punish). Nevertheless, it seems clear that on this alternative reading, "must" and "right" are not modal but deontic judgments, and so the proposed "reduction" of deontic concepts to modal concepts fails.

From a philosophical point of view, these connections between deontic predicates and alethic modal concepts seem to involve a *naturalistic* commitment, that can be shown by means of a similar argument to the so-called

---

[26] For analysis and criticism of the reductive approach developed by Kanger, see Aqvist 1984: 147–264 and McNamara 2006: 220.

[27] See Anderson 1958: 100–103.

[28] As we shall see, if $M{\sim}S$ and the definitions of deontic concepts were added to a normal modal system, that is, one in which we have as an axiom $N(\alpha \to \beta) \to (N\alpha \to N\beta)$, and is closed under *modus ponens* and the necessitation rule, the standard system of deontic logic would be obtained.

open question introduced by Moore against naturalism in ethics.[29] Even if the infringement of obligations were always followed by a sanction, it would make perfect sense to question whether the punished behavior was in fact obligatory. The argument can hardly be regarded as decisive, but is useful to stress that some relevant aspect of our concept of obligation resists this kind of reduction and requires additional explanations.

Be that as it may, the analysis that has proved to be the most profitable to deal with the analogies between deontic, modal, and quantified statements is the one that offers a reduction of the first two into the third. From this point of view, alethic modal statements can be translated to quantification by means of Leibniz's idea that the truth of a statement is necessary if the statement is true in every *possible world*, and that the truth of a statement is possible if there is at least one *possible world* in which it is true.[30]

$$N p(w) = \text{T iff } \forall w'(Rww' \rightarrow v(p, w') = T)$$

$$M p(w) = \text{T iff } \exists w'(Rww' \wedge v(p, w') = T)$$

This means that p is necessarily true in a world w if and only if for every possible world w' standing in a certain relation with w (usually called the *accessibility relation*), the truth-value of p in w' is T (true). And p is possibly true in a world w if and only if there is at least one possible world w' accessible to w, and the truth-value of p in w' is T (true). From a logical point of view, it is unnecessary to take sides on the nature of possible worlds; they may be conceived as propositions, states of affairs, existing independent entities, or ways the world might have been had things gone different, among other possibilities.[31]

In the case of deontic statements, as we shall see, the same idea can be equally introduced with a slight variation in the relation under consideration. There is, however, one problem that should be seriously considered regarding deontic statements. The semantic analysis of deontic logic in terms of quantification over possible worlds seems to involve a commitment to the idea that deontic statements qualifying certain actions or states of affairs as obligatory, prohibited or permitted, are capable of truth-values, although not by reference to what is the case in the actual world but in certain normatively ideal worlds relative to the actual world. And this is, as we shall see, a highly controversial claim.

---

[29] See Moore 1903: 15–17.
[30] See Leibniz 1672: 466. The brilliant development of this idea for the formal analysis in modal logic is attributable to Kripke (see Kripke 1959).
[31] See Rönnedal 2010: 99.

1.4. MAIN SYSTEMS OF DEONTIC LOGIC

We have already presented some significant analogies that hold between modal, existential and normative concepts such as "obligatory," "prohibited," and "permitted." These latter notions are called *deontic operators* or *deontic modalities*. Deontic operators can be interdefined; using O to represent obligation, PH to represent prohibition, and P to represent permission:

$$O \text{ primitive:} \qquad P \text{ primitive:}$$
$$PHp = O{\sim}p \qquad Op = {\sim}P{\sim}p$$
$$Pp = {\sim}O{\sim}p \qquad PHp = {\sim}Pp$$

This means that we may, for instance, formulate a norm that imposes an obligation in terms of prohibition or permission, and *vice versa*. Thus, to say "Paying taxes is obligatory" is equivalent to saying "Not paying taxes is prohibited," and to saying "Not paying taxes is not permitted."

In his seminal article "Deontic Logic," G. H. von Wright begins by pointing out the definitional analogies between normative concepts and alethic modal concepts,[32] and adds to them the existence of analogous laws of distribution between modal and deontic operators. Possibility and permission operators are distributive over disjunction, and necessity and obligation operators are distributive over conjunction:

$$M(p{\vee}q) \leftrightarrow (Mp{\vee}Mq) \quad P(p{\vee}q) \leftrightarrow (Pp{\vee}Pq)$$
$$N(p{\wedge}q) \leftrightarrow (Np{\wedge}Nq) \quad O(p{\wedge}q) \leftrightarrow (Op{\wedge}Oq)^{[33]}$$

Of course, the outlined analogies should not hide the important differences that remain between modal and deontic concepts. Probably the most important and uncontroversial of them is that for most interpretations of modal concepts, the following two implications are valid:

$$\vdash Np \rightarrow p \quad \vdash p \rightarrow Mp$$

But the deontic counterparts of those laws seem strongly counterintuitive, because their acceptance would mean that everything that is obligatory is in fact true $(Op{\rightarrow}p)$; and that if something is true, then it is permitted $(p{\rightarrow}Pp)$.

Another point at which von Wright's deontic systems depart from alethic modal logic is in the interpretation he ascribes to the "things" which are pronounced obligatory, forbidden, or permitted. Variables p, q, and so on are

---

[32] von Wright 1951; see also von Wright 1989.

[33] Regarding the PH operator, neither of these two laws of distribution hold, but the following equivalence is valid: $PH(p{\vee}q) \leftrightarrow (PHp{\wedge}PHq)$.

understood as names of classes of actions or *generic actions* – such as smoking, walking, and so on – that can be performed in different circumstances.[34] They are neither names of individual acts, nor of states of affairs. Such generic actions have, according to von Wright, performance-values analogous to truth-values.

Two important consequences follow from this background: (1) deontic operators cannot be iterated, and (2) *mixed* formulas are not well-formed. On the one hand, a formula such as OOp is not well formed, because Op is not the name of a generic action and so cannot be under the scope of a deontic operator. On the other hand, a formula such as $(p{\rightarrow}Oq)$ would be ill-formed, because as variables are used under this interpretation to represent names of generic actions, p cannot be the antecedent of a conditional statement. As we show, the most common systems of deontic logic interpret variables p, q, and so on, as descriptions of states of affairs, thereby approximating more closely alethic modal systems.

It may be said that the different systems of deontic logic are based on the analogies between norms and modal propositions. However, the discrepancies in vocabulary (i.e., well-formed expressions within the system), axioms, and rules of inference of the different systems of deontic logic are a by-product of the greater or lesser degree of philosophical distrust regarding those analogies between norms and modal propositions. Von Wright characterizes a *minimal system* of deontic logic in the following way:[35]

- Tautologies of PC are valid when propositional variables are replaced by deontic formulas.
- There is only one specific deontic axiom: $P(\alpha \vee \beta) \leftrightarrow (P\alpha \vee P\beta)$.
- Prohibitions and obligations are defined in terms of permissions (i.e., $PH\alpha = {\sim}P\alpha$ and $O\alpha = {\sim}P{\sim}\alpha$).
- The rules of inferences are not only substitution and *modus ponens* but also a specific rule: provably equivalent PC-formulas are intersubstitutable *salva veritate* in deontic formulas.

According to the last clause, from $p{\leftrightarrow}q$, we can derive $Op{\leftrightarrow}Oq$. This rule is often called the *rule (principle) of extensionality*, and is reproduced in many systems of deontic logic. Its intuitive justification arises from the fact that the logical equivalence between two variables (e.g., p and q) assures that they both refer to the same thing (action or state of affairs). Thus, to predicate a

---

[34] By contrast, *individual actions* are instances of generic actions – that is, particular cases of a certain act-category. See von Wright 1963a: 36.

[35] See von Wright 1983: 102.

normative qualification of a certain variable is equivalent to the attribution of such qualification to any other logically equivalent variable.

This minimal system of deontic logic is an alternative to other stronger deontic systems, and it represents a somewhat skeptical view of the analogy between deontic logic and alethic modal logic. In the minimal system, $(Pp\rightarrow Pq) \rightarrow (\sim Pq\rightarrow \sim Pp)$ is obtained replacing propositional variables by deontic sentences as an application of *modus tollens*, which von Wright claims is "valid for any sentence, whether deontic or not."[36] In such a system, however, some specific deontic inferences cannot be proved, such as $(Op\wedge O(p\rightarrow q)) \rightarrow Oq$. Although this formula *resembles* an application of *modus ponens*, it is not valid in the minimal system.[37]

In his first contribution to deontic logic, von Wright elaborated a stronger system of deontic logic, with the additional axiom $Pp\vee P\sim p$.[38] This formula is equivalent to Bentham's Law: $Op\rightarrow \sim PHp$ – that is, an obligatory action cannot be prohibited as well. The incorporation of Bentham's Law into the minimal system generates what has been called the *classical system* of deontic logic. The well-formed formulas of the system are:

- A deontic operator P or O, followed by an elementary or compound act-formula, is a wff.
- A wff preceded by the negation-symbol is a wff.
- Two wffs connected by $\wedge$, $\vee$, $\rightarrow$ or $\leftrightarrow$ constitute a wff.

Von Wright claimed that "the existence of logical truths which are peculiar to deontic concepts is what makes the study of deontic logic interesting."[39] Accordingly, he pointed out three principles as the foundations of the classical system of deontic logic:

Principle of deontic distribution: If an act is the disjunction of two other acts, then the permission of the disjunction of those acts is equivalent to the disjunction of the permission of the first act and the permission of the second act: $P(p\vee q) \leftrightarrow (Pp\vee Pq)$.

Principle of permission: An act p is either permitted or its negation is permitted, i.e. $Pp\vee P\sim p$.

Principle of deontic contingency: The principle of permission and the principle of distribution jointly entail $P(p\vee \sim p)$ – that is, tautological acts are permitted or, what amounts to the same, contradictory acts are not obligatory. But what is the status of $PH(p \wedge \sim p)$ and $O(p\vee \sim p)$? Von Wright claims that

---

[36] See von Wright 1957: 62.
[37] See von Wright 1957: 63.
[38] See von Wright 1957: 63–67.
[39] Von Wright 1957: 63.

tautologous acts are not necessarily obligatory, and contradictory acts are not necessarily forbidden.[40]

In the presentation of the classical system, von Wright assumed that deontic formulas were capable of truth-values. Thus, based on the three afore-mentioned principles, von Wright developed a decision method in terms of truth tables to determine which formulas are deontic tautologies within the system.

Although von Wright initially did not formulate an axiomatic presentation of the classical system, later he suggested a possible axiomatization in the following terms:[41]

(A_0) All tautologies of PC (with wffs substituted for the variables).
(A_1) $P\alpha \leftrightarrow \sim O \sim \alpha$
(A_2) $P(\alpha \vee \beta) \leftrightarrow P\alpha \vee P\beta$
(A_3) $P\alpha \vee P \sim \alpha \ (= Pt)$

Rules of inferences:

(R_1) *Modus Ponens* (if $\vdash \alpha$ and $\vdash (\alpha \to \beta)$, then $\vdash \beta$)
(R_2) *Rule of Extensionality*: Provably equivalent formulas of PC are inter-substitutable in wffs of the deontic calculus – for example, from $\vdash (p \leftrightarrow q)$ it follows $\vdash (Op \leftrightarrow Oq)$).

A_1 expresses the interdefinability between permission and obligation. A_2 expresses the principle of deontic distribution of the P-operator over disjunction. A_3, in its turn, expresses the principle of permission, equivalent to the principle that $O\alpha$ implies $P\alpha$. In this presentation, A_1 guarantees the validity of two important theorems that are particularly relevant for legal theory: the *principle of normative consistency* (i.e., $\sim(O \sim p \wedge Pp)$) and the *principle of normative completeness* (i.e., $O \sim p \vee Pp$). According to this system, therefore, and considering any action p, it cannot be the case that p is permitted and prohibited (NCons), and either p is prohibited or permitted (NComp). Their proofs are extremely simple:

Principle of normative consistency (NCons): $\sim(O \sim p \wedge Pp)$
Proof:

(1) $Pp \to \sim O \sim p$ implication from left to right of A_1.
(2) $O \sim p \to \sim Pp$ contraposition in (1) $((p \to q) \to (\sim q \to \sim p))$
(3) $\sim(O \sim p \wedge Pp)$ definition of conditional in terms of conjunction in 2
                            $((p \to q) \leftrightarrow \sim(p \wedge \sim q))$

---

[40] See von Wright 1957: 69.
[41] See von Wright 1967: 136; also von Wright 1968:s chapter 1 §4.

Principle of normative completeness (NComp): $O{\sim}p \vee Pp$
Proof:

(4) ${\sim}O{\sim}p \rightarrow Pp$ implication from right to left of A_1.
(5) $O{\sim}p \vee Pp$ definition of conditional in terms of disjunction in (4)
     $((p \rightarrow q) \leftrightarrow ({\sim}p \vee q))$

Legal scholars and legal philosophers have often been tempted to take these principles as a proof that, for logical reasons, law is a complete and consistent normative system.[42] However, let us examine this point in more detail. As Soeteman remarks,[43] taking any of those operators and using negations, four normative alternatives emerge:

i) Op iii) ${\sim}O{\sim}p$

ii) $O{\sim}p$ iv) ${\sim}Op$

As (iii) ${\sim}O{\sim}p$ and (iv) ${\sim}Op$ are, respectively, equivalent to Pp and $P{\sim}p$, and Fp is equivalent to $Pp \wedge P{\sim}p$, in virtue of the principle of normative completeness, we have in fact only three basic or elementary jointly exhaustive and mutually exclusive normative situations:

$$Op \vee PHp \vee Fp$$

In fact, it is possible to conceive of a fourth normative situation; that in which – with regards to p – no norm has been given. We may call that situation *normative neutrality*. However, the classical system, as well as stronger systems of deontic logic, limits their field of application to norms and their relations. For this reason, situations of normative neutrality, where no norms have been issued, are suppressed a priori. We later explore whether the existence and relevance of normative *gaps* require taking this possibility seriously.[44]

The analogies between deontic logic and alethic modal logic are still closer in the so-called *standard system* of deontic logic.[45] The *standard system* (SDL) is an extension of the classical system. Only two modifications are required to obtain the standard system from the classical system. First, the replacement of the rule of extensionality by a stronger rule, such as the modal rule of necessitation (in deontic context: if $\vdash \alpha$, then $\vdash O\alpha$). Second, deontic operators are prefixed to propositions rather than to generic actions.

The standard system is a normative interpretation of the normal alethic modal system *KD* (also called *D*), which is an extension of the more basic

---

[42] A detailed analysis of this claim will be offered in Chapter 5.
[43] See Soeteman 1989: 93.
[44] See Soeteman 1989: 97.
[45] See Hansson 1969: 373–398.

normal modal system K. A system of modal logic designed as an extension of propositional logic is called normal if and only if (1) it contains the distribution schema $N(\alpha \rightarrow \beta) \rightarrow (N\alpha \rightarrow N\beta)$, and (2) it is closed under *modus ponens* and the following necessitation rule:

$$\frac{\vdash \alpha}{\vdash N\alpha}$$

The system KD can be obtained adding to K an axiom D:

$$N\alpha \rightarrow M\alpha$$

Therefore, *KD* is also a normal modal system. The standard system of deontic logic (SDL) may be presented axiomatically as follows:

(A_1) All tautologies of PL
(A_2) $O(\alpha \rightarrow \beta) \rightarrow (O\alpha \rightarrow O\beta)$ (OK)
(A_3) $O\alpha \rightarrow \sim O \sim \alpha$ (OD)

(RI_1) If $\vdash \alpha$ and $\vdash (\alpha \rightarrow \beta)$, then $\vdash \beta$ (*Modus Ponens*)
(RI_2) If $\vdash \alpha$, then $\vdash O\alpha$ (*O-Necessitation*)

One of the main virtues (or defects, according to the point of view) of the standard system is that on account of its proximity to alethic modal logic, it allows a semantic presentation in terms of possible worlds. Between the 1950's and 1960's, different possible-worlds semantics for deontic logic were offered by several scholars.[46] Here we will confine ourselves to explain briefly one of those models, for its importance on subsequent studies on deontic logic: The Kripkean model.

A Kripkean *frame* is a structure composed of three elements $<W, w^*, R>$, where W is a non-empty set of possible worlds, w^* is a given element of W (that may be identified with the actual world), and R is a dyadic relation of relative possibility (more usually referred to as *deontic alternativeness* or *deontic accessibility*). Intuitively, we may read this relation as follows: a possible world w that satisfies R with the actual world w^* is such that within it everything that is obligatory in the actual world is in fact the case. A Kripkean *model* is a frame so defined, with a valuation function (v), which assigns values T or F (true or false) to the formulas of a given language L.

The basic idea for the development of systems of deontic logic consists in the following truth-clauses for deontic statements:

$$v(Op, w^*) = T \text{ iff } \forall w(Rw^*w) \rightarrow v(p, w) = T)$$

$$v(Pp, w^*) = T \text{ iff } \exists w(Rw^*w \land v(p, w) = T)$$

---

[46] See Kanger 1957; Hintikka 1957; Montague 1960, and Kripke 1963. For an excellent review of the origins of possible-worlds semantics for deontic logic, see Woleński 1990.

This means that a norm such as Op is true in the actual world if and only if in every possible world that is deontically accessible from the actual world p is true; and a norm such as Pp is true in the actual world if and only if there is at least one deontically accessible world from the actual world in which p is true. Kripke observed, regarding alethic modal logic, that different formal properties over the relation of accessibility between worlds give rise to different logical systems. In the case of deontic logic, it is equally possible to obtain different systems imposing different constraints over the relation R. For instance, if we take into account the class of all the frames (i.e., if no restriction is imposed over the relation of deontic accessibility), the result will be a weak system of deontic logic, characterized by the axiom $O(p{\rightarrow}q) \rightarrow (Op{\rightarrow}Oq)$.

Notice that, if in the actual world both $O(p{\rightarrow}q)$ and Op are true, then in every world that is deontically accessible from the actual world, both $p{\rightarrow}q$ and p are true. From this, and simple propositional calculus, it follows that in every deontically accessible world q is also true, and so in the actual world Oq also holds. However, it is possible to take into account only certain classes of frames, for instance, the class of all the frames in which relation R is *serial* (i.e., $\forall w \exists w'(wRw')$). This constraint over relation R guarantees that for all the possible worlds in W, there is at least one deontically accessible world. By reference to such class of frames we obtain the standard system of deontic logic, characterized by the axiom: $Op{\rightarrow}Pp$.[47]

That this is so can be explained as follows. Suppose that in the actual world Op holds but Pp does not hold. In such a case, in all deontically accessible worlds regarding the actual world p is true, but in fact there are no deontically accessible worlds in which p is true. Contrary to appearances, these two claims are compatible, because the statement that for every possible world, if it is deontically accessible regarding the actual world, p is true in it, is a general and conditional claim that may be true vacuously (i.e., whenever there are no deontically accessible worlds regarding the actual world). But we have assumed that the relation of deontic accessibility is serial, so there has to be at least one deontically accessible world for each possible world. Thus, if it is true that in all deontically accessible worlds regarding the actual world p is true, and there is at least one deontically accessible world regarding the actual world, then in that world p has to be true. Consequently, in the class of all the

---

[47] Just as has been shown regarding quantified statements, the only relations that hold without additional assumptions are those of contradiction between the pairs Np-$M{\sim}p$, and Ip-Mp, in the case of modal concepts, and between the pairs Op-$P{\sim}p$, and PHp-Pp, in the case of deontic concepts. All the others only hold under the assumption, in the case of modal concepts, that there is at least one possible world accessible to the actual world, and in the case of deontic concepts, that there is at least one deontically ideal world relative to the actual world.

frames in which the relation R is serial, there is no possible world in which $Op \rightarrow Pp$ does not hold.

As this example shows, with these relatively simple and elegant resources, possible-worlds semantics provides a rich and theoretically powerful framework to represent various systems of deontic logic.[48]

Modal Systems	Deontic Systems
1) K	1') OK
PC +	PC +
KA $N(\alpha \rightarrow \beta) \rightarrow (N\alpha \rightarrow N\beta)$	OKA $O(\alpha \rightarrow \beta) \rightarrow (O\alpha \rightarrow O\beta)$
Df. M $M\alpha =_{df} \sim N \sim \alpha$	Df. P $P\alpha =_{df} \sim O \sim \alpha$
NR $\dfrac{\vdash \alpha}{\vdash N\alpha}$	ONR $\dfrac{\vdash \alpha}{\vdash O\alpha}$
(No constraints over the accessibility relation.)	
2) KD	2') OKD *(Standard System)*
K +	OK +
DA $N\alpha \rightarrow M\alpha$	ODA $O\alpha \rightarrow P\alpha$
The accessibility relation is serial ($\forall w \exists w'(wRw')$).	
3) M	3') OM
K +	OK +
M $N(N\alpha \rightarrow \alpha)$	OM $O(O\alpha \rightarrow \alpha)$
The accessibility relation is secondarily-reflexive ($\forall ww'\ (wRw' \rightarrow w'Rw')$).	
4) T	4') OT
K +	OK +
TA $N\alpha \rightarrow \alpha$	OTA $O\alpha \rightarrow \alpha$
The accessibility relation is reflexive ($\forall w\ (wRw)$).	
5) $S4$	5') $OS4$
T +	OT+
S4A $N\alpha \rightarrow NN\alpha$	OS4A $O\alpha \rightarrow OO\alpha$
The accessibility relation is reflexive ($\forall w\ (wRw)$) and transitive ($\forall ww'w''$ $((wRw' \wedge w'Rw'') \rightarrow wRw'')$).	
6) $S5$	6') $OS5$
T +	OT+
S5A $M\alpha \rightarrow NM\alpha$	OS5A $P\alpha \rightarrow OP\alpha$
The accessibility relation is reflexive ($\forall w\ (wRw)$), transitive ($\forall ww'w''$ $((wRw' \wedge w'Rw'') \rightarrow wRw'')$), and symmetric ($\forall ww'\ (wRw' \rightarrow w'Rw)$).	

Let $w \in W$ be such that w^*Rw – that is, w satisfies the relation of deontic accessibility regarding w^* (is a deontic alternative to w^*, or is deontically

[48] For example, Åqvist develops ten systems of deontic logic according to different properties over the relation of deontic accessibility (see Åqvist 1984).

permissible regarding w^*). As previously explained, the intuitive idea is that in a such case w is a world in which all obligations in w^* are actually fulfilled. In virtue of that it may be said that w is a *deontically ideal world* regarding w^*. According to this characterization, being a deontically ideal world is a relative notion (relative to a given world, not necessarily distinct from itself).[49]

This idea of a deontically ideal world should be clearly distinguished from what may be called a *deontically perfect world*. Jakko Hintikka offered a very interesting comparison of the idea of deontically accessible worlds with the Kantian idea of a kingdom of ends.[50] The notion of deontic alternativeness or deontic accessibility may be read as a weaker and relativized variant of the Kantian notion of a kingdom of ends. It is weaker because it makes no reference to a particular moral principle, such as the categorical imperative or any other; it is also relativized because the notion of deontic alternativeness is relative to a certain possible world taken as a point of reference, as has already been indicated. In addition, whereas the Kantian kingdom of ends seems to be conceived as unique, it is ordinarily accepted that there may be various deontically accessible worlds regarding a certain world. But what seems most interesting about this comparison is that Hintikka suggests that under this understanding of the idea of a kingdom of ends as a deontic alternative to the actual world, such an alternative should be conceived as a *deontically perfect world* (i.e., a world in which *all* obligations, not only those that hold for the actual world but also the ones that hold in that alternative world, are fulfilled).[51] Thus, the idea of a deontically perfect world may be defined as follows:

$w \in W$ is a deontically perfect world iff wRw, i.e. iff $Op \rightarrow p$ holds in it.

In other words, a possible world is deontically perfect if and only if it is deontically ideal regarding itself (i.e., whenever the relation of deontic accessibility is reflexive, validating the principle $Op \rightarrow p$). Now, of course, the validity of this principle cannot be accepted as a valid principle of deontic logic, in the sense that a system of deontic logic based on the class of all frames in which the relation R is reflexive seems inadequate. However, there is a weaker system that corresponds to the idea suggested by Hintikka: a system of deontic logic based on the class of all frames in which the relation of deontic accessibility is secondarily-reflexive (i.e., $\forall ww' (wRw' \rightarrow w'Rw')$).

---

[49] As we see in the following discussion, not all those who accept possible-worlds semantics for deontic logic agree with this interpretation in terms of deontically ideal worlds.

[50] See Hintikka 1971.

[51] See Hintikka 1971: 73.

In such frames, if a possible world w' is deontically ideal regarding another world w, then w' is deontically ideal regarding itself (i.e., it is deontically perfect). The resulting system, usually identified as *DM* or *dT'*, is an extension of the standard system of deontic logic characterized by the validity of the axiom:

$$O(Op \rightarrow p)$$

Suppose that $O(Op \rightarrow p)$ were invalid in a given world w within a model based on a secondarily-reflexive frame. In such case, there should be a world w' deontically ideal regarding w in which $Op \rightarrow p$ did not hold, and so Op would be valid in w' while p false. But because the frame is secondarily-reflexive, we should have $w'Rw'$, and consequently $Op \rightarrow p$ holds in w', which amounts to a contradiction. Therefore, there cannot be a world within a secondarily-reflexive frame in which $O(Op \rightarrow p)$ does not hold.[52]

$O(Op \rightarrow p)$ is a widely discussed principle in deontic logic because it is one of the few principles that may be admitted in it that has the structure $O\alpha$, where α is not trivial,[53] and seems a sound principle for deontic logic at least if we take as normative reference deontically perfect worlds, that is, if we limit our consideration to those deontically ideal worlds that are deontically perfect worlds, in the sense that all obligations (whether in the actual or in those ideal worlds) are fulfilled, and no prohibition is transgressed. Moreover, it is rather difficult to grasp in what sense a world w may be deemed as deontically ideal regarding the actual world if the obligations that hold in w are not entirely obeyed.

There is, however, a rather awkward consequence that should be noticed, were this point of view accepted as a basis for designing a system of deontic logic. In our world – the actual world – not all obligations are fulfilled and not all prohibitions respected, so it is far from being a deontically perfect world in the sense defined. But then, as Chellas points out, if there is at least one action p such that p is not the case in the actual world in spite of being obligatory, under the assumption that deontically ideal worlds should be deontically perfect, our world cannot be deontically ideal regarding any other world.[54] This seems to force us to choose between one of these two alternatives: Either we give up the idea of evaluating deontic logic by reference to deontically perfect worlds, and thus to take $O(Op \rightarrow p)$ as an axiom, or we have to accept that, because the actual world cannot be deontically ideal regarding

---

[52] See Rönnedal 2010: 132.
[53] See Chellas 1980: 193.
[54] See Chellas 1980: 193–194.

any other possible world, we live in one of the worst of all worlds, in the sense that no possible world would be deontically worse than ours.

The wide variety of systems of deontic logic, and their corresponding semantic readings, is an incessant source of both conceptual inspiration and philosophical perplexity. On the one hand, those different systems are an indispensable tool to analyze the relations between families of normative concepts, and to exhibit their theoretical assumptions. On the other hand, however, the proliferation of systems of deontic logic also casts some doubts on the philosophical adequacy of the discipline. In this sense, disagreements arising from the different proposals of systems of deontic logic tend to generate a kind of skepticism concerning the possibility of justifying a genuine logic of norms. As is shown in the following discussion, at the roots of this skepticism lie some serious difficulties in giving an adequate explanation of the relations between norms, truth and propositions.

1.5. THE POSSIBILITY OF DEONTIC LOGIC

Although it is a controversial issue whether all norms owe their existence to the formulation of certain expressions in language (i.e., whether all norms are linguistic expressions which determine what ought to be done by explicitly *saying* what ought to be done),[55] at least regarding those norms that indeed have a linguistic formulation, language is used with the aim of directing the conduct of the addressee in a certain way. Hence, language in those cases does not play the same function as in the formulation of descriptive statements (i.e., assertions capable of being considered as true or false). In fact, even those norms that lack a canonical formulation in language cannot be assimilated to mere descriptions of regularities of conduct, because this would be tantamount to dissolving the difference between *is* and *ought*.[56] These remarks suggest that the dimension of norms and that of truth run separate ways or, in other words, that norms do not lend themselves to the assignment of truth-values.

Now, if norms express propositional attitudes different from assertions and, therefore, are not capable of truth-values, there is a major difficulty in the foundation of deontic logic and the very possibility of accepting logical relations between norms. This difficulty, often analyzed in moral philosophy, is closely connected to the so-called *Frege-Geach problem*.[57]

---

[55] See infra, Chapter 2. On the impossibility to reduce the realm of norms to those explicitly formulated in language, see Brandom 1994: 19 ff.

[56] See Brandom 1994: 26–30.

[57] See Geach 1965; Dummett 1973: 295 ff; Hurley 1989: 175 ff.; Gibbard 2003: 41 ff.

In his writings on negation, Frege rejected the idea that negation could be conceived as a propositional attitude different from assertion (i.e., that if someone asserts and denies the same proposition, the content of the speech act will be the same in both cases, the difference being only the kind of speech act performed, the *force* [the pragmatic aspect] of each expression).[58] According to Frege, whenever someone negates p, she is performing the same kind of speech act as the one she performs when asserting p, asserting the truth of the proposition contradictory to p. The argument Frege uses to justify his position runs as follows. Consider these two argument-schemas:

(1) If p, then q;
     p.
     Therefore, q.

(2) If not p, then not q;
     not p.
     Therefore, not q.

In both cases, the reasoning seems to operate in the same way (i.e., *modus ponens*). But this would not be the case if negation were a speech act different from assertion (i.e., if it were a special kind of linguistic act coordinated with that of assertion, but with an opposite valence). The reason is that (1) allows inferring, from the truth of a conditional statement and the truth of its antecedent, the truth of its consequent. In other words, because the content of the second premise matches the content of the antecedent of the conditional, it is possible to detach the truth of the consequent. If (2) were to operate the same way, to derive not q from the truth of the conditional statement "if not p, then not q," the content of the second premise should match the content of the antecedent of the conditional statement. However, if negation were a propositional attitude different from that of assertion, even though the assertoric force of the first premise would apply to it as a whole, as in (1), in the second premise the negation will be absorbed by the act of negation, and the content of that premise will be simply p, so it will no longer match the content of the antecedent of the conditional statement (not p). Thus, the inference of the conclusion cannot be explained in the same way as in (1), and this contradicts the intuition that both inference-patterns operate in the same way.

The argument may be used as a criterion to evaluate whether a given sentence indeed expresses a propositional attitude different from that of assertion

---

[58] See Frege 1919.

and, consequently, if it makes sense to predicate truth-values of it. This criterion would be to consider whether such interpretation is able to account for the
fact that certain inferences operate in the simple way in which schemas such
as (1) actually operate. This is the reason why an analogous argument was used
by Geach to challenge non-cognitivist conceptions of moral judgments, that
is, those theories that defend the idea that moral judgments are not descriptive
in nature (and therefore not capable of truth-values), but involve other uses of
language (expressive, prescriptive, and so on).

Geach uses as a criterion to reject different proposals for interpreting words
or phrases as signs of force – including the non-cognitivist interpretation of
"wrong" as expressing a condemnation of certain actions – their occurrence in
the antecedent of conditional statements.[59] According to Geach, expressions
such as "it is true that . . . " or " . . . is wrong" cannot bear a special force because
modus ponens works in the same way with premises such as "if it is true that *p*,
then *q*" and "if gambling is wrong, then getting someone to gamble is wrong."
Those conditional premises would neither assert *p* nor condemn gambling.
Consider the following argument-schemas:

(3) If it is true that and object is *F*, then it is *G*;
     It is true that *a* is *F*.
     Therefore, *a* is *G*.

(4) If doing *x* is wrong, then getting your little brother to do it is wrong;
     a is wrong.
     Therefore, getting your little brother to do *a* is wrong.[60]

In (3) and (4), "it is true that . . . " and " . . . is wrong" should mean the same
in every occurrence in order for the inferences to operate in the same way. But
then "it is true that . . . " and " . . . is wrong" cannot work as indicating the force
of the expressions in which they occur, because under such understanding the
second premises of both arguments will not allow detaching the consequent
of the conditional statements of the first premises on account of the lack of
correspondence with their antecedents.

Although, as already observed, Geach uses this argument to challenge non-
cognitivist conceptions of moral judgments, a similar objection may be raised
against the possibility of logical relations between deontic concepts, if they
are interpreted as expressing propositional attitudes different from assertions.

---

[59] See Geach 1965: 449–465.
[60] See Geach 1965: 463–464.

This is so because (4) might be easily reformulated using deontic expressions, such as:

(5) If doing x is forbidden, then getting your little brother to do it is forbidden;
a is forbidden.
Therefore, getting your little brother to do a is forbidden.

The example shows that, from a logical point of view, arguments containing deontic expressions seem to behave in close analogy to those exclusively composed of descriptive statements, and this suggests that norms should be interpreted after all as capable of truth-values. In fact, it is a widespread practice to infer certain norms from other norms, a clear example of that being the justification of legal decisions. Judges are required to justify their normative decisions in valid general norms, in the sense that an adjudicative decision in the legal domain is regarded as justified only to the extent that it can be reconstructed as logically valid reasoning, where both its conclusion and – at least one of – the premises are norms. However, it seems problematic to explain such logical relations between norms if they were conceived as incapable of truth-values.

In general terms, we might say that the attempts to apply formal logic as a tool for the analysis of normative discourse require giving an answer to a primary difficulty that forces us to reconcile certain pre-analytic intuitions that seem to be in conflict. On the one hand, it seems natural to think that norms lack truth-values. But, on the other hand, logic has been traditionally associated with the notion of truth, in the sense that the concept of logical consequence, as well as that of contradiction, and the meaning of logical connectives, have been traditionally defined in terms of truth.[61] Yet, arguments in which at least one of the premises is a general norm and the conclusion another norm are not uncommon. Moreover, there seems to be no substantial difference in the use of logical connectives in descriptive and prescriptive discourse.[62]

Jørgensen presented this problem in the form of a dilemma, and it may be said that the different answers that have been offered to it mark the historical

---

[61] For instance, one of the reasons Kelsen adduces against the applicability of logical principles to norms is that "[t]he basic presupposition of the principles of traditional logic concerning the truth of statements is that there are true and false statements. . . . But norms are the meaning of acts of will directed to the behavior of others, and so are neither true nor false. Consequently they are not subject to the principles of traditional logic, since these are related to truth and falsity" (Kelsen 1979: 211). For a detailed analysis of Kelsen's ideas on the topic, see Chapter 2, Section 2.3.

[62] See Bulygin 1995: 129–142.

evolution of deontic logic[63]: under the assumption that norms are neither true nor false, there are only two possible alternatives regarding the applicability of logic to normative discourse. Either the notion of logical consequence, and logical connectives, are defined in terms of truth, in which case there is no possibility for a logic of norms; or a logic of norms is possible, but then the scope of logic has to be wider than descriptive discourse, and the notion of logical consequence as well as logical connectives should not be defined in terms of truth, which contradicts a firmly established tradition.

The problem is that, on the one hand, the meaning of logical connectives does not seem to vary depending on their occurrence in descriptive and prescriptive statements, which is an indication that their contribution to the truth-values of descriptive statements is not the only relevant component of their meaning. And, on the other hand, the usual way in which we understand normative expressions seems to suggest that logical relations among norms are possible. All this would justify the rejection of the first horn of Jørgensen's dilemma. However, this alternative represents a fundamental challenge to the logical approach which gives primacy to semantics. In other words, the possibility of a logic of norms gives rise to a crisis concerning the traditional thesis that the logical domain is confined to that of truth and that there is a strong connection between validity and truth.

---

[63] See Jørgensen 1937–8: 288–296. Although an overview of the different alternatives that have been suggested to overcome this difficulty will be offered infra, for a thorough analysis of the issue see Soeteman 1989: chapters 3 and 4.

2

Paradoxes and Shortcomings of Deontic Logic

Almost since its origins, deontic logic has been threatened by several *paradoxes*, elaborated by theorists to highlight different shortcomings that seem to derive from its fundamental axioms. The discovery of such paradoxes led some deontic logicians toward an attitude of general skepticism about the discipline, for as Rescher remarked, "it is . . . only fair to say that there is virtually no issue in the field upon which a settled consensus has been reached."[1]

However, no area of logic is free from paradoxes. One of the main impulses at the beginnings of alethic modal logic was a certain sort of discomfort with material implication – for example, the rather counterintuitive consequence that stems from tautologies such as $(p \rightarrow q) \vee (q \rightarrow p)$. But these new developments in modal logic did not generate a skeptical attitude toward it; instead, they were regarded as opportunities for clarifying the properties of logic itself. And in fact, the same goes for deontic logic: from a technical point of view, paradoxes provided a decisive impetus toward sharpening the basic concepts of deontic logic. Thus, even if some of these paradoxes expose serious obstacles for deontic systems, their discussion, as much as the answers that have been offered for each of them, made a significant contribution to the progress of this area of logic. As Russell rightly noticed, paradoxes and puzzles play a crucial role in testing a logical theory.[2]

The expression "paradox" is used in this context in a rather loose sense.[3] Some of the so-called paradoxes of deontic logic are no more than counterintuitive results emerging from possible interpretations of valid formulas of deontic systems. That seems to be the case with Prior's paradox of derived

---

[1] Rescher 1966: 7.
[2] See Russell 1905.
[3] On the concept of paradox, see Sainsbury 1987.

obligations and McLaughlin's paradox.[4] By contrast, others are rather genuine paradoxes in a strict sense – that is, they generate logical contradictions from sets of seemingly consistent premises, such as Chisholm's paradox of contrary-to-duty obligations.[5] Here we do not try to offer an exhaustive presentation of them all.[6] Instead, we restrict our attention to some of the most famous cases, with particular attention to those that pose specific problems for the application of deontic logic to legal theory.

2.1.1. *Ross's Paradox*

In propositional calculus p is equivalent to $(p \lor q) \land (p \lor \sim q)$; thus, in the standard system of deontic logic, applying the extensionality rule, Op is equivalent to $O((p \lor q) \land (p \lor \sim q))$. With the aid of the principle of distribution for the O-operator $(O(p \land q) \leftrightarrow (Op \land Oq))$, we obtain $Op \leftrightarrow (O(p \lor q) \land O(p \lor \sim q))$, from which the following implication is derivable:

(1) $Op \rightarrow O(p \lor q)$[7]

Ross's paradox, taking its name from the Danish philosopher Alf Ross, is concerned with this theorem, for which Ross offered the following problematic reading: "If it is obligatory to mail the letter, it is obligatory to mail the letter or burn it."[8] This sounds rather odd given that the obligation to mail the letter or burn it is undoubtedly fulfilled by burning the letter. But by burning the letter we violate the obligation to mail it. Therefore, it seems that the obligation to mail the letter or burn it cannot be logically derivable from the obligation to mail it.

Ross's Paradox has inspired many articles, and although some theorists, such as von Wright[9] and Weinberger,[10] have taken it as a serious challenge for deontic systems, many others disqualify it as a genuine objection. The fundamental reason for this latter attitude is that the fact that by burning the letter we comply with the obligation to mail the letter or burn it, but violate the obligation to mail it, does not allow concluding that the former obligation does not follow logically from the latter. If someone mails a letter, she complies with the obligation to mail the letter, and thus, in virtue of the rules of ordinary propositional logic, also complies with the obligation to mail the letter or

---

4   See below 2.1.3.
5   See below 2.2.2; Nute and Yu 1997: 3–7.
6   For an excellent technical analysis of deontic paradoxes, see Åqvist 1984: 161 ff.
7   See von Wright 1968: 20.
8   See Ross 1941.
9   See von Wright 1968: 21–22.
10 See Weinberger 2001: 138.

burn it. But from this it does not follow, in virtue of any logic (propositional or deontic), that burning the letter is obligatory, or even permitted. In other words, the possibility to derive $O(p\vee q)$ from Op in no way implies that we are allowed to say anything concerning the deontic status of q alone; in fact, q might be obligatory, forbidden, or facultative.

In a similar line of thought, Føllesdal and Hilpinen claim that Ross's paradox disappears in a proper interpretation of the semantics of the standard system of deontic logic. According to it, the paradox only proves that if "p is true in all deontically perfect worlds, $p\vee q$ is also true in all deontically perfect worlds. This is no more paradoxical than the fact that $p\vee q$ is a logical consequence of p."[11] Héctor Neri Castañeda defends the same idea when he writes that "there is . . . no paradox, only confusion between the disjunctive character of a practical thought content and the existence of a genuine choice of courses of action."[12] $O(p\vee q)$ only implies that to observe such a disjunctive obligation, it is necessary to instantiate $p\vee q$. Therefore, this difficulty would be at least partially related to the fact that logical connectives are purely extensional and, thus, do not reflect exactly the meanings of their counterparts in natural language.[13]

2.1.2. *Paradox of Derived Obligation*

By substituting p with $\sim p$ in Ross's paradox, we get $O\sim p\to O(\sim p\vee q)$. Now, from the definition of material implication in terms of disjunction and the extensionality rule, we get in the standard system:

(2) $O\sim p\to O(p\to q)$

Prior's paradox of derived obligation is related to this theorem.[14] The story goes that in his 1951 paper on deontic logic, von Wright claimed that the formula $O(p\to q)$ could be understood as representing *normative commitment* (i.e., that the performance of p commits us to perform q). Against this idea, Prior observed that $O\sim p\to O(p\to q)$ implies the counterintuitive assertion that to do a forbidden act would commit us to do any other act. In an example, "If it is forbidden to kill a person, then it is obligatory that if I kill her, then I steal something from her."[15]

Another possible formulation is the following. Let p mean "John Doe impregnates Suzy Mae," and q "John Doe marries Suzy Mae." Under that

---

[11] Føllesdal and Hilpinen 1971: 22.
[12] Castañeda 1981: 64–5.
[13] See Soeteman, 1989: 116.
[14] See Prior 1954.
[15] See Prior 1954.

reading, the formula under consideration would yield the validity of the following sentence: "If it is obligatory that John Doe not impregnate Suzy Mae, then it is obligatory that if John Doe impregnates Suzy Mae, John Doe marries Suzy Mae." Now, as q in $O{\sim}p{\to}O(p{\to}q)$ is any proposition whatsoever, it could also be read as "John Doe does not marry Suzy Mae," in which case the following sentence would also be true: "If it is obligatory that John Doe not impregnate Suzy Mae, then it is obligatory that if John Doe impregnates Suzy Mae, John Doe does not marry Suzy Mae," which seems in some sense contradictory to the previous interpretation. Even worse, if we read q as "John Doe kills Suzy Mae," we would also have: "If it is obligatory that John Doe not impregnate Suzy Mae, then it is obligatory that if John Doe impregnates Suzy Mae, John Doe kills Suzy Mae."

The formula (2) is a consequence of the O-necessitation rule applied to the valid PC formula ${\sim}p{\to}(p{\to}q)$. As in PC, it is also valid that $p{\to}(q{\to}p)$, the following formula also holds in the standard system of deontic logic:

(3) $Op \to O(q \to p)$

Reading here p as "John Doe marries Suzy Mae" and q as "John Doe kills Suzy Mae," this leads to admit the validity of the implausible consequence: "If it is obligatory that John Doe marries Suzy Mae, then it is obligatory that if John Doe kills Suzy Mae, John Doe marries Suzy Mae," which seems to contradict the principle that *ought* implies *can*.

It is important to recall that Prior did not conclude from the statement of the paradox that von Wright's original system (the same could be said of the standard system) had counterintuitive consequences, and for that reason should be abandoned. Instead, his own conclusion was that normative commitment could not be properly represented as $O(p{\to}q)$.

Prior's paradox and Ross's paradox are intimately connected to the paradoxes of material implication of PC. Hence, many scholars have suggested that their apparently odd conclusions lie in the ambiguities of normative expressions in natural language.[16] In the case of Prior's paradox, $O(p{\to}q)$ cannot be taken as equivalent to the conditional expression "If p then it is obligatory that q"; instead, as we saw, $O(p{\to}q)$ is equivalent to $O({\sim}p{\vee}q)$, and consequently Prior's paradox is no more than an alternative formulation of Ross's. For this reason, and following this tendency to deprive the paradox of its counterintuitive force, Åqvist has claimed that if we stick to the strict meaning of material implications "and, most importantly, do not 'read into' them anything 'beyond' it, their counterintuitive appearance will simply vanish."[17]

[16] See Nute and Yu 1997: 3–7.
[17] See Åqvist 1984: 183; see also Hintikka 1971: 88.

2.1.3. *McLaughlin's Paradox*

We have seen that in the standard system of deontic logic it is possible to derive $Op \rightarrow O(p \lor q)$. By transposition of this formula, $\sim O(p \lor q) \rightarrow \sim Op$ is obtained. Applying the definition of the P-operator in terms of the O-operator, we get $P \sim (p \lor q) \rightarrow P \sim p$. Now, as in PC, $\sim(p \lor q)$ is equivalent to $\sim p \land \sim q$, it is easy to derive:

(4) $P(p \land q) \rightarrow Pp$

and, similarly, $P(p \land q) \rightarrow Pq$.

Let p be read as walking in a public place and q as wearing clothes. Then $P(p \land q) \rightarrow Pp$ could be interpreted, as McLaughlin suggests,[18] as: "If walking in a public place and wearing clothes is permitted, then walking in a public place is permitted." But this seems to imply that walking in a public place is permitted even if clothes are not worn!

McLaughlin assumes in this inference an inadmissible interpretation of the P-operator, and that generates the apparently counterintuitive conclusion. Even though from $P(p \land q)$ it follows Pp, from this it is not possible to derive $P(p \land \sim q)$. The reason for this is that an authorization to perform p does not mean that p may be performed in any way. "Parking in this place is allowed" means that an action describable as parking in the indicated place, as such, is not prohibited. But it would be absurd to suppose that such authorization involves an equal authorization to park in that place a vehicle loaded with explosives.[19] Thus, as von Wright remarks, "the fact that an act is permitted does not mean that doing it in conjunction with anything were permitted."[20]

2.1.4. *Free Choice Permission Paradox*

In a common understanding of the phrase "it is permitted," the formula $P(p \lor q)$ seems to imply $Pp \land Pq$. If someone says, "It is permitted to work or to study," this ordinarily means that the norm-addressee has an authorization to study *and* also to work.[21] Von Wright calls the disjunctive permission for which it holds that each alternative is permitted *free choice permission*, and *paradoxes of free choice permission* to the difficulties related to the formula:

(5) $P(p \lor q) \rightarrow (Pp \land Pq)$

---

[18]   See McLaughlin 1955.
[19]   See Soeteman 1989: 110.
[20]   von Wright 1956: 508.
[21]   See von Wright 1968: 21–26.

Nonetheless, this formula is not a theorem in the standard system of deontic logic. And in case it were admitted as valid, it would lead to unacceptable consequences, because within the standard system the axiom or theorem $Op \rightarrow Pp$ is also accepted. Additionally, we have seen that in the standard system it is possible to derive $Op \rightarrow O(p \lor q)$. Therefore, from Op we would get $O(p \lor q)$; from $O(p \lor q)$ it is possible to derive $P(p \lor q)$; if this permission is interpreted as a free choice permission, we would get $Pp \land Pq$; and from $Pp \land Pq$, by simplification, we obtain Pq. Thus, we would have $Op \rightarrow Pq$ (i.e., that if something is obligatory, then any other thing is permitted). This is absurd, and has the additional consequence that in such case nothing can be obligatory.[22]

The problem might be solved by claiming that although the permission $P(p \lor q)$ usually concurs with the conjunction $Pp \land Pq$, this is not a logical need. Nevertheless, this answer is not completely satisfactory, for there is an evident connection between this paradox and Ross's paradox; it is because in ordinary systems of deontic logic the apparently counterintuitive formula $Op \rightarrow O(p \lor q)$ is provable that the intuitively reasonable formula $P(p \lor q) \rightarrow (Pp \land Pq)$ cannot be accepted.

Consequently, there should be a system of deontic logic in which permission has the character of a free choice permission, but in such a system the formula that gives rise to Ross's paradox should not be validated, because that would lead to absurd results. To show that such a system is possible, von Wright explored different concepts of permission and obligation to prove that paradoxes such as the one examined here are nothing but the product of a confusion of some of those different concepts.[23]

2.2. MORE SERIOUS CHALLENGES

2.2.1. *Good Samaritan Paradoxes*

There is a family of paradoxes known as the Good Samaritan paradoxes. In Prior's original version, it can be presented as follows:[24]

(1) It is forbidden to rob anyone.
(2) If the Good Samaritan helps one who has been robbed, then someone has been robbed. Therefore,

---

[22] $Op \rightarrow Pq$ implies $Op \rightarrow P{\sim}p$; additionally, $Op \leftrightarrow {\sim}P{\sim}p$ implies $Op \rightarrow {\sim}P{\sim}p$. Both conjoint derivations are equivalent to $Op \rightarrow (P{\sim}p \land {\sim}P{\sim}p)$, which by PC implies ${\sim}Op$.

[23] See von Wright 1968: 24.

[24] See Prior 1958.

(3) It is forbidden that the Good Samaritan helps the one who has been robbed.

The most problematic version of this group of paradoxes was presented by Forrester, and is known as the Gentle Murder paradox.[25] Consider these statements:

(4) It is obligatory that Smith not kill Jones.
(5) If Smith does kill Jones, then it is obligatory that Smith kill him gently.
(6) Smith does kill Jones.
(7) That Smith kills Jones gently implies that Smith does kill Jones.

If p stands for "Smith kills Jones gently" and q for "Smith does kill Jones," a possible formalization of these four statements would be:

(4') $O \sim q$
(5') $q \rightarrow Op$
(6') q
(7') $p \rightarrow q$

Here (7') represents a stronger conditional (strict conditional) than the simple material conditional. Now, from (5') and (6') it follows:

(8) Op

From (7') and the inheritance principle (i.e., if $\vdash p \rightarrow q$, then $\vdash Op \rightarrow Oq$), it follows:

(9) $Op \rightarrow Oq$

And from (4'), (8) and (9), it follows:

(10) $O \sim q \land Oq$

But (10) contradicts the principle of deontic consistency $\sim(Op \land O \sim p)$, and if we apply the equivalent implication $Op \rightarrow \sim O \sim p$ to (10), we obtain a genuine contradiction:

(11) $Oq \land \sim Oq$[26]

---

[25] See Forrester 1984.

[26] Another well-known paradox related to this group was presented by Åqvist, known as the *paradox of epistemic obligation*, and is based on the principle that knowledge implies truth: (1) It is obligatory for the police to know that Smith has robbed Jones; (2) If the police knows that Smith has robbed Jones, then Smith has robbed Jones. Therefore, (3) It is obligatory that Smith robs Jones. See Åqvist 1967.

The approaches that try to offer a solution to the gentle murder paradox, and more generally to all the Good Samaritan paradoxes, have taken fundamentally two different paths. Many authors try to dissolve these paradoxes by pointing that the grammatical structures involved in their premises are ambiguous, specifically in relation to the scope of the deontic operators in them. In this sense, it has been indicated that the deontic operator in a statement such as "Smith kills Jones gently" should only affect "gently," but not "kill."[27] Sinnott-Armstrong, for instance, formalizes (5) as:

(5") $\exists x(Mxsj) \rightarrow \exists x(Mxsj \land OGx)$

instead of

(5"') $\exists x(Mxsj) \rightarrow O\exists x(Mxsj \land Gx)$

Here, quantification operates over acts, $Mxsj$ represents the killing of Jones by Smith, and Gx the gentle character of the act. According to (5"), what is obligatory is merely the gentle character of the act and not the act of killing itself, and thus the conclusion that it is obligatory that Smith kill Jones is avoided.

Nevertheless, this kind of approach has not received unanimous approval. Several authors agree in diagnosing that the problem here is attributed to the acceptance of the inheritance principle (if $\vdash p \rightarrow q$, then $\vdash Op \rightarrow Oq$).[28] In fact, this principle seems to play an important role in some of the other paradoxes already noted, such as Ross's paradox or Prior's paradox of derived obligation, because both $Op \rightarrow O(p \lor q)$ and $O{\sim}p \rightarrow O(p \rightarrow q)$ may be taken as consequences of the PC tautologies $p \rightarrow (p \lor q)$ and ${\sim}p \rightarrow (p \rightarrow q)$, and the application of the inheritance principle in deontic logic. The importance of this principle for deontic paradoxes was summarized by von Wright when he claimed that in a deontic logic that rejected the left to right implication of the equivalence $O(p \land q) \leftrightarrow (Op \land Oq)$, but preserving the implication from right to left, the paradoxes would not appear. In virtue of the inter-substitutivity of equivalent sentences, the left to right implication of that equivalence is identical with the inheritance principle.[29]

However, the problem with this proposal is that the inheritance principle has a strong intuitive appeal, because it merely seems to demand that agents take responsibility for the consequences of what they have committed to do.[30]

[27] See Sinnott-Armstrong 1985; see also Castañeda 1986.
[28] See Jackson 1985; Hansson 1988, 2001: 141.
[29] See Hansson 2001: 142–143.
[30] See Nute and Yu 1997: 3–7.

2.2.2. *Contrary-to-Duty Paradoxes*

A paradox of deontic logic that probably has received more attention in the specialized literature than any other is related to the so-called contrary-to-duty obligations[31] – that is, those that arise whenever another obligation has been violated. The most famous of them is Chisholm's paradox,[32] which may be presented by the following set of sentences:[33]

(12) It ought to be that a certain man goes to the assistance of his neighbors.
(13) It ought to be that if he does go, he tells them he is coming.
(14) If he does not go, then he ought not to tell them he is coming.
(15) He does not go.

This set of sentences seems, at least at first sight, non-redundant and consistent. A possible formalization of it according to the standard system of deontic logic is the following:

(12') Op
(13') $O(p \rightarrow q)$
(14') $\sim p \rightarrow O \sim q$
(15') $\sim p$

However, because Oq is derivable from (12') and (13'), and from (14') and (15') we get $O \sim q$, this set allows to derive the conjunction $Oq \wedge O \sim q$, which contradicts the principle of deontic consistency. Of course, an alternative way to symbolize the sentences is either to replace (13') with:

(13") $p \rightarrow Oq$

or to replace (14') with:

(14") $O(\sim p \rightarrow \sim q)$

In either case, $Oq \wedge O \sim q$ is no longer derivable. However, (13") is a trivial consequence of (15'), and (14") is a trivial consequence of (12') – in each case by a different application of the principle ex falso sequitur quodlibet $((p \wedge \sim p) \rightarrow q)$ – and this contradicts the intuitive non-redundancy of the set

---

[31] See Carmo and Jones 2002: 265–343; Hilpinen 2001: 168–173; Makinson and Van der Torre: 2000 and 2001.
[32] McNamara writes: "[I]f von Wright launched deontic logic as an academic specialization, Chisholm's Paradox was the booster rocket that provided the escape velocity deontic logic needed from subsumption under normal modal logics, thus solidifying deontic logic's status as a distinct specialization" (McNamara 2006: 241).
[33] See Chisholm 1963.

(12) through (15). Hence, it seems that the standard system of deontic logic has no resources to represent the original set of sentences in a way that preserves both its consistency and non-redundancy.

The fundamental problem this paradox exposes consists in the difficulties involved in the formalization of conditional norms. In the standard system of deontic logic there are two obvious candidates: $O(p{\rightarrow}q)$ and $p{\rightarrow}Oq$, and each validates without restrictions a different form of modus ponens: $(O(p{\rightarrow}q) \wedge Op) \rightarrow Oq$ and $((p{\rightarrow}Oq) \wedge p) \rightarrow Oq$, respectively. Thus, different strategies have been suggested to restrict these forms of inference so as to avoid contradictions such as the one Chisholm's paradox reveals.[34]

The challenges involved in these, as well as in a number of other paradoxes we have not surveyed here, have generated several refinements and alternative proposals to the standard system of deontic logic. Yet, it seems fair to conclude that those paradoxes that have received more attention basically put in question: (1) the interdefinability of permission in terms of prohibition and obligation – and the very characterization of permission, (2) the principle of deontic consistency, (3) the representation of conditional norms, and (4) the inheritance principle.

In the next chapter, we have much more to say regarding the first three problems; therefore, we add nothing more about them at this time. Suffice it to advance now that we intend to show that the difficulties involved in the interdefinability between deontic operators and the objections raised against the principle of deontic consistency can be clarified by taking into account the difference between a genuine logic of norms and a logic of norm-propositions, and that the problems in the representation of conditional norms lose at least part of their strength if different concepts of "conditional duties" are distinguished, validating each of them different forms of inference.

Concerning the inheritance principle, Sven Ove Hansson has observed that its acceptance in the standard system of deontic logic is a consequence of conceptualizing deontic logic by reference to a set of deontically ideal worlds, in the sense defined in the previous chapter.[35] Because in a normatively ideal world nobody would do anything wrong, nobody will have to avoid wrongdoings or compensate potential victims of wrongdoings. Thus, if we shape our obligations in the actual world by reference to ideal worlds, our actual obligations to avoid wrongdoings or to compensate victims of our wrongdoings will

---

[34] Contrary to the suggestion in the text, Prakken and Sergot argue that contrary-to-duty obligations are not instances of defeasible or non-monotonic reasoning. See Prakken and Sergot 1996.

[35] See Hansson 2006.

lack an adequate ground. Therefore, information about ideal worlds would be insufficient for determining what our obligations are, and focusing our attention exclusively on ideal worlds would have counterintuitive consequences for deontic logic, as Ross's, Prior's, Åqvist's, and the Good Samaritan paradoxes show.

Hansson suggests that for an adequate determination of our obligations we should also take into account sub-ideal worlds, because the sole reference to deontically ideal worlds would recommend us to act as if we actually lived in that kind of world, and that would not always be good advice.[36]

It seems uncontroversial that the standard system of deontic logic, with its semantic interpretation in terms of deontically ideal worlds, cannot give an adequate account of all the subtleties of normative discourse, in particular of our obligations in sub-ideal circumstances. By reference to ideal worlds there is no chance to represent obligations that stem from the failure to comply with other obligations. Nonetheless, this is still not a sufficient reason to disqualify the recourse to deontically ideal worlds, or to abandon the standard system altogether. This framework is useful to give a reasonably adequate explanation of at least a first level of intuitions concerning the logical relations between norms – interdefinability between deontic operators, the idea that obligation implies permission, the distributivity of deontic operators over disjunctions and conjunctions, and so on. Moreover, the necessity to consider sub-ideal worlds is not only insufficient to disqualify normatively ideal worlds, but rather presupposes some previous notion of ideality. Hence, the argument shows the need of greater complexity and refinement, not of a change of framework.[37]

In fact, the inheritance principle is a consequence of the rule of inference of the standard system known as the O-necessitation rule (i.e., $\vdash p$, then $\vdash Op$) and the axiom KO, according to which $O(p{\rightarrow}q) \rightarrow (Op{\rightarrow}Oq)$. Now, the axiom KO is an intuitive application of modus ponens in deontic logic, and has not been the object of serious attacks. By contrast, the O-necessitation rule has indeed been hotly debated, because its acceptance commits us to accept that every tautology is obligatory and every contradictory state of affairs is forbidden. As we have already seen, in von Wright's original system, he adopted the principle of deontic contingency, and thus, rejected this rule.[38] And later he claimed that the incorporation of a deontic rule of necessitation seemed to him "highly counterintuitive, sheer nonsense."[39]

---

[36] See Hansson 2006: 332–333.
[37] In Chapter 3, we see that an adequate way to deal with at least one sense of subideality is to distinguish a logic of norms and a logic of norm-propositions.
[38] See von Wright 1951a; also, Prior 1955: 222.
[39] von Wright 1983: 105.

In any case, this pessimistic attitude has to face the strong reasons that also have been offered to support the validity of $O(p \vee \sim p)$ – or, equivalently, $\sim P(p \wedge \sim p)$ – as well as the O-necessitation rule.[40] As Soeteman shows, the contingency of $\sim P(p \wedge \sim p)$ leads to problematic consequences. He claims that, were $\sim P(p \wedge \sim p)$ invalid, $P(p \wedge \sim p)$ would be valid. Because q is propositionally equivalent to $q \vee (p \wedge \sim p)$, Pq is equivalent to $P(q \vee (p \wedge \sim p))$. By the principle of distribution of the P-operator over disjunction, this is equivalent to $Pq \vee P(p \wedge \sim p)$. As we assumed that $P(p \wedge \sim p)$ is valid, $Pq \vee P(p \wedge \sim p)$ will also be valid, and consequently Pq itself will be valid, because it is equivalent to that disjunction. Therefore, the validity of $P(p \wedge \sim p)$ commits us to accept that all random acts will be permitted and, thus, nothing will be prohibited. Additionally, the adoption of $\sim P(p \wedge \sim p)$ (or $O(p \vee \sim p)$) as an axiom in deontic logic would be completely harmless because by logical necessity we have no option but to obey the obligation to perform tautologous acts and the prohibition to perform contradictory acts.[41]

Be that as it may, the fact is that all these doubts concerning the inheritance principle and the O-necessitation rule are ultimately doubts concerning the scope and strength of the analogies between deontic logic and alethic logic. Perhaps the main philosophical assumption that underlines those analogies is the following: Applying a modal operator such as N to a proposition p produces another proposition (Np) and, consequently, applying a deontic operator such as O to a proposition p should also result in another proposition (Op). But then norms would be proposition-like entities! However, if norms were not propositions, what would be the "nature" of deontic logic? How could we justify the claim that a norm N_1 logically entails another norm N_2? It is time to turn to these questions.

2.3. FACING JØRGENSEN'S DILEMMA

The paradoxes we have briefly noted in the preceding sections are not the only difficulties deontic logic has to face. As already seen, the very possibility of deontic logic has been put into question. Soeteman rightly claims that if validity means that the truth of the conclusion of an argument follows necessarily from the truth of its premises, and norms are neither true nor false, the very possibility of normative reasoning is controversial.[42] This is just another way to formulate Jørgensen's dilemma[43]: under the assumption that norms are neither true nor false, either the notion of logical consequence, and

[40] See, for instance, Stenius 1963: 253; Anderson 1956: 181–183; Åqvist 1984: 157.
[41] See Soeteman 1989: 101. For a counterargument, see Woleński 1990: 280–281.
[42] See Soeteman 1989: 47.
[43] See Jørgensen 1937–8: 288–296.

logical connectives, are defined in terms of truth, and there is no possibility for a logic of norms; or a logic of norms is possible, but then the notion of logical consequence as well as the logical connectives should not be defined in terms of truth.[44]

Jørgensen's dilemma is the most significant philosophical problem of deontic logic. In Makinson's words, the "fundamental problem of deontic logic" is to offer a reconstruction of deontic logic taking due account of the idea that norms are devoid of truth-values.[45] And like any other dilemma, it leaves open three alternatives to face it. The first consists in accepting the consequences of the first horn and recognizing that deontic reasoning is only an appearance of logical reasoning, giving an adequate explanation of this appearance.[46] Alternatively, we may assume the second horn and try to show that deontic logic is possible because of the fact that logic extends beyond the realm of truth. Or, finally, we may reject the assumption that gives rise to the dilemma and accept that norms are, after all, capable of truth-values.

The first alternative can be exemplified by Hans Kelsen's posthumous book, *General Theory of Norms*, which constitutes one of the best examples of deontic skepticism in legal theory.[47] Like many other philosophers, Kelsen was ambivalent about the possibility of deontic logic. In an early stage of his philosophical production, Kelsen believed that this new branch of logic would be an adequate ground for his ideas on coherence and completeness of law,[48] but later – especially after 1960 – he rejected the possibility of a genuine logic of norms.[49] More than one half of his *General Theory of Norms* is, directly or indirectly, concerned with the possibility of a logic of norms, and Kelsen devotes several pages to criticize a wide range of philosophers who tried to justify such an endeavor. According to Hartney,[50] Kelsen's criticism focused on four proposals: (1) the equivalence between prescriptions and ordinary statements (Klug, Bohnert); (2) the idea that a logic of norms is possible to the extent that it focuses on the descriptive contents of norms (Wellman, Moritz,

---

[44] "According to a generally accepted definition of logical inference, only sentences which are capable of being true or false can function as premises or conclusions in an inference; nevertheless it seems evident that a conclusion in the imperative mood may be drawn from two premises, one of which or both of which are in the imperative mood" (Jørgensen 1937–8: 290). Although Jørgensen only discussed imperatives, his worries may be extended to norms and normative reasoning in general.

[45] See Makinson 1999: 30.

[46] For a thorough analysis of the different alternatives to overcome Jørgensen's dilemma, see Soeteman 1989: chapters 3 and 4.

[47] See Kelsen 1979: 211–270.

[48] See von Wright 1985: 269.

[49] See Hartney 1991; Paulson 1992: 265–274.

[50] See Hartney 1991: xlv–xlvii.

Ayer, and others); (3) the suggestion that there is a correspondence between prescriptions and a certain type of descriptive statements, and that logic can be indirectly applied to prescriptions (Dubislav, Frey, and others), and (4) the substitution for "truth" of other predicates such as "satisfaction" (Hofstadter and McKinsey) or "validity" (Klug, Schreiber).

We do not recite here the details of Kelsen's discussion but concentrate on his main arguments against deontic logic. Those arguments focus on two problems: the principle of contradiction and the rules of inference in deontic logic. Kelsen maintains, on the one hand, that if the principle of contradiction were applicable to norms, then two conflicting norms could not be valid in the same system. This conclusion parallels the results that contradictions produce in (propositional) logic – that is, a proposition and its negation cannot both be true. In the case of normative discourse, this would mean that *for logical reasons* one of the conflicting norms cannot be a valid norm. On the other hand, if classical rules of inference were applied to norms, from the validity of a certain general norm plus a given set of facts, the validity of a particular norm would be derivable in a normative system.

However, after the second edition of his *Pure Theory of Law*, Kelsen embraced a sort of "normative irrationalism"[51]: logic cannot be applied to norms. This deontic skepticism is based on the assumption that norms lack truth-values, reinforced in the case of legal norms by an ontological argument. According to Kelsen, legal norms are positive norms: they are created by authorities to regulate human behavior. Therefore, the validity of legal norms (i.e., their specific existence as norms) requires the performance of certain acts of prescription. Insofar as there is no *ought* without a *will*, individual norms must also be established by an act of will (i.e., a prescription). Unlike factual statements – which remain true or false even if they are not stated by anybody – an *act* of will mediates between the validity of a general norm and the validity of an individual norm derivable from it. Even if it were true that all thieves must be imprisoned, and that Schulze is a thief, the individual norm "Schulze must be imprisoned" would not be legally valid without an adjudicative decision.[52]

Kelsen's logical argument reproduces Jørgensen's dilemma in the legal domain:

(1) Logic presupposes truth-values.
(2) Legal norms are neither true nor false.
(3) Logic does not apply to legal norms.

---

[51] This expression was coined by Weinberger (see, Weinberger 1986: 194).
[52] For an illuminating discussion on both arguments, see Hartney 1991: xlii–liii.

On the other hand, his ontological argument may be summarized as follows:

(1') Legal norms depend on an act of will for their validity.

(2') Individual legal norms, although logically derivable from general norms plus certain facts, are not valid without an institutional decision.

(3') Logic does not apply to legal norms.

Although both arguments lead to the same conclusion, it is clear that the first is plainly independent from the second. Moreover, as Hartney rightly claims, even if the "ontological argument" were sound, it would provide no support for Kelsen's deontic skepticism, because whereas the question whether logic applies to norms is a question of logic, the question whether the existence of one norm entails the existence of another is not.[53]

Therefore, beyond Jørgensen's logical argument, there are no compelling reasons in Kelsen's *General Theory of Norms* in favor of his deontic skepticism. In fact, even Kelsen seems to be committed to recognize something like an underlying logic of norms, for at least three reasons. First, Kelsen stresses the differences between static and dynamic normative systems. In Kelsen's characterization, static normative systems involve the possibility of deriving the content of one norm from the content of another, which amounts to a logical inference.[54] Thus, Kelsen cannot reject logical relations among norms and, at the same time, claim that some systems (e.g., moral systems) are static normative systems.[55] Second, Kelsen is forced to accept the possibility of at least some logical relations among norms if they are to fulfill any guiding function. For instance, if someone states that no one should intentionally kill another being, she is also saying that no one should intentionally kill another being on working days. The issue at stake here is the meaning of those sentences by which an act of will is expressed. At this level, an expression of will is abstracted from the factual psychological act of will. By contrast, Kelsen's rejection of logical relations among norms deprives general norms of any direct guiding function.[56] Third, Kelsen in fact seems to admit logical relations between norms, at least between two general norms that differ exclusively in their degree of generality, where the most general implies the less general.[57]

To avoid deontic skepticism, with its counterintuitive consequences – we do infer norms from other norms – several proposals have been offered in

---

[53] See Hartney 1991: xliv.

[54] See Kelsen 1960: 195–196.

[55] For an interesting discussion of this problem in Kelsen's writings, see the contributions published in Gianformaggio 1991.

[56] See Hartney 1991: xlix–l.

[57] See Kelsen 1979: 249.

contemporary deontic logic to show that norms, although incapable of truth-values, admit other bivalent values that make logical relations possible among them. Here is a brief sketch of some the most salient ideas of this line of thought.

2.3.1. *Satisfaction*

As we have seen in Chapter 1, logical consequence is usually explained in terms of the hereditary property of truth. In classical logic, the relation of logical consequence is considered truth-preserving (i.e., a sound reasoning guarantees in the conclusion the truth of its premises). Some philosophers have claimed that, although norms are not capable of truth-values, there are other hereditary properties that can display a similar role than truth in normative reasoning, such as satisfaction.[58]

Following Ross, in a logic of satisfaction the logical values ascribed to norms are "satisfied" and "not-satisfied," which correspond respectively to the values "true" and "false,"[59] and a norm is said to be satisfied when the proposition describing the required action is true. For instance, Op is satisfied when p is true.[60]

Statements of satisfaction are ordinary propositions that assign a factual property to a certain norm; they are not normative statements, but descriptions of the fact that norms are satisfied. This parallelism between statements of satisfaction and indicatives was taken by some authors as an adequate ground for defining the relation of consequence between norms. For example, according to Hofstadter and McKinsey – the pioneers of the attempt to build deontic logic on the idea of satisfaction – $O(p \lor q)$ follows logically from Op because of the *satisfaction* of $O(p \lor q)$ in all worlds in which Op is satisfied.[61] In other words, relations between norms are relations between the satisfactions of those norms.

Although a system such as this is perfectly conceivable and sound, there is a huge difference between *a logic of the satisfaction of norms* and a genuine *logic of norms*. A few examples will be enough to illustrate what we mean:[62]

(i) In spite of the strong analogies between alethic modal logic and deontic logic, a point at which both fields diverge is in the different relations between

---

[58] This opinion has been defended by many authors. Apart from the ones mentioned here; see, for example, von Wright 1983; Schreiber 1962: 108–113; Klug in Kelsen-Klug 1981: 66.

[59] In the case of general norms, the absolute concept of satisfaction defined here is usually replaced by the weaker and gradual notion of *effectiveness*, understood as "the fact that a rule . . . which requires certain behavior is obeyed more often than not" (Hart 1961: 103).

[60] See Ross 1968: 174 ff.

[61] See Hofstadter and Mckinsey 1939.

[62] See Soeteman 1989: 80–81.

states of affairs and modalities, alethic and deontic: whereas Np implies p, and p implies Mp, it would be odd to assume in a logic of norms that whatever is obligatory is in fact the case, or that whatever is the case is permitted. Thus, neither Op should imply p, nor p should imply Pp.

Now, the logic of satisfaction reverses, without preserving any reasonable intuition, the relations that hold between alethic modalities and states of affairs. Because in case p is true, Op is satisfied, in the logic of satisfaction p implies Op, and by transposition, $\sim Op$ implies $\sim p$, which is tantamount to saying that Pp implies p. Moreover, by transitivity Pp implies Op, conversely of what seems wise to assume in a logic of norms.

(ii) In a logic of satisfaction, $\sim Op$ is equivalent to $O\sim p$, because when Op is not satisfied, $\sim p$ is performed, and so $O\sim p$ is satisfied, and vice versa. In a logic of norms, by contrast, although $O\sim p \rightarrow \sim Op$ seems acceptable, the converse does not hold: it may be the case that p is not obligatory and $\sim p$ is not obligatory either. In such a case, p would be facultative for the norm-subject. As a result of this, in a logic of satisfaction, there are only two logical possibilities, $Op \lor O\sim p$ (i.e., an action may be obligatory or prohibited); whereas in a logic of norms, we have three alternatives: $Op \lor PHp \lor Fp$.

(iii) In a logic of satisfaction, $Op \lor Oq$ is equivalent to $O(p \lor q)$. But in deontic logic, although $(Op \lor Oq) \rightarrow O(p \lor q)$, the converse does not hold: $O(p \lor q)$ is compatible with $\sim Op$ and $\sim Oq$.

The moral of these remarks seems clear. Satisfaction cannot provide a sound foundation for a proper deontic logic because, as Ross remarks, internal deontic negation, disjunction, and implication distinguish norms from their indicative counterparts.[63] These difficulties are not "internal shortcomings;" instead, they indicate that, irrespective of its merits, an adequate explanation of logical relations among norms cannot be reconstructed through a logic of satisfaction.

2.3.2. *Validity as Binding Force*

Although many philosophers think it abnormal to predicate truth-values of norms,[64] there are other properties usually assigned to them. One salient among such properties is *validity*, which in fact seems to operate as a surrogate of truth in normative discourse. Thus, it is not surprising to find several theoretical efforts to explain logical relations among norms in terms of validity.

---

[63] See Ross 1968: 175.

[64] For example, see von Wright 1957: vii: "Deontic logic gets part of its philosophic significance from the fact that norms and valuations, though removed from the realm of truth, yet are subject to logical law."

Although this conceptual strategy seems to be promising, most of its plausibility derives from the ambiguity of the term "validity." Scholars use "validity" with several meanings, some of which are plainly inadequate as a foundation of a logic of norms. For example, in some of his works, Alf Ross defends a subjective conception of validity, reducing it to psychological facts on the part of the normative authority or on the part of the norm-receiver.[65] Hence, deontic logic is accordingly reduced to a logic for statements concerning the existence of psychological facts. This reduction renders invalid many sound normative forms of inference. For instance, the fact that someone accepts a general norm to the effect that promises should be kept, and the fact that she has made a certain promise, does not guarantee that she will accept the validity of the conclusion that she has to keep her promise, because that is just an empirical matter.[66]

Besides this subjective notion, to evaluate whether "validity" can substitute "truth" as a suitable property to explain logical relations between norms, two other concepts of validity should be clearly distinguished. On the one hand, to say that a norm is valid is sometimes a way to assign *binding force* to it (i.e., to claim that the norm has to be obeyed). On the other hand, validity is also used as a synonym of *membership in a normative system*. Both senses of validity are frequently confused because it is quite natural to assume that a norm is binding if and only if it belongs to a certain normative system. However, we will see that this confusion has been the source of many problems, particularly in legal theory.[67]

Both of the latter two concepts of validity have been employed as explanations of the nature of norms and the possibility of a genuine logic of norms. Let us briefly consider both approaches, beginning with validity as binding force. To claim that a norm is valid in this sense is to endorse a prescription: to prescribe the duty to obey it. Hence, validity as binding force can be seen as a hereditary property similar to "truth" in ordinary (assertoric) reasoning. According to this reconstruction, validity as binding force meets Tarski's convention T for truth, according to which a materially adequate definition of truth should validate all instances of the schema "'p' is true if, and only if, p".[68] Something similar happens with validity as binding force: a norm prescribing that promises must be kept is valid if, and only if, promises must be kept.[69]

---

[65] Ross 1941.
[66] See Soeteman 1989: 54.
[67] See Chapter 4.
[68] See Tarski 1931.
[69] See Celano 1999: 35–77.

The question to pose here is whether predicating validity in this sense of a given norm is different from predicating truth of it. For instance, Soeteman argues that a normative judgment is valid if: (1) it is tautological; (2) it is contingent and valid according to a material standard of validity; or (3) it can be deduced from valid normative judgments, whether or not together with true alethic statements.[70] But he defines a tautological statement as a statement that is true irrespective of how its non-logical terms are interpreted.[71] So it is not quite clear how this can be taken as a "replacement" of "truth" by "validity," for even if the words are different, this amounts to the assumption that deontic logic is possible because norms can be true or false.[72]

2.3.3. *Validity as Membership in a Normative System*

An alternative use of "validity" is to identify it with membership in a normative system. Membership is a *relation* between an individual and a set; consequently, validity as membership is also a relational concept: to say that a norm is valid in this sense is to say that it belongs to a given normative system.

In some of his works, Weinberger seems to defend the idea that validity as membership in a normative system can provide an adequate ground for a logic of norms.[73] He claims that validity can be taken as a general concept, applicable both to norms and propositions. In his view, the statement "norm N is valid" means "N belongs to a certain system NS," and the statement "the proposition p is valid" means "p belongs to a propositional system S, and it is true in S." Given this analogy, Weinberger believes that the notion of logical consequence can be defined in terms of this hereditary property as a surrogate of truth.

The problem, however, is that not every hereditary property is able to perform the task that truth plays in logical inferences, and the mere membership in a system cannot guarantee that the relations between the elements that belong to it are logical in character.[74]

---

[70] See Soeteman 1989: 65.
[71] See Soeteman 1989: 7.
[72] See Alchourrón and Martino 1990.
[73] See Weinberger 1981: 97.
[74] As Bulygin argues: "[W]e have no criterion for distinguishing between logical and non-logical or ad-hoc rules of inference, for all of them fulfill Weinberger's requirement: all of them preserve validity and so validity is hereditary in relation to them. But Weinberger quite explicitly rejects certain rules of inference 'Op, so $O(p \lor q)$' or '$O(p \land q)$, so Op.' What are the grounds for this rejection? These rules certainly preserve validity, yet they are rejected as logical rules of inferences" (Bulygin 1985: 156–157).

Perhaps the intuition that Weinberger attempts to articulate is the analogy between truth and validity *in a certain type of system*; a deductive system. Following Tarski, this kind of system can be defined as the entire set of logical consequences of a set of sentences. But in such a case, as Bulygin points out, to say that logical rules preserve the property of being valid would be vacuous, for it is analytic regarding these notions of system and membership. By contrast, to say that logical rules preserve truth is far from being analytic, because truth is defined independently from the notion of a system.[75]

2.3.4. *The Indirect Application of Logic to Norms*

According to the previous analysis, neither satisfaction nor validity, under their different senses, is able to substitute truth as a hereditary property that explains logical relations between norms. Thus, some philosophers and deontic logicians have suggested as a solution to the problem of the foundation of deontic logic the idea that ordinary logic can be "indirectly" applied to norms.[76] As an example of this approach, in the second edition of the *Pure Theory of Law*, Kelsen defended a non-cognitivist conception of norms: norms are conceived of as entities incapable of truth-values. Therefore, he wrote that logic cannot be applied directly to norms, because this discipline only deals with true or false propositions. But although logical principles would not be applicable to norms, they certainly can be applied to the statements that describe norms (like legal statements), and through them indirectly to norms.[77]

This solution to the problem of the foundation of deontic logic rightly distinguishes between norms and propositions about (the existence of) norms (i.e., norm-propositions). Indeed – as we try to show[78] – this distinction is so fundamental that no sound reconstruction of the logical aspects of normative discourse can ignore it. However, the explanation of the differences between norms and norm-propositions is still an open philosophical problem. Kelsen's solution – as well as other philosophical approaches that follow the same path – actually assumes the existence of a strong isomorphism between norms and

---

75 See Bulygin 1985: 157.
76 This is also Jørgensen's solution to Jørgensen's dilemma. In his view, regarding every imperative sentence there is a corresponding indicative sentence, the content of which is that which is ordered by the imperative sentence. Thus, the rules of logic would indirectly apply to imperative sentences through their application to the corresponding indicative sentences. Now, apart from this wishful consideration, it remains obscure how it would be even possible to transpose the logical relations among indicative sentences to imperative ones.
77 See Kelsen 1960: 74.
78 See Chapter 3.

norm-propositions, in the sense that the differences between norms and norm-propositions would only be given by the fact that norm-propositions are either true or false, whereas norms lack truth-values. In other aspects, both discourses would be similar in their relevant logical features. For example, according to Kelsen, a norm-proposition describing a legal norm N such as "If A, ought to be S" would have a conditional structure. Under this view, norm-propositions would be like paraphrasing of norms, and even though they are susceptible of truth-values, they would be descriptive "ought-statements."[79]

However, contrary to Kelsen, it seems plain that a statement that describes a conditional norm does not need to be itself a conditional statement. Although norm N has a conditional structure, the norm-proposition "Norm N is valid in system S" is not a conditional assertion. In fact, if legal norms are conceived of as general norms, no legal statement will have the same structure as the corresponding legal norm; for legal norms will have a universal character, and legal statements describing their membership in a legal system will be existential statements.

The confusion between the logical characteristics of norms and norm-propositions reveals itself more dramatically when Kelsen's solution is projected onto the analysis of normative conflicts. Let NP_1 and NP_2 be norm-propositions that describe, respectively, norms N_1 and N_2. According to Kelsen, both norms would be logically inconsistent if the propositions that describe them were inconsistent. Of course, a pair of inconsistent propositions cannot be both true; however, if the norms N_1 and N_2 are in conflict (e.g., Op and PHp), the propositions that describe their membership in a legal system ("Op belongs to S" and "PHp belongs to S") are perfectly consistent, and if the norm-propositions themselves are in conflict (e.g., "Op belongs to S" and "Op does not belong to S"), they cannot describe a pair of norms in conflict. In other words, it is perfectly possible to provide a consistent description of an inconsistent normative system, and an inconsistent description of a normative system is no reason to think that the system is itself inconsistent.

A more refined proposal that also explores the analogy between descriptive and prescriptive aspects of normative discourse can be found in some of von Wright's works. Von Wright remarks that any deontic statement, such as "it is obligatory to do p," is ambiguous because it may be interpreted as a prescription, but also as a description of a norm in force.[80] For example, the statement "you must not park here" can be either an order issued by

---

[79] For a further examination of this Kelsenian category of descriptive ought, see Chapter 4.
[80] For example, von Wright 1963a: 119.

a competent authority or a proposition that describes the fact that a certain norm has been issued that prohibits parking in that place. In *Norm and Action*, von Wright explores at length this ambiguity and concludes that deontic logic can be seen as a logic for normative expressions interpreted descriptively (norm-propositions).[81]

This approach resembles Kelsen's ideas on the indirect application of logic to norms. Both philosophers focus on the application of logic to descriptions of norms (i.e., norm-propositions), but they clearly differ in their view of the relations between norms, propositions, and logic. Whereas Kelsen believes that logic can be indirectly applied to norms because it is directly applicable to norm-propositions, von Wright argues that the validity of the principles of a logic of norm-propositions actually depends on the logical relations between norms. Another interesting analogy between Kelsen and von Wright is the connection between logic and ontology. Similar to Kelsen, von Wright draws certain conclusions regarding the logic of norms in virtue of certain ontological commitments. For example, the notions of self-consistency and consistency defended by von Wright are plausible only to the extent that the existence of norms is explained as a normative relation between authorities and addressees.

Prescriptions (a specific type of norm) come into existence through normative actions, which can be paradigmatically seen as verbal actions; they consist in the use of deontic statements to regulate behavior. Although prescriptions are formulated in a certain language, the existence of norms must not be confused with the promulgation of a certain norm-formulation. The existence of a prescriptive norm not only depends on normative actions performed by authorities but also requires a certain capacity on the part of the addressees (norm-subjects). Prescriptive norms exist only if the addressee "receives" the norms, in which case a normative relation is established between authorities and subjects.[82] This "ontology" of prescriptive norms has some important consequences. For example, according to von Wright, conflicting norms cannot exist because if someone commands another, for instance, to open the window and leave it closed, one of the commands annihilates the other, so "they cannot exist together 'in logical space.' "[83] However, he also claims that there is no inconsistency between "incompatible" norms created by different authorities.[84] This surprising consequence is not a minor point because the

---

[81] See von Wright 1963a: 151.
[82] See von Wright 1963a: 118.
[83] von Wright 1963a: 148.
[84] See Alchourrón and Bulygin 1989: 676.

idea of deontic logic would be of little interest if there were no normative conflicts.[85]

Like Kelsen's approach, the one suggested by von Wright is infected by confusion between logic and ontology. Therefore, an easy solution would be to abandon the ontological commitments and preserve only the logical reconstruction. However, regardless of other problems stemming from such a solution, von Wright – again, like Kelsen – also assumes a strong and unwarranted isomorphism between the logic of norms and the logic of propositions about norms. However, as we see in the next chapter, this is wrong. Although the logic of norms and the logic of norm-propositions have a strong parallelism, only under certain conditions are they isomorphic.

2.4.1. *Deontic Logic with Truth*

A radical solution to Jørgensen's dilemma is to reject the assumption that constitutes its starting point; that norms do not bear truth-values. Many philosophers – prominently Kalinowski[86] – have argued that norms, as well as value judgments, do have truth-values. Just as certain facts make descriptive statements true or false, there are also "normative facts," more or less independent from our normative beliefs that make norms true or false. Presented in this way, the obvious disadvantage of this proposal is that it grounds deontic logic on a highly controversial ontological assumption.[87]

Special attention within this line of thought deserves to be given the most extended semantic approach to deontic logic (i.e., possible-worlds semantics). Almost all contemporary developments of deontic logic assume this semantic background as an attempt to reconcile truth and norms. According to this, as we have seen, it is possible to predicate truth or falsity of norms, not by reference to the actual world, but in relation to certain possible and ideal worlds that may be understood as those worlds the normative authority intends to actualize. To say that the norm Op is true in the actual world would mean that, in all possible worlds which are normative alternatives to the actual world, it is the case that the duty imposed by the norm is fulfilled.

---

[85] As von Wright himself says, "if no two norms can logically contradict one another, then there can be no logic of norms either. There is no logic, we might say, in a field in which everything is possible" (von Wright 1963a: 148).

[86] See Kalinowski 1967: 149ff.

[87] See Vernengo 1986.

In spite of the elegance and technical fruitfulness of possible-worlds semantics, it also seems to carry with it the heavy weight of strong ontological commitments: the existence of possible worlds as real as the actual world. However,
within the theory of possible worlds, there is still an open controversy concerning what the right answer is to a fundamental problem. It seems that whoever
seriously assumes the idea of possible worlds has to commit herself to the
existence of a plurality of possible worlds but, on the other hand, she also
has to maintain the idea that only one of those worlds is real, and the others
merely possible. Nonetheless, merely possible things do not exist; therefore,
in contradiction to the first idea, only one possible world would exist.[88]

The controversy arises here fundamentally between two positions, which
have been called possibilism and actualism. Both argue that the problem under
consideration derives from a fallacy of equivocation, because the assertions
(1) there are many possible worlds, and (2) only one of them is real, are both true
in a certain sense. Now, each of these positions identifies the equivocation in
different places. According to possibilism, the equivocation rests on the domain
of quantification. The claim that there are many possible worlds would be true
if the domain of the quantifier in this phrase were unrestricted. Nevertheless,
in many occasions, we restrict the domain of quantifiers to proper subsets of
what exists (the things that *really* exist) and, in such cases the statement would
say something different.[89] Following Quine's idea that our ontology depends
on what we decide to recognize as the domain of quantification, from this point
of view all possible worlds exist in the same sense in which the real world exists;
only that the real world is our world. On the contrary, according to actualism,
what exists coincides with what is real, and thus unrestricted quantification is
equivalent to quantification over what is real. The equivocation rests, under
this view, in the class of things to which one refers when using the expression
"possible world." When we say that there are many possible worlds, we would
be referring to possible states of the world, to the different configurations the
world may take. When we say that only one world exists – the actual world –
we would be referring to something that is in one of those possible states.
There are many ways the world might be, and those ways really exist, but only
one of them is instantiated.[90]

As seems evident, possibilism – or modal realism – adopts in fact a robust
ontological assumption: possible worlds exist in the same sense as does the
real world. The "reality" of the actual world would exclusively depend on a

[88] See Stalnaker 2003: 6–7.
[89] See Lewis 1986: 1–50.
[90] See Stalnaker 2003: 7.

restriction on our domain of quantification. Actualism also takes the idea of possible worlds seriously, but does not endorse such heavy ontology. From this perspective, only the actual world exists; alternative possible worlds to the actual world are merely theoretical devices, conceivable representations of how the world might be if it were different from what it is. From this point of view, for example, to say that p is necessarily true in the actual world depends on figuring out how the actual world might be if it were different from the way it is, and that in all those representations p were true, which does not mean assigning any existence at all to other worlds. Consequently, contrary to appearances, the adoption of possible-worlds semantics does not necessarily imply a commitment with any controversial ontology.

Additionally, it should be noted that recourse to the theory of possible worlds as a semantic framework for deontic logic does not inevitably lead to the attribution of truth-values to norms. As we will soon see, this conclusion mainly depends on the conception of norms that we have in mind in our reconstruction of deontic logic.

2.4.2. *Deontic Logic Without Truth*

Another radical solution to the dilemma under consideration is to reject the view that logic is restricted to the domain of truth. In "Deontic Logic," von Wright did not take account of the problem of how a logic of norms could even be possible, in spite of the fact that, because of his philosophical background, he regarded norms as culture-dependent, subjective, and relative, and thus as entities removed from the realm of truth and falsity. He proceeded as if the possibility of building a formal calculus with plausible axioms were the only requirement needed to satisfy the demands of logic. When later he reflected on the problem, his conclusion was "that logic . . . has a wider reach than truth."[91] However, he soon realized that in the absence of a careful foundation, this remark about the wider scope of logic was nothing more than wishful thinking.

However, in one of his final writings on deontic logic, he introduced the idea that deontic logic can be interpreted as a logic for a "rational legislator."[92] Under this reading, logical relations between norms are defined in terms of rational norm-giving activity. Thus, logical incompatibility between a pair of norms (e.g., Op and $O\sim p$, means that a rational authority should not require at the same time both p and $\sim p$). The same idea can explain other logical relations without resorting to the notions of truth and falsity. Consequently,

[91] von Wright 1957: vii.
[92] See von Wright 1983: 132, 140–141.

from this perspective the domain of logic can be extended to non-descriptive phenomena.[93]

Carlos Alchourrón tried to develop this point of view, facing Jørgensen's dilemma through its second horn.[94] His thesis is that it would be nothing but a philosophical prejudice to believe that logic is confined to descriptive discourse, and that its main notions should be defined in terms of truth and falsity. Thus, he outlines a logical system independent of the notions of truth and falsity that characterize (either direct or indirectly) syntactic and semantic approaches. According to Alchourrón, the kernel of logic is the notion of consequence, so a rational reconstruction of this notion should provide a good starting point. Alchourrón focuses on an abstract notion of logical consequence, a way to reconstruct the common features of the syntactic and the semantic characterizations of logical consequence. These common features are, in his view:[95]

(1) Inclusion: Every set is included in the set of its own consequences ($\alpha \subseteq Cn(\alpha)$);

(2) Idempotence: The consequences of the consequences are also consequences ($Cn(Cn(\alpha)) = Cn(\alpha)$); and

(3) Monotonicity: When the premises are increased, the consequences obtained from a smaller set must be maintained (if $\alpha \subseteq \beta$, then $Cn(\alpha) \subseteq Cn(\beta)$).

Here, Alchourrón borrows some ideas from Belnap[96] and Gentzen.[97] Particularly, he claims that Gentzen's sequent calculus – with some minor modifications – makes it possible to define deontic operators by means of rules of introduction and elimination.[98] This approach results in a kind of sequential logic, and derivations are expressed by schemes such as $\alpha \vdash \beta$ (β is a consequence of α), where the formula on the left is called prosequent, and the formula on the right postsequent. The symbol $\vdash$ (often called Gentzen's

---

[93] In the same line, Hart argued that "[a]lthough considerable technical complexities are involved, several more general definitions of the idea of valid deductive inference that render the notion applicable to inferences the constituents of which are not characterized as either true or false have now been worked out by logicians" (Hart 1983: 100).

[94] See Alchourrón and Martino 1990; Alchourrón 1995.

[95] These properties have been pointed out by Tarski in his meta-linguistic characterization of a *function* of deductive consequence in a certain language L, but he also adds the requirement of *compacticity* (i.e., if $b \in Cn(\alpha)$, then $b \in Cn(\alpha')$ for some finite subset $\alpha' \subseteq \alpha$). This axiom is abandoned in the abstract notion defended by Alchourrón (see Alchourrón 1995: 37–38).

[96] See Belnap 1962.

[97] See Gentzen 1934.

[98] See Alchourrón and Martino 1990: 61 ff; Alchourrón 1995: 41–42.

connector) does not represent a logical connective; it makes no sense to introduce it inside formulas in the prosequent or postsequent. The main function of Gentzen's connector is to indicate a relation between sets of premises (even possibly empty sets). The intuitive meaning of this connector is to represent deductive relations.

The only axiom needed is a sequence such as $\alpha \vdash \alpha$; other sentences are obtained by the application of rules of derivation. These rules of derivation are of two different kinds: on the one hand, rules that define the context of deducibility, that is, closely related to the notion of logical consequence, and on the other hand, operative rules, such as the rules of introduction and elimination of logical connectives in a system of natural deduction. This abstract conception of logical consequence does not require the notion of truth to explain why a certain proposition β follows from a set of propositions α. The meaning of logical connectives and operators are provided by rules for their use. Accordingly, it is possible to stipulate the rules that govern the logical behavior of propositional connectives – such as conjunction, disjunction, and so on – by rules of introduction and elimination in inferential patterns, and the same goes for deontic operators. For instance, the introduction of the O (obligation) operator is presented through the following rule:

Rule O
$$\frac{\alpha_1, \ldots, \alpha_n \vdash \beta}{O\alpha_1, \ldots, O\alpha_n \vdash O\beta}$$

where $\alpha_1, \ldots, \alpha_n$ is any set (it can be the empty set) and where β is a sentence or an empty sequence, but can never be a sequence with more than one sentence. All the operations that can be applied to sentences can also be here applied, such as, for example, negation; the rule may be read as saying that whatever is inferred from a set of duties is a duty.[99]

This abstract conception seems to offer a powerful analytical device. However, the particular way in which Alchourrón presents deontic logic on the basis of this abstract notion of logical consequence has raised objections. As Zuleta remarks, deontic systems exclude the validity of a formula such as $Op \lor O{\sim}p$, but $Op \lor {\sim}Op$ is a theorem in the standard system. Unfortunately, such theorem is not validated by Alchourrón's proposal.[100] Zuleta also points out that in rule O the O-operator simultaneously appears in the prosequent and postsequent, and thus it cannot be regarded as a genuine rule of

---

[99] See Alchourrón and Martino 1990: 62.
[100] See Zuleta 2008: 69.

introduction because, according to Gentzen, operators must only appear in the postsequent of rules of introduction.[101]

It should be noted that even if Zuleta's technical arguments against the way of introducing deontic operators seem compelling, they do not invalidate either the general proposal of Alchourrón[102] (i.e., that if we abandon the idea that logic is restricted to truth, the most problematic obstacle for the development of deontic logic has been removed), or the idea of an abstract notion of logical consequence underlying the traditional syntactic and semantic notions of it.

This brief overview of the different theoretical alternatives offered as an escape from Jørgensen's dilemma seems to indicate that there is no way out through the substitution of the concept of truth by any plausible surrogate, because all the suggested alternatives (satisfaction, validity as binding force or as membership in a legal system, and so on) either lead to unsatisfactory results or involve no more than a substitution in label. Nor is any form of indirect application of logic to norms feasible for building on it a genuine logic of norms. Were these conclusions sound, the only open alternatives for dealing with Jørgensen's dilemma would be the two radical views just examined; either accepting that, after all, norms are proposition-like entities, and thus, susceptible of truth-values, or abandoning the idea that logic is restricted to the realm of truth. And, as we will presently see, the difference between these two views reflects two fundamentally different conceptions of norms.

2.5. CONCEPTIONS OF NORMS: TWO ALTERNATIVES FOR DEONTIC LOGIC

If we accept the idea that all language phenomena have a syntactic, a semantic, and a pragmatic dimension, and that norms are at least expressible in language,[103] we should also accept that these same three dimensions have a correlate in the case of norms. However, the relevant question here is in which of these dimensions are norms distinguishable from other linguistic expressions.

Sometimes norms are identified with their formulations in language. The linguistic formulation of a norm is a deontic sentence – what von Wright

---

[101] See Zuleta 2008: 66.

[102] A similar approach to face Jørgensen's dilemma is offered by Ota Weinberger in Weinberger 1991: 284–307.

[103] This is not meant to endorse the strong thesis that norms owe their existence to certain linguistic formulations, which in fact we believe mistaken (see, for instance, Ferrer Beltrán and Rodríguez 2011: 27 ff).

proposed to call *norm-formulation* – containing normative terms such as "obligatory," "forbidden," "permitted," and so on.[104] For instance, legal scholars usually use the term "norm" to refer to each and every article or paragraph in an official text (e.g., all formulations contained in the Criminal Code); that is, they identify norms with norm-formulations.

This linguistic practice has, of course, nothing objectionable as such. However, it does not constitute a secure ground for the identification of norms, at least for the following reason: Norms cannot be identified at a mere syntactic level because the very same linguistic expression can be used to express either a norm (if enacted by an authority) or a norm-proposition – that is, a sentence that describes the existence of a norm (if uttered by someone who is not an authority).[105] Thus, von Wright maintains that whether a given sentence is a norm-formulation or not can never be decided on "morphic" grounds (i.e., depending on signs alone).[106]

But once norm-formulations are distinguished from the norms they express, the question remains regarding what kind of entities we call norms are, along with their relation to language (i.e., their connection with norm-formulations). Regarding this issue, there are two basic conceptions of norms; the *pragmatic* and the *semantic* conception. To illustrate the differences between them, it seems useful to adapt Anscombe's famous example of a shopping list.[107] Imagine a man who is sent by his wife to the supermarket with a shopping list. Let us also suppose that the wife hires a detective to follow him and make a record of anything he does. The man enters the supermarket and, trying to follow his wife's list, places different articles in the cart. A few steps behind, the detective writes down everything the man does in another list. Therefore, we have two lists; the wife's list (W-list) and the detective's list (D-list). Suppose now that there is a difference between the W-list and the contents of the cart. The W-list says "oranges," but the husband picked up grapefruits. In such a case, there is no ground for considering the W-list mistaken in any intelligible sense, because it is an instruction, a directive; its main function is to guide the husband's behavior. So, in cases of discrepancies between the content of W-list and the content of the cart, the mistake is not in the list but in what the husband did. Following Anscombe, we may say that this list has a *direction of fit* world-to-language, in the sense that it is the world that has to fit with the language and not vice versa. In cases of discrepancies

---

[104] See von Wright 1963a: 109.
[105] See von Wright 1963a: 109.
[106] See von Wright 1963a: 102.
[107] See Anscombe 1957: 56.

between prescriptions and actions, the problem is not in the instruction but in the world (i.e., in our actions).

Suppose now that the discrepancy is between the content of the cart and the D-list. For example, following the W-list, the husband puts a bottle of Chardonnay in the cart, but the detective writes in his list "liquid detergent." Here the mistake is in what the detective inscribes; the detective has to make an accurate description of what happens and, therefore, to record correctly all the products the man puts in the cart. If there are differences, it is the D-list that has to be corrected, not the content of the cart. The D-list has an opposite direction of fit with respect to the W-list; it goes from the language to the world (i.e., in case of discrepancies the problem is not in the world but in the language).

At first sight, we might say that when the language is used descriptively, as in the case of the D-list, we intend to represent accurately the reality, to make a picture of the world, as Wittgenstein puts it in the *Tractatus*.[108] If the world is correctly reflected, then what the sentence expresses will be true; otherwise it will be false, and we will have to correct it for the intended purpose. This kind of "correspondence" between language and world is the kernel of the old idea that truth is correspondence to reality. However, when the language is used prescriptively, as in the case of the W-list, it attempts to influence a certain agent's conduct. If the behavior of the addressee of the prescription does not correspond to what it prescribes, there is no reason at all to correct the prescription, because here it is behavior that should fit the prescription. This is the explanation of norms chosen by supporters of the *pragmatic conception* of norms; the difference between asserting that p is the case and prescribing that p ought to be the case lies in the use of language, in the different propositional attitude we adopt in each case. Norms are an instance of the prescriptive use of language, where the direction of fit is from the world to the language.

According to the *pragmatic* conception, norms are the outcome of the prescriptive use of language. One and the same proposition can be asserted, prescribed, questioned, and so on, and consequently each of those acts will produce a different result: an assertion, a norm, a question, and so on. For example, the proposition that Peter closes the window can be used to make an assertion ("Peter closes the window"), a question ("Does Peter close the window?"), or a command ("Peter, close the window!"). Normally, those pragmatic differences are marked by certain auxiliary symbols (e.g., "?" or "!"), but such symbols do not affect the propositional meaning of the expressions

---

[108] See Wittgenstein 1921: 3.01.

in which they appear. These pragmatic differences may be illustrated as follows:

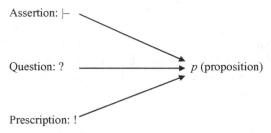

From this perspective, norms can only be identified at the pragmatic level.[109] By contrast, according to the *semantic conception*, norms are the meaning of certain statements (norm-formulations), and therefore they behave as proposition-like entities.[110] The semantic approach assumes that norms are a certain type of propositions (i.e., deontic propositions), just like alethic formulations state propositions. Thus, in this sense, the differences between norms and non-modalized propositions cannot be explained in terms of different normative acts, but by their different propositional contents. Those differences can be represented as:

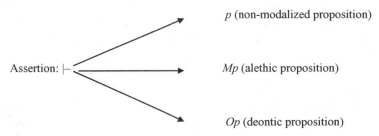

Partisans of the semantic conception of norms need to offer a solution to a crucial problem: how can norms be distinguished from non-modalized propositions? As we said, from this point of view both are meanings, but

---

[109] From this point of view, von Wright writes: "[T]okens of the same types are sometimes used prescriptively, sometimes descriptively. When used prescriptively they order or permit something; when used descriptively they state that something has been ordered or permitted. In the second case only do the sentences mean or say something which is either true or false" (von Wright 1984: 22).

[110] A possible intermediate position between a purely syntactic conception of norms and a purely semantic conception is conceivable. According to such view, norms are linguistic entities *under a certain interpretation*. Thus, neither a simple linguistic formulation *is* a norm, but rather the relationship between them (see Alchourrón and Bulygin 1971; Moreso and Navarro 1993: 30–31). At least for the sake of simplicity, we take this alternative as a sophisticated variant of the semantic conception.

non-modalized propositions are descriptive meanings, whereas norms are pre-scriptive meanings. Now, the explanation of the difference between both types of meanings cannot be that non-modalized propositions are the meaning of descriptive *sentences* and norms are the meaning of prescriptive *sentences*, because in that case we would be ultimately locating the difference at the syntactic level, and that would demand a clear criterion to identify descriptive from prescriptive sentences. But, as we have already seen, it is impossible to offer such criterion, as sentences such as "it is obligatory that *p*" are system-atically ambiguous; they may express norms or propositions describing the existence of norms. Nor is it possible to differentiate both types of meanings as differences in the uses of language, as it would be tantamount to collapsing this conception of norms into the alternative pragmatic conception.

From a semantic point of view, the most plausible way to distinguish norms from non-modalized propositions seems to be in terms of possible-worlds semantics. Whereas what determines the truth or falsity of the proposition that *p* is the case is something that occurs in the actual world, what determines the truth or falsity of the proposition that *p* ought to be the case is something that occurs, not in the actual world, but in those possible worlds that may be taken as deontic alternatives to the actual world. Thus, as we have seen, the norm "it is obligatory that *p*" will be true in the actual world if *p* is true in all possible worlds that are deontic alternatives to the actual world.[111] Unquestion-ably, this way of explaining the difference involves accepting the possibility of assigning truth-values to norms, although not by reference to the actual world.[112]

According to the previous analysis, either we interpret that the direction of fit of a linguistic utterance that expresses a norm such as "it is obligatory that *p*" is language-to-world, and therefore the statement seeks to record what happens in certain normatively ideal worlds related to the actual world, and will be true or false depending on the accuracy of the description, or the direction of fit of an expression such as "it is obligatory that *p*" is world-to-language, the expression lacks truth-values, and its difference with non-modalized propositions is pragmatic and not semantic. Therefore, either we choose the semantic conception of norms and also accept that norms are true or false, or we favor the pragmatic conception and reject the attribution of truth-values to norms. There seems to be no conceptual room for assuming the semantic conception and denying that norms do have truth-values.

---

[111] For a defense of this point of view, see for instance Zuleta 2008: 82 ff.

[112] Contrary to this idea, Alchourrón and Bulygin have claimed that partisans of the semantic conception of norms may accept or reject assigning truth-values to norms (see Alchourrón and Bulygin 1981). For the reasons exposed in the text, there is no way to reconcile the semantic conception with the rejection of truth-values to norms.

The ultimate reason that justifies these conclusions is that behind the distinction between the semantic and pragmatic conceptions of norms, there are in fact two different views of meaning; one according to which meaning is explained exclusively in terms of truth-conditions, and the other in which the pragmatic aspects of language participate in meaning.[113] From the first point of view, norms will have a direction of fit from the language to the world and will be capable of truth values; from the second, norms will have a direction of fit from world to language and lack truth-values.

These two conceptions of norms have profound implications for the way one faces Jørgensen's dilemma. Under the first approach, Jørgensen's dilemma is avoided, and it is easy to justify the possibility of logical relations among norms, but only because within this perspective norms are conceived of as proposition-like entities, and therefore, are capable of truth and falsehood. By contrast, under the second approach, the idea that norms have truth-values is unacceptable, so either we reject the existence of logical relations among norms, or we have to face Jørgensen's dilemma through its second horn and, contrary to the traditional view, concede that the scope of logic is not limited to truth. It is apparent that each of the two more plausible ways to escape the dilemma that we explored earlier corresponds to a different conception of norms.

In what follows, we assume the pragmatic conception of norms, fundamentally because of three independent reasons. First, as we have shown, the alternative conception is committed to the counterintuitive assumption that norms are proposition-like entities and, thus, capable of truth-values. Second, although from the pragmatic conception norms are incapable of truth-values, using the framework designed by Alchourrón of an abstract notion of logical consequences, it is possible to maintain that logic goes beyond truth, and consequently, that deontic logic is possible even from the point of view of the pragmatic conception. Third, despite appearances to the contrary, even within the pragmatic conception of norms, it is possible to preserve the powerful formal apparatus of possible-worlds semantics.

We have seen that under the standard reading of possible-worlds semantics for deontic logic – which assumes the semantic conception of norms – Op is true in the actual world if p is true in all possible worlds that are deontic alternatives to the actual world. Now, under the pragmatic conception of norms it could be argued that prescribing that p is obligatory in the actual world is tantamount to *preferring* or *selecting* as normatively ideal with respect to the actual world those possible worlds in which p is true. Under this alternative

---

[113] For a brief comment on the objections directed against the traditional limits among syntax, semantics, and pragmatics, following ideas of Wittgenstein, Austin, and Sellars, and their consequences on legal interpretation, see Canale and Tuzet 2007.

reading, the norm itself is constitutive of which possible worlds the norm-giver considers normatively ideal in relation to the actual world.

It is important to notice that, just as strong analogies hold between deontic statements and alethic and quantified statements, there are equally strong – or even stronger – analogies between deontic statements and the dyadic relations of preferences. Taking as basic the notions of strong preference ("... is better than ..." ($\succ$)) and weak preference ("... is at least as good as ..." ($\succcurlyeq$)), the following analogies hold:[114]

NORMS

$Op =_{df} {\sim}P{\sim}p$

CONTRARIETY

PREFERENCES

$(p \succ {\sim}p) =_{def} {\sim}({\sim}p \succcurlyeq p)$

CONTRARIETY

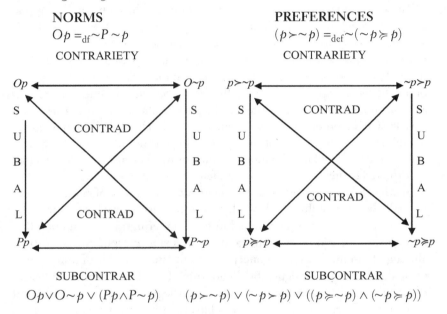

SUBCONTRAR

$Op \vee O{\sim}p \vee (Pp \wedge P{\sim}p)$

SUBCONTRAR

$(p \succ {\sim}p) \vee ({\sim}p \succ p) \vee ((p \succcurlyeq {\sim}p) \wedge ({\sim}p \succcurlyeq p))$

First, the interdefinitions between $\succ$ and $\succcurlyeq$ are similar to those between O and P. Second, the relations in the square of opposition are strictly the same in the case of preference concepts, with $\succ$ operating like O, and with $\succcurlyeq$ operating like P. Thus, for instance, $p \succ {\sim}p$ implies $p \succcurlyeq {\sim}p$ – subalternation – just like Op implies Pp; and $p \succ {\sim}p$ is contradictory regarding ${\sim}p \succcurlyeq p$ just like Op is contradictory regarding $P{\sim}p$. Third, the "logical space" in the case of preference concepts allows three alternatives: either p is better than ${\sim}p$, or ${\sim}p$ is better than p, or p is at least as good as ${\sim}p$ and ${\sim}p$ is at least as good as p (they are indifferent), just as in the case of deontic statements (p is either obligatory, or prohibited, or facultative).

<hr />

[114] See von Wright 1963b; Rodríguez 2002: 211–240. To show the parallelisms more clearly, we take preferences to hold, not between two arbitrary alternatives, but between a certain state of affairs and its negation.

In fact, there is at least one aspect in which the analogies between deontic statements and preferences are even closer than those that hold between deontic, alethic, and quantified statements, because, though in the case of the two latter we have:

$$\vdash \forall x Hx \rightarrow Ha \rightarrow \exists x Hx$$

$$\vdash Np \rightarrow p \rightarrow Mp$$

their corresponding translations in deontic and preference logic do not hold:

$$\nvdash Op \rightarrow p \qquad\qquad \nvdash p \rightarrow Pp$$

$$\nvdash (p \succ \sim p) \rightarrow p \qquad \nvdash p \rightarrow (p \succcurlyeq \sim p)$$

Of course, norms cannot be so easily identified with preferences, and the idea of relating deontic logic with the logic of preferences is not new. For instance, recently Sven Ove Hansson developed a system of deontic logic in different works based on preferences between possible worlds under the idea that predicates of obligation are *counternegative* regarding the relation of weak preference ($\succcurlyeq$-counternegative).[115] In a nutshell, instead of a direct assimilation of norms to preferences – as the previous analogies may suggest – Hansson claims that the O-operator satisfies the following property: For any p and q,

$$(Op \wedge (\sim p \succcurlyeq \sim q)) \rightarrow Oq$$

We do not examine the plausibility of such a system here.[116] The only thing we would like to point out is that inasmuch as the relations of preference between possible worlds are taken as already fixed, and norms are interpreted as describing those preferences, we would still be within the confines of the semantic conception of norms. Moving toward the pragmatic conception requires norms to be read as performing a selection of normatively ideal worlds. Let W be a non-empty set of possible worlds, w^* an element of W (the actual world), and $S(w^*,W)$ a selection function that correlates w^* with a subset of W (the normatively ideal worlds regarding w^*). Norms that hold in w^* specify the scope of $S(w^*,W)$ in the following way:

$$O(w^*)p =_{df} \forall w \in W \, (w \in S(w^*, W) \rightarrow v(p, w) = T)$$

$$P(w^*)p =_{df} \exists w \in W \, (w \in S(w^*, W) \wedge v(p, w) = T)$$

[115] See Hansson 2001: 146 ff; 2004 and 2006.

[116] Suffice it to note, as a possible shortcoming, that Hansson's approach seems to bring what is obligatory too close to what is merely preferable. For example, from the obligation to pay off a debt of $5, and the fact that not paying off the $5 debt is no worse than not conveying a needed benefit worth more than $5, according to the $\succcurlyeq$-counternegative character of obligations it would follow that one ought to convey a needed benefit worth more than $5, what seems at least rather counterintuitive.

According to this, to say that it is obligatory to perform p in w^* means that all possible worlds that this norm selects as normatively ideal are such that in them p is true, and to say that performing p is permitted in w^* means that there is at least one possible world within the set of normatively ideal worlds selected by this norm in which p is true.

The pragmatic conception of norms involves assuming that norms express a propositional attitude different from assertions. However, as we have seen, there is an apparently powerful argument derived from Frege's and Geach's ideas against this view. Consider again the following schemas:

(1) If p, then q;

p

Therefore, q.

(2) If not p, then not q;

not p.

Therefore, not q.

(3) If an action is forbidden, then attempting to perform it is forbidden;

Murder is forbidden.

Therefore, attempting to murder is forbidden.

Frege's argument against negation as a propositional attitude different from assertion is that in (1), the conclusion seems to be derivable from the premises because the content of the second premise matches the antecedent of the first. But if negation were a special kind of propositional attitude different from assertion, in the second premise of (2) negation would be absorbed by the force of the expression, and the content of that premise (p) would no longer match the content of the antecedent of the first premise. Thus, to preserve the intuition that (2) operates as (1) we have to reject the thesis that negation is a special kind of propositional attitude. Geach's argument against non-cognitivist interpretations of moral concepts, easily translatable as an objection against the pragmatic conception of norms, states exactly the same thing but regarding arguments such as (3).

It is important to notice that Frege's and Geach's arguments depend crucially on two assumptions, that we may call *uniformity* and *general scope*. According to the former, all these inference-patterns operate in the same way. According to the latter, the force of a linguistic expression, regardless of its degree of complexity, applies to it as a whole, and consequently the force of an expression cannot significantly occur inside a clause that is part of a more complex expression. Both assumptions seem to reflect strong intuitions, but of course neither of them is uncontroversial.

Suppose first we give up uniformity.[117] In such a case, taking ⊢ to represent an indicator of assertoric force; ⊣ to represent an indicator of negatory force, and ! to represent an indicator of prescriptive force, we may reconstruct the preceding inference-patterns as:

(1') $\vdash (p \rightarrow q)$
    $\underline{\vdash p\qquad\quad}$
    $\vdash q$

(2') $\vdash (\sim p \rightarrow \sim q)$
    $\underline{\dashv p\qquad\qquad}$
    $\dashv q$

(3') $!(p \rightarrow q)$
    $\underline{!p\qquad\quad}$
    $!q$

There is a clear difference here between (2') and (3'). In the case of negation, if we stick to the intuition of general scope, it is difficult to claim that in an expression such as "if ~p, then ~q", the linguistic force of the whole expression is not assertive. But in such a case, even if there were reasons to justify that an inference-pattern such as (2') is defensible to justify the conclusion, we would have to face not only that, contrary to our intuitions, (1) and (2) are two distinct kinds of inference, but also that negation has two senses: when it appears inside complex expressions it would be part of the content of what is asserted, and when it is the principal connective it would express a different kind of propositional attitude. By contrast, in the case of an expression such as "if an action is forbidden, then attempting to perform it is forbidden," it is possible, as (3') shows, to claim that its force is prescriptive and not assertive, and this renders (3') much more plausible than (2').[118] And although under this reconstruction (3') is not identical to (1'), the only difference between them is the propositional attitudes involved in each case, so it is even questionable that uniformity has not been preserved.

However, it could be objected that !($p \rightarrow q$) is not an adequate representation of the first premise of (3), and that, in close analogy with (2'), we should have something such as $\vdash (Op \rightarrow Oq)$. But, contrary to what happens with negation, in the case of normative expressions, there are indeed two interpretations of them, one descriptive and one genuinely prescriptive, as we have already noted and explore more carefully in the next chapter. Therefore, in case the first premise of (3) were interpreted as a norm-proposition and not a genuine norm, we should represent it as:

(3") $\vdash (Op \rightarrow Oq)$
$\underline{\vdash Op}$
$\vdash Oq$

Here, each occurrence of the O-operator expresses a norm-proposition, not a genuine norm, so that (3") would be just a special case of (1') – that is, *modus ponens* – and thus we would have preserved the intuition of uniformity.

Be that as it may, preserving or rejecting the intuition of uniformity is not the real issue here. Suppose we forget all about conditional expressions and *modus ponens*, and simply take into account complex expressions such as:

(4) Tomorrow it will be cold and raining.
(5) Tomorrow it will not be cold and will not rain.
(6) It is forbidden to murder and to attempt to murder.

If the intuition of general scope is to be maintained, then in each case the scope of the linguistic force has to apply to these expressions as a whole. Hence, (5) could not be represented as:

(5') $\dashv p \land \dashv q$

but as:

(5") $\vdash (\sim p \land \sim q)$

And this would be enough to show that negation has to be understood as part of the content of the expressions in which it occurs, and not as a different kind of linguistic force, merely for "arithmetical reasons," so to speak.

Clearly, $\sim(p \land q)$ is different from $(\sim p \land \sim q)$ as they do not have the same truth values. Therefore, under the assumption of general scope, either we accept that negation is not a different kind of propositional attitude, or we accept that negation has two different senses according to its occurrence inside or outside complex expressions, which seems unjustified.

But what happens if we reject the intuition of general scope? There is in fact a significant argument against it: $\vdash(p \land q)$ does not seem equivalent to $\vdash p \land \vdash q$. It is one thing to assert the conjunction of two propositions, and quite another the conjunction of the assertions of two propositions. Under the assumption of general scope, these two expressions are undistinguishable. But if general scope is given up, we may represent (1), (2), and (3) as:

(1") $\vdash p \to \vdash q$
$$\frac{\vdash p}{\vdash q}$$

(2") $\dashv p \to \dashv q$
$$\frac{\dashv p}{\dashv q}$$

(3"') $!p \to !q$
$$\frac{!p}{!q}$$

Here, the intuition of uniformity would be preserved in each case. But, of course, it is difficult to maintain that logical connectives can be applied to locutionary acts. It is difficult, without a doubt, but not impossible. At least if we are disposed to accept that logic has a wider range than truth.

3

Norm-propositions, Conditional Norms, and Defeasibility

3.1. LOGIC OF NORMS AND LOGIC OF NORM-PROPOSITIONS

So far we have been dealing with the problem of the foundations of deontic logic, particularly with the controversial relation between propositions and norms. And although the thesis that norms are proposition-like entities is highly controversial (we have, in fact, rejected that point of view), there is no disputing the propositional character of the discourse *about* norms. It is unreasonable to deny the possibility of formulating true or false descriptive statements about the norms that belong to a certain normative system.

The difference between genuine norms and statements about norms is quite apparent. However, as previously noticed, the problem is that the very same words (e.g., "Parking is not allowed here") may be used, depending on the context, either to formulate a norm (when the speaker is a norm-authority) or to express a norm-proposition (about the norms issued by a certain authority). Perhaps this ambiguity helps to explain the unfortunate reason why, although the distinction with different names has been noticed by several authors,[1] it has received little attention in the analysis of the logic of normative discourse.[2]

What is the canonical structure of norm-propositions? Von Wright characterizes norm-propositions as propositions "that such and such a norm exists."[3] But because norms usually exist as a part of complex systems of norms, the grammatical form of deontic statements expressing norm-propositions often hides a relevant part of their conceptual content.[4] Thus, a statement such as

---

[1] See Bentham 1872; Hedenius 1941; Wedberg 1951; Hansson 1969, among others.
[2] See von Wright 1999: 20.
[3] Von Wright 1963a: 106.
[4] Referring to the legal domain, Hart observes that "[t]here is frequent occasion for lawyers to describe what they might call the 'legal position' in relation to some subject without referring to the particular enactments or regulations or other sources of the relevant law, though of course

"Parking is not allowed here," understood as a norm-proposition, although apparently referring to the deontic status of an action without qualifications, is in fact a *relative* statement that reports the deontic status of an action *according to a particular normative system*. Norm-propositions are thus true or false depending on the set of norms taken as relevant. Therefore, the structure of norm-propositions may be represented as:

$$Op \in S$$

where Op is the norm that is being *mentioned* (not *used*) by this norm-proposition, and S is the normative system to which the proposition says that Op belongs.

The differences between norms and norm-propositions suggest that there should be a corresponding difference between a genuine logic of norms and a logic of norm-propositions. In Chapter 1, it was remarked that the standard system of deontic logic validates the principle of normative consistency (namely, that no action can be both prohibited and permitted), and the principle of normative completeness (namely, that every action is either prohibited or permitted). Now, does this system give an adequate reconstruction of the logical relations among normative expressions such as "obligation," "prohibition," and "permission"? To answer this question it is necessary to keep in mind the systematic ambiguity of those expressions, which may appear as formulations either of genuine norms or of norm-propositions.

In Chapter 2, we advanced the idea that it is wrong to assume that logical relations among norm-propositions are equivalent to those that hold among norms themselves. A simple way to explain the differences between a genuine logic of norms and a logic of norm-proposition is to take due notice of the different ways in which negation affects the former and the latter. When applied to norms, negation seems to behave in close analogy to descriptive discourse: the negation of a norm (e.g., Op) is also a norm $(P{\sim}p)$;[5] for each norm there is only one norm that is its negation; a norm and its negation are reciprocal (if $P{\sim}p$ is the negation of Op, then Op is the negation of $P{\sim}p$).[6] Moreover, a norm and its negation are mutually exclusive and jointly exhaustive, because ${\sim}(Op{\wedge}P{\sim}p)$ and $Op{\vee}P{\sim}p$ are valid formulas in a logic of norms.

it would be always understood that 'the legal position' thus described is that arising under the laws of a particular system, and a more accurate formulation would make this explicit by including such words as 'according to English law'" (Hart 1983: 329).

[5] See Alchourrón and Bulygin 1988: 231.

[6] The expression "negation-norm" was coined by von Wright (see von Wright 1983: 130–209).

But the negation of norm-propositions is more problematic. "In normative system S, act p is prohibited" is a complex metalinguistic statement that asserts that a certain norm belongs to a normative system. Therefore, its negation can be understood in two different ways: "In system S, act p is not prohibited" may be read as expressing that S does not contain a norm prohibiting p, in which case the negation operates over the *membership* of the norm in the system (i.e., the norm-proposition is negated); or it may be read as expressing that S does contain a norm not-prohibiting p (i.e., a norm permitting p), in which case the negation affects the *norm* referred to in the statement.

To make this distinction clear, it is necessary to introduce two notions of negation for norm-propositions: *external negation* (represented as $\sim$) and *internal negation* (represented as $\neg$). Whereas external negation of a norm-proposition is an operation that switches the value of membership of a given norm in a normative system, internal negation of a norm-proposition is an operation that leads to another norm-proposition asserting the membership in the system of the negation of the original norm. For example:

External negation: $\sim PH_S p =_{df.} PH p \notin S$
Internal negation: $\neg PH_S p =_{df.} \sim PH p \in S =_{df.} Pp \in S$

Here, the external negation of the proposition according to which p is pro-hibited in normative system S is a proposition that negates the membership of a norm prohibiting p in system S, whereas the internal negation of such a proposition is a proposition asserting the membership in S of a norm to the effect that p is not prohibited (i.e., a norm permitting p).

Accordingly, "permission" is an expression that may appear in a genuine norm, or in a norm-proposition. In the first case (i.e., under a prescriptive interpretation), to say that an action is permitted is unambiguously equivalent to saying that it is not prohibited. By contrast, when "permission" appears in a norm-proposition, it becomes ambiguous, because there are two alternative senses in which an action can be said to be permitted according to a set of norms: a *negative sense* (there is no norm in the set prohibiting it) and a *positive sense* (there is a norm in the set permitting it). We may call these two notions negative permission ($P^-_S p$) and positive permission ($P^+_S p$):

Negative permission: $P^-_S p =_{df.} PH p \notin S$
Positive permission: $P^+_S p =_{df.} \sim PH p \in S =_{df.} Pp \in S.$

It is easy to see that the negative permission of p is equivalent to the external negation of the prohibition of p, whereas the positive permission of p is equiv-alent to the internal negation of the prohibition of p. Negative permission merely indicates the absence of a norm; positive permission, on the contrary, depends on the existence of a certain norm.

The difference between these two notions of permission perhaps can be better understood in the following way. Suppose we focus on those norms which depend for their existence on an action by some authority (prescriptions). If an action p is permitted in the negative sense in a normative system, and an authority decides to prohibit it, no conflict will arise. As a result of the prohibition, action p, which was not regulated before, will now become prohibited in the system. But if the same action was permitted in the positive sense, and the authority decides to prohibit it, the result will be the introduction of a normative conflict in the system: p will be permitted and prohibited at the same time.

Although the ambiguity of the term "permitted" was detected by von Wright, he initially considered that positive permission had a normative character, and negative permission did not.[7] In other words, von Wright distinguished only two concepts of permission, because he identified prescriptive permission with positive descriptive permission. And as he thought that positive permission implied negative permission, he called the former "strong permission" and the latter "weak permission." However, as seen previously, there are in fact three concepts of permission, one prescriptive and two descriptive (positive and negative). Moreover, in a logic for norm-propositions we can use as a basis the O-operator (or the PH-operator) and define two descriptive concepts of permission from it, but we may also use as a basis the P-operator and define two concepts of prohibition and two of obligation from it:

O-based:

(1) $O_S p =_{df.} Op \in S$

(2) $PH_S p =_{df.} O{\sim} p \in S$

(3) $P^+{}_S p =_{df.} {\sim}O{\sim}p \in S$

(3') $P^-{}_S p =_{df.} O{\sim}p \notin S$

(4) $F^+{}_S p =_{df.} {\sim}Op \in S \wedge {\sim}O{\sim}p \in S$

(4') $F^-{}_S p =_{df.} Op \notin S \wedge O{\sim}p \notin S$

P-based:

(1") $O^+{}_S p =_{df.} {\sim}P{\sim}p \in S$

(1') $O^-{}_S p =_{df.} P{\sim}p \notin S$

(2") $PH^+{}_S p =_{df.} {\sim}Pp \in S$

(2') $PH^-{}_S p =_{df.} Pp \notin S$

(3") $P_S p =_{df.} Pp \in S$

(4") $F_S p =_{df.} Pp \in S \wedge P{\sim}p \in S$

The formulas identified with numbers followed by quotation marks are equivalent to the formulas with numbers without quotation marks of the alternative presentation, and the formulas with numbers with single quotation marks have no equivalence in the alternative version. Consequently, from a formal point of view, considering the two senses negation assumes when it operates on norm-propositions, *all deontic notions turn ambiguous* (i.e., it is possible

---

7 See von Wright 1963a: 102.

to distinguish the following four pairs of concepts, with their corresponding equivalences):[8]

$$(1'')\ O^+_S p = {\sim}P^-_S{\sim}p = \neg P^+_S{\sim}p \qquad (1')\ O^-_S p = {\sim}P^+_S{\sim}p = \neg P^-_S{\sim}p$$
$$(2'')\ PH^+_S p = {\sim}P^-_S p = \neg P^+_S p \qquad (2')\ PH^-_S p = {\sim}P^+_S p = \neg P^-_S p$$
$$(3)\ P^+_S p = {\sim}PH^-_S p = {\sim}PH^+_S p \qquad (3')\ P^-_S p = {\sim}F^+_S p = \neg F^-_S p$$
$$(4)\ F^+_S p = {\sim}O^-_S p \wedge {\sim}O^-_S{\sim}p = \qquad (4')\ F^-_S p = {\sim}O^+_S p \wedge {\sim}O^+_S{\sim}p =$$
$$\neg O^+_S p \wedge \neg O^+_S{\sim}p \qquad\qquad\qquad \neg O^-_S p \wedge \neg O^-_S{\sim}p$$

The first presentation of the differences between a genuine logic of norms and a logic of norm-propositions was put forward by Carlos Alchourrón, and later developed in work co-authored with Eugenio Bulygin.[9] Their proposal can be set out axiomatically as follows:

System of logic of norm-propositions (LNP):

$$(A_1)\ O_S(\alpha \wedge \beta) \leftrightarrow (O_S\alpha \wedge O_S\beta)$$
$$(A_2)\ O_S\alpha \to P^+_S\alpha$$
$$(A_3)\ P^+_S(\alpha \wedge \beta) \to P^+_S\alpha$$

(RI_1) From $\vdash (\alpha \leftrightarrow \beta)$, it follows $\vdash (O_S\alpha \leftrightarrow O_S\beta)$
(RI_2) From $\vdash (\alpha \leftrightarrow \beta)$, it follows $\vdash (P^+_S\alpha \leftrightarrow P^+_S\beta)$[10]

If we compare this system with the standard system of deontic logic, we should notice first that norm-propositions are relative to a given normative system, and that is reflected in the subscripts $(_S)$ in the formulas. By contrast, the expressions of the logic of norms do not refer to any particular normative system, because they represent absolute concepts. Second, in the system of logic for norm-propositions, there is nothing like the principle of $Pp \leftrightarrow {\sim}O{\sim}p$,[11] which is accepted as valid in deontic logic. This is so because, as we have seen, there are two forms of negation of norm-propositions, which give rise to two descriptive concepts for each of the deontic operators. And although external negation satisfies all the properties that we expect from ordinary negation – the same five principles that were enunciated in analogous formulation as

---

[8] Although the differences between positive and negative permission seem to have correlates in ordinary language, there are no corresponding uses of the concepts of negative prohibition (PH^-_S) and negative obligation (O^-_S). That is why the usual presentation of the logic of norm-propositions is based on the O-operator, and the only concept that has a positive and a negative reading is permission. See Alchourrón and Bulygin 1971: 124 n. 10.

[9] See Alchourrón 1969: 242–268, Alchourrón and Bulygin 1971.

[10] See Alchourrón 1993: 46.

[11] In the system LNP, there is also an axiom and a rule of inference $(A_3$ and $RI_2)$ that are not found in the usual systems of deontic logic. This is, however, a minor difference; were it possible to add to LNP an analogue to the principle $Pp \leftrightarrow {\sim}O{\sim}p$, A_3 and RI_2 would be superfluous because they would be derivable from the other axioms and rules.

satisfied by the negation of norms – that is not the case with internal negation. A norm-proposition and its internal negation can both be true (in which case the system will be inconsistent) as well as both false (in which case the system will be incomplete).[12] That is why the equivalence expressed in $Pp \leftrightarrow \sim O \sim p$, although valid in the logic of norms (LN), is not valid in the logic of norm-propositions.

In spite of these differences, it can be proven that under certain assumptions, LNP and LN are equivalent, and consequently, that positive permission P^+ will be equivalent to negative permission P^-. And that is so because an analogue of the principle $Pp \leftrightarrow \sim O \sim p$ is indeed valid in LNP under the conditions of consistency and completeness of the normative system taken into account:

(5) $\sim(O_S \sim p \wedge P^+_S p)$ $(\mathrm{Cons}_S p)$
(6) $O_S \sim p \vee P^+_S p$ $(\mathrm{Comp}_S p)$

It is important to see that the conjunction of (5) and (6) – that is,

(7) $\sim(O_S \sim p \wedge P^+_S p) \wedge (O_S \sim p \vee P^+_S p)$

is equivalent to

(8) $P^+_S p \leftrightarrow \sim O_S \sim p$

Proof:

(5) $\sim(O_S \sim p \wedge P^+_S p)$
(9) $\sim(P^+_S p \wedge O_S \sim p)$ commutativity of conjunction in (5)
(10) $P^+_S p \rightarrow \sim O_S \sim p$ definition of conditional in (9)
(11) $\sim(O_S \sim p \wedge P^+_S p) \rightarrow (P^+_S p \rightarrow \sim O_S \sim p)$ introduction of conditional from (5) to (10)

(6) $O_S \sim p \vee P^+_S p$
(12) $(\sim O_S \sim p \rightarrow P^+_S p)$ definition of conditional in (6)
(13) $(O_S \sim p \vee P^+_S p) \rightarrow (\sim O_S \sim p \rightarrow P^+_S p)$ introduction of conditional from (6) to (12).

Therefore, it follows that:

(14) $((\mathrm{Cons}_S p) \wedge (\mathrm{Comp}_S p)) \leftrightarrow (P^+_S p \leftrightarrow \sim O_S \sim p)$

---

[12] See Bulygin 1995: 135, 137.

and because by the definitions already seen, $\sim O_S \sim p$ is equivalent to $P^-_S p$, then:

(15) $((\text{Cons}_S p) \wedge (\text{Comp}_S p)) \leftrightarrow (P^+_S p \leftrightarrow P^-_S p)$

In other words, under the assumptions of completeness and consistency of the normative system taken as point of reference, LNP is equivalent to LN. It could be said that the logic of norms aims to reconstruct the rationality of the activity of enacting norms, the rationality of the legislator,[13] so to speak, and a rational lawgiver should neither introduce contradictions in a normative set, nor leave actions normatively unregulated.[14] By contrast, the logic of norm-propositions aims to reconstruct the logical consequences of a given set of norms. Therefore, we should assume from this point of view neither completeness nor consistency of the normative system under consideration, because in fact real normative systems may be non-ideal (i.e., may not be the product of rational norm-giving).[15]

Some further consequences that can be proven regarding consistency and completeness in LNP are:

(A) If a normative system is inconsistent in relation to an action p, it is complete in relation to that same action: $(\sim(\text{Cons}_S p) \rightarrow (\text{Comp}_S p))$.

(16) $O_S \sim p \wedge P^+_S p$
(17) $O_S \sim p$ simplification in (16)
(18) $O_S \sim p \vee P^+_S p$ introduction of disjunction in (17)
(19) $(O_S \sim p \wedge P^+_S p) \rightarrow (O_S \sim p \vee P^+_S p)$ introduction of conditional
from (16) to (18)

(B) If a normative system is incomplete in relation to an action p, it is consistent in relation to that same action: $\sim(\text{Comp}_S p) \rightarrow (\text{Cons}_S p)$.

(20) $\sim(O_S \sim p \vee P^+_S p)$
(21) $\sim O_S \sim p \wedge \sim P^+_S p$ De Morgan in (20)
(22) $\sim O_S \sim p$ simplification in (21).

---

[13] See von Wright 1983: 132. Similarly, it is frequently assumed that ideal or critical morality is also complete and consistent – even though the existence of their norms does not depend on the prescription of any authority.

[14] It should be noted that if an action is permitted, it is not unregulated, because permissions are regulations in the relevant sense.

[15] This gives a reason to doubt the objection against the inheritance principle grounded on the need to take into account sub-ideal situations (see Chapter 2, Section 1).

(23) $O_S{\sim}p \wedge P^+{}_S p$ assumption.

(24) $O_S{\sim}p$ simplification in (23).

(25) $O_S{\sim}p \wedge {\sim}O_S{\sim}p$ introduction of conjunction (24, 22)

(26) ${\sim}(O_S{\sim}p \wedge P^+{}_S p)$ introduction of negation (23–25)

(27) ${\sim}(O_S{\sim}p \vee P^+{}_S p) \rightarrow {\sim}(O_S{\sim}p \wedge P^+{}_S p)$ introduction of conditional (20–26).

These two demonstrations may be generalized in virtue of the application of the principle *ex falso sequitur quodlibet* $((p \wedge {\sim}p) \rightarrow q)$ as follows:

(C) If a normative system is inconsistent in relation to a certain action, it is complete in relation to any action $(\exists x \sim(\mathrm{Cons}_S x) \rightarrow \forall x\,(\mathrm{Comp}_S x))$.

(D) If a normative system is incomplete in relation to a certain action, it is consistent in relation to any action $(\exists x \sim(\mathrm{Comp}_S x) \rightarrow \forall x\,(\mathrm{Cons}_S x))$.[16]

Normative systems may be logically defective, suffering from inconsistency or incompleteness. One of the most attractive consequences of the distinction between a logic of norms and a logic of norm-propositions is that it offers the necessary resources to account for this. Moreover, the distinction shows that some usual objections directed against the standard system of deontic logic are nothing more than the result of confusing these two levels of analysis, especially the doubts concerning the interdefinability between permission on the one hand, and obligation and prohibition on the other, which hold in the standard system of deontic logic, and the fact that it excludes the possibility of normative conflicts or moral dilemmas.

All systems of deontic logic, with greater or lesser accuracy, aim to provide a reconstruction of a genuine logic of norms, not of a logic of norm-propositions. By contrast, it is the logic of norm-propositions, and not the logic of norms, that offers the most appropriate theoretical framework for exploring the consequences of existing normative systems, and so, the one with greater practical applications.

3.2. AN APPARENT DILEMMA FOR A LOGIC OF NORM-PROPOSITIONS

In spite of the virtues just summarized, the distinction between a genuine logic of norms and a logic of norm-propositions, and even the very difference

---

[16] For alternative systems of logic for norm-propositions where normative conflicts and normative gaps are avoided "whenever possible," see Beirlaen and Straßer 2013.

between norms and norm-propositions, have to face a serious philosophical challenge, and that may be the reason that explains why they have not received the attention they deserve in the analysis of normative discourse.

Alchourrón and Bulygin have claimed that, on the semantic conception of norms, it would be possible to affirm or deny that norms have truth-values, and in either case a genuine logic of norms would be distinguishable from a logic of norm-propositions.[17] However, in Chapter 2 we showed that according to the semantic conception, norms are necessarily proposition-like entities and, therefore, are capable of truth-values. Consequently, there is no logical space to assume the semantic conception and deny that norms are true or false. Now, an important corollary of this point of view is that, precisely because of this characteristic, the distinction between norms and norm-propositions cannot be maintained within the semantic conception of norms, because *norms themselves are propositions about what ought to be the case.*

Of course, even from this point of view it would be possible to draw a distinction between propositions about what ought to be the case and metalinguistic propositions about them. This, however, will not be a substantial distinction of two different kinds of entities, but one restricted only to the level of language. Closer to – but not identical with – the norm/norm-proposition distinction would be that between the assertion that p is obligatory according to the norms of a certain normative system, and the assertion that p is obligatory *simpliciter* – that is, between *relative* norm-propositions (relative to what ought to be the case according to a certain set of norms) and *absolute* norm-propositions (all things considered).[18]

By contrast, according to Alchourrón and Bulygin, from the standpoint of the pragmatic conception, norms would be conceived as acts of prescription, and thus they would neither be capable of truth-values, nor of logical relations. Therefore, a genuine logic of norms would be impossible.[19] Logical relations would only be admissible between norm-propositions (i.e., between descriptive statements about the existence of norms). Now, the challenge for this point of view consists in offering a system of logic for norm-propositions that does not presuppose logical relations among norms themselves.

In other words, Alchourrón and Bulygin's valuable contribution in comparing a logic of norms and a logic of norm-propositions was that, even in the

---

[17] See Alchourrón and Bulygin 1981.
[18] The distinction between absolute and relative norm-propositions was suggested by Jan-R. Sieckmann in a personal communication.
[19] See Alchourrón and Bulygin 1981.

case that a logic of norms were possible, and normative systems were understood as closed under logical consequence, a logic of norm-propositions would only be equivalent to a logic of norms under strong additional assumptions (consistency and completeness).

But now it seems that either we assume the semantic conception of norms and admit that they are proposition-like entities, in which case the very distinction between norms and norm-propositions vanishes (and there is no way to distinguish a logic of norms from a logic of norm-propositions), or we assume the pragmatic conception of norms, where the distinction between norms, that lack truth-values, and true or false norm-propositions is possible to delineate; but because there is no logic of norms, again the contrast between a logic of norms and a logic of norm-propositions is unsustainable, not to mention that the very possibility of a logic of norm-propositions without logical relations among norms seems quite difficult to justify.

Alchourrón and Bulygin explored a way out of this dilemma by claiming that, on the pragmatic conception of norms, normative discourse would not be condemned to an absolute irrationalism because rationality could be preserved in a logic of norm-propositions. In a series of papers in which they examined the pragmatic conception, there is an attempt to design a system of logic for norm-propositions under the assumption that there are no logical relations among norms.[20] However, such a system was substantially identical to the one they had previously developed from the alternative conception (i.e., the semantic conception); both systems basically coincide with the model described in the previous section (LNP).

However, in one of his final papers, von Wright presented a different proposal to reconstruct the logic of norm-propositions.[21] According to this system, the schematic form of deontic statements is represented as:

(i) a variable for statements or molecular compound of variables for statements preceded by a deontic operator O or P, or

(ii) a molecular compound of statements defined as in (1).

Under a descriptive reading, deontic statements express norm-propositions, and the laws of classic propositional calculus hold for them, as well as a

---

[20] Basically, in Alchourrón and Bulygin 1979, 1981, and 1984. After those explorations, however, they returned to the semantic conception, because they found it very difficult to surmount some of the limitations of the expressive conception, particularly, regarding a satisfactory reconstruction of conditional norms. See Alchourrón and Bulygin 1991: chapters 27 and 28.

[21] See von Wright 2000.

principle according to which logically equivalent compounds of variables are substitutable *salva veritate*. No special logical truths for norm-propositions is assumed and, more specifically, several formulas that are supposed to be valid in a prescriptive reading (i.e., in a logic of norms) are not logically true. Among them

(1) $\sim O\sim p \to Pp$
(2) $Pp \to \sim O\sim p$
(3) $Pp \lor P\sim p$
(4) $O(p \land q) \to \sim P\sim p$
(5) $P(p \land q) \to \sim O\sim p$

It is easy to notice that, as von Wright himself points out, (1) is equivalent to the principle of completeness and (2) to the principle of consistency. As we examined earlier, in the LNP system, neither of these two principles was accepted as valid without qualifications, because both are contingent characteristics of normative systems. Therefore, up to this point there is no difference with LNP. However, as von Wright also points out, (2) is equivalent to $Op \to \sim P\sim p$ and (3) to $\sim P\sim p \to Pp$. Therefore, by transitivity they jointly imply $Op \to Pp$, a principle whose satisfaction by a normative system under this view would also be contingent. Here Pp should be interpreted, in the proposed descriptive reading, as $P^+_s p$ (i.e., as positive permission). Yet, this conflicts with the assumption in LNP of the axiom A_2. The principle expressed in (4), in turn, in conjunction with (1) and (2) implies $O(p \land q) \to (Op \land Oq)$, in correspondence with axiom A_1 of LNP. And (5) in conjunction with (1) implies $P(p \land q) \to Pp$ (i.e., axiom A_3 of LNP). Consequently, as von Wright suggests, if none of these formulas were admitted as logically valid, none of the axioms that Alchourrón and Bulygin assume for a logic of norm-propositions would be left!

Although such a conclusion may seem at first sight rather surprising, things are exactly as they should be, because as von Wright warns, in his system *there are no special logical truths for norm-propositions*. What is remarkable and deserves an explanation is the significant difference of approach that characterizes each of these systems.

The reason why in the systems of logic for norm-propositions developed by Alchourrón and Bulygin – either under the assumption of the semantic or the pragmatic conception of norms – there are special logical truths for norm-propositions is that the normative set accepted as relevant is understood as *closed* under the notion of logical consequence. In other words, a logic of norm-propositions is understood as a logic of descriptive statements relative to a normative system that is not solely composed of those norms explicitly enacted by certain normative authorities, but also of all those norms that are logically derivable from them. The reason for this is that, even though from the pragmatic conception there would be no logical relations between norms, the "normative system" is understood by Alchourrón and Bulygin as a set of norm-contents, and this set is closed under logical consequence.[22] Thus, the two versions of the logic of norm-propositions converge on LNP.[23]

To justify this point of view, Alchourrón and Bulygin introduce the idea of "implicit commands." They argue that in a non-psychological sense, the assertion of a certain proposition is tantamount to assert implicitly all its logical consequences, and the same would happen with norms.[24] But "in a non-psychological sense," (i.e., in a logical sense), if Carla asserts "John kissed Mary," even if it is true that she asserts the proposition that John kissed Mary and, that this logically implies that Mary was kissed by John, this does not imply that Carla had also asserted that Mary was kissed by John, *unless we assume that there are logical relations among acts of assertion.* Alchourrón and Bulygin in fact acknowledge that "the person in question surely has not thought" of all the logical consequences of what she has asserted, and that "hence, she did not have the intention to assert them."[25]

Of course we may say that the proposition that Mary was kissed by John follows from the content of what Carla asserted. But if an implicit assertion is an assertion in "a non-psychological sense," and if an assertion in such sense encompasses all its logical consequences, this idea does not justify the claim that a proper reconstruction of the set of those propositions that were in fact asserted by Carla, that is, the propositions that were the object of acts of assertion by Carla (characteristically voluntary acts), is necessarily closed under the notion of consequence; instead, it presupposes it. And the same is true for "implicit commands": if an authority x commands p, even if p implies p or q, it does not follow that x has commanded p or q, *unless we assume that there are logical relations among acts of prescription.*

---

[22] See Alchourrón and Bulygin 1981: 101.
[23] David Makinson has claimed that the logic of norm-propositions proposed by Alchourrón and Bulygin from the pragmatic conception of norms does not presuppose logical relations among norms; particularly, that in their system Op does not imply Pp (see Makinson 1999: 34). But the authors themselves have argued instead that, although they did not examine the question, it would be possible to explore the acceptance or rejection of such principle as alternative possibilities (see Alchourrón and Bulygin 1984: 462–463).
[24] See Alchourrón and Bulygin 1981.
[25] See Alchourrón and Bulygin 1981.

In LNP, as we have seen, there are specific logical truths for norm-propositions. For example:

- The obligation of p in a system S implies the positive permission of p in S;
- The conjunction of the obligation of p and the obligation of q in S is equivalent to the obligation of the conjunction of p and q in S;
- Positive permission of the conjunction of p and q in S implies positive permission of any of them in S.

But if we think of a logic of norm-propositions relative to a system that does not include all its logical consequences, all these principles would be merely contingent, as contingent as the satisfaction of completeness and consistency. This is exactly what happens in the system sketched by von Wright. Unlike Alchourrón and Bulygin, von Wright takes into consideration norm-propositions relative to a system not closed under the notion of logical consequence, but only composed of norms explicitly enacted by certain authorities. Von Wright's system only describes normative acts, and from the fact that, for instance, the norm Op has been issued in S it does not follow that another norm to the effect that Pp has also been issued in S. In the logic of norms, Op may be defined as $Pp \wedge {\sim}P{\sim}p$, and certainly Op implies Pp. But the descriptive operator $O_S p$ (p is obligatory in system S) is equivalent to $(Op \in S)$, and from $(Op \in S)$ it does not follow $(Pp \in S)$, unless we assume that S is closed under logical consequence $(Cn(S) = S)$. And the same goes for the distribution of obligation and permission over conjunction and disjunction.

It could be thought that these two alternative reconstructions of the logic of norm-propositions are the consequences of two different conceptions of normative systems: one according to which they are reconstructed as exclusively containing explicitly enacted norms, and the other as including all the consequences that follow from a set of explicitly enacted norms. Thus, even in the case in which there were no logical relations among norms, it might be possible to choose between these two interpretations of the logic of norm-propositions. But that would be wrong. Under the assumption that a genuine logic of norms is impossible, it is inconsistent to maintain the idea that normative systems are closed under logical consequence. In other words, either we claim that there are special laws in a logic of norm-propositions, in which case normative systems cannot be understood as exclusively composed of those norms explicitly enacted by certain authorities, but including all the logical consequences of such norms according to some presupposed system of logic of norms; or we reject the possibility of a genuine logic of norms, in which case each normative system will be exclusively composed of explicitly enacted norms, and for an adequate description of such normative systems nothing more than ordinary logic will be needed, so that there will be no special truths of an alleged logic of norm-propositions. In short, either a logic of norm-propositions presupposes a genuine logic of norms, or it is no more than ordinary logic applied to the analysis of normative systems.[26]

There is no need to say here much about our own position on this issue. In the Chapter 2 we offered a set of arguments to justify our option for the pragmatic conception of norms, and the possibility of accepting the existence of logical relations between norms, facing Jørgensen's dilemma through its second horn (i.e., that logic has a broader scope than truth). From this point of view, the logic of norm-propositions neither collapses into ordinary logic, nor into a logic of norms, and thus it is possible to preserve the enriched formal framework presented in the previous section, eluding this apparent dilemma for a logic of norm-propositions.[27]

3.3. CONDITIONAL NORMS

The most complex and discussed issue in deontic logic concerns the way to represent conditional norms, for it combines the difficulties involved in developing a logic of norms with the problems of the nature of conditional statements.[28] Remember Chisholm's paradox of contrary-to-duty obligations, where a set of sentences like

(1) Op

(2) $O(p \rightarrow q)$

(3) $\sim p \rightarrow O\sim q$

(4) $\sim p$

---

[26] See Rodríguez 2003; in the same line, see Weinberger 1985: 165–198 and Zuleta 2008: 57. The systems of deontic logic developed in Makinson 1999 and Makinson and van der Torre 2000, 2001, and 2003, although presented as a logic for norm-propositions without presupposing logical relations among norms themselves, do not elude this objection. In them, normative systems are taken as a "black box" that receives as *inputs* information about factual circumstances, and produces as *outputs* normative consequences. But in the different models offered for the *outputs*, all the logical consequences that follow from the factual circumstances and the norms of the system are taken into account, and that is tantamount to presupposing logical relations among norms themselves.

[27] In the final chapter of the book, we return to the central question that divides the various reconstructions of the logic of norm-propositions. There we evaluate reasons for accepting or rejecting the idea that normative systems, especially legal systems, contain all their logical consequences.

[28] The study of conditional norms is of paramount importance for the analysis of legal systems, because most legal norms seem to have a conditional structure, correlating normative consequences to classes of situations.

allows us to derive:

(5) $Oq \wedge O{\sim}q$

The main problem the paradox exposes is that the two forms of inference that lead to this inconsistency – that is, $(O(p{\rightarrow}q) \wedge Op) \rightarrow Oq$ and $((p{\rightarrow}Oq) \wedge p) \rightarrow Oq$ are not easily combined, and each of them is connected to one of the two main alternatives that has been evaluated as candidates to represent conditional norms (or *deontic commitment*).

On the one hand, what has been called the *insular conception* of conditional norms, according to which both the antecedent and the consequent of a conditional expression are within the scope of the deontic operator (with schemas of the kind of $O(p{\rightarrow}q)$). Under this representation, it is easy to derive, from the obligatoriness of the antecedent, the obligatoriness of the consequent.

On the other hand, what has been called the *bridge conception* of conditional norms, according to which the deontic operator only affects the consequent of a conditional expression (with schemas such as $p{\rightarrow}Oq$). Under this representation, by contrast, it seems easy to derive, from the *truth* of the antecedent, the obligation in the consequent.[29]

Neither of these two ways of representing conditional norms as they appear in natural language is free from difficulties. For instance, we have already seen that the insular conception is subject to another paradox: Prior's paradox of derived obligation. From $O{\sim}p$ follows $O(p{\rightarrow}q)$, which may be interpreted as the counterintuitive inference that if an action is forbidden; then doing it would commit us to doing anything whatsoever. The bridge conception, in turn, has been criticized because expressions such as $p{\rightarrow}Oq$ seem to be hybrids that combine a descriptive antecedent with a prescriptive consequent. The partisans of each of these alternative formalizations have proposed, in an attempt to overcome objections such as these, replacing the material conditional with other connectives, some of them stronger (strict conditionals or generalized conditionals), others weaker (subjunctive conditionals, counterfactuals conditionals or defeasible conditionals).

Remember that in von Wright's original system of deontic logic, a formula such as $p{\rightarrow}Oq$ would be excluded as ill-formed, because variables within the scope of deontic predicates are taken to represent generic actions.[30] Hence, only in cases in which deontic expressions are interpreted as operators over

---

[29] The names "insular" and "bridge" conception were introduced in Alchourrón 1996: 8.
[30] See von Wright 1951a.

variables representing states of affairs it is sound to read $O(p{\rightarrow}q)$ and $p{\rightarrow}Oq$ as two alternatives to represent conditional norms.

In an interesting paper, Carlos Alchourrón remarked that two basic objections have been raised against the formalization of conditional norms as $O(p{\rightarrow}q)$ – or, in an abbreviated representation, $O(q/p)$.[31] The first points to the unrestricted validity of the principle known as *strengthening of the antecedent* (SA):

(6) $O(q/p) \rightarrow O(q/p \wedge r)$

According to SA, if it is obligatory that q under circumstances p, then it is obligatory that q under circumstances p in conjunction with any other circumstances. The underlying intuition in this objection is that there are conditional norms for which the principle of strengthening of the antecedent should not hold. These norms, which he calls *defeasible*, are such that they can be cancelled when some exceptional event occurs. Representing conditional norms in a way that validates the principle of strengthening of the antecedent without any restrictions does not seem adequate to offer an account of defeasible norms, because according to this principle no conditional norm can be defeated by any fact.

From a different point of view, the standard system of representation of conditional norms as $O(p{\rightarrow}q)$ has also been objected to because it lacks something such as the following form of inference, which Alchourrón calls deontic *modus ponens*:

(7) $O(q/p) \rightarrow (p{\rightarrow}Oq)$

Here, the underlying intuition would be that there are conditional norms, which Alchourrón calls *indefeasible*, from which it should be possible to derive actual or categorical obligations from the truth of its respective antecedents.

The first objection generated systems such as the ones developed by Hansson and Lewis (*HL*-systems),[32] in which conditional obligations are represented by a dyadic deontic operator $O(/)$ that does not validate the principle of strengthening of the antecedent, and in which a monadic operator Op is introduced by definition as an equivalent to $O(p/T)$, T being any tautology.

According to Alchourrón, the problem with these systems is that, although they offer an adequate answer to the first objection, the second remains as

[31] See Alchourrón 1996: 5–8. Alchourrón uses $O(q/p)$ as an abreviated representation both of $p \rightarrow Oq$ and $O(p \rightarrow q)$.

[32] See Hansson 1969 and Lewis 1973 and 1974; also Føllesdal and Hilpinen 1971; van Fraassen 1972 and Åqvist 1987.

deontic *modus ponens* is not admitted in them, and consequently indefeasible norms cannot be represented. Moreover, Alchourrón suggests that so long as we stay within the domain of the insular conception of conditional norms (as is the case with the dyadic operator of *HL*-systems), the representation of indefeasible norms is impossible.

Alchourrón's way out consists in embracing the less popular bridge conception of conditional norms. From this perspective, the usual procedure is to use material conditionals to represent conditional norms, with schemas such as $p \rightarrow Oq$. Alchourrón proposes instead to replace the material conditional by a strict conditional ($\Rightarrow$). This would allow, on the one hand, overcoming some philosophical difficulties that arise from the interpretation of expressions such as $p \rightarrow Oq$ and, on the other hand, introducing the idea of defeasibility by adding a revision operator (f) to the antecedent of such conditionals, defining a defeasible conditional connective as:

(8) $(p > q) =_{\text{df}} (fp \Rightarrow q)$

where the revision operator selects a certain subset of cases p, the "normal" ones. With this tools, Alchourrón claims that from the bridge conception of conditional norms, both indefeasible ($p \Rightarrow Oq$) and defeasible norms ($p > Oq$) could be represented, and that would show the superiority of this approach over the insular conception.

More precisely, in the system proposed by Alchourrón (which he calls *AD*, because both actual and defeasible norms might be represented in it), the following five types of duty-imposing norms are distinguished:

(9) Op Actual or categorical obligation
(10) $p \Rightarrow Oq$ Indefeasible conditional obligation
(11) $p > Oq$ Defeasible conditional obligation
(12) $T \Rightarrow Op$ Indefeasible unconditional obligation
(13) $T > Op$ Defeasible unconditional obligation ($O_d p$)

Here, (10) implies (11), and (12) implies (13) (i.e., indefeasible duties imply the correlative defeasible duties, whereas the converse does not hold). However, none of the following implications would be valid:

(14) $Op \rightarrow O_d p$
(15) $O_d p \rightarrow Op$

This means that, although an indefeasible conditional obligation of doing q in circumstances p implies a defeasible conditional obligation of doing q in circumstances p, an actual obligation of doing p neither implies nor is implied by a defeasible obligation of doing p.

According to Alchourrón, in *HL*-systems, the dyadic operator $O(q/p)$ is read as a normative interpretation of a defeasible conditional (i.e., it works as $p>q$), whereas *AD* takes as basic the monadic operator O representing an actual obligation, and defeasible conditional norms are represented as $p>Oq$. Alchourrón claims that his system *AD* preserves all sound intuitions the *HL*-systems intend to capture, and excludes some (in his view) counterintuitive consequences of them. The most significant differences between both systems (apart from the impossibility of representing those norms that admit deontic *modus ponens* in *HL*-systems) are the following:

(i) HL-systems assume the principle of identity:

(16) $O(p/p)$

In its non-normative reading (i.e., as $p>p$), this principle is not problematic because it would expresses that p is true in the most normal worlds in which p is true. But under its normative reading it says that p is obligatory when it is the case that p, which sounds rather odd. By contrast, in *AD* it is not possible to derive:

(17) $p > Op$

(ii) Although defeasible conditionals do not satisfy the principle of strengthening of the antecedent, they do satisfy the following restricted form, known as *rational monotonicity* (RM):

(18) $((p > q) \land \sim(p > \sim r)) \to ((p \land r) > q)$

which is propositionally equivalent to:

(19) $((p > q) \land \sim((p \land r) > q)) \to (p > \sim r)$

On account of (19), the deontic interpretation of the defeasible conditionals made in *HL*-systems renders the following principle valid:

(20) $(O(q/p) \land \sim O(q/p \land r)) \to O(\sim r/p)$

In *AD*, by contrast, taking the monadic *O*-operator as basic to represent actual obligations and replacing q by Oq in (19), we get:

(21) $((p > Oq) \land \sim((p \land r) > Oq)) \to (p > \sim r)$

As it is easy to see, there is a significant difference between the consequences that follow from (19) in both systems. According to (20), in *HL*-systems, if it is prima facie obligatory to do q in case p, but it is not prima facie obligatory to do q in case p and r, this implies that r is prima facie forbidden in case p.[33] According to (21), in AD, if it is prima facie obligatory to do q in case p, but it is not prima facie obligatory to do q in case p and r, then it follows that in the most normal p-worlds, r is false. As Alchourrón explains, the second conclusion seems far more plausible than the first. In an example, if it is prima facie obligatory for judges to impose sanctions on murderers, but it is not prima facie obligatory for them to impose sanctions on murderers who acted in self-defense, from that it does not follow (as (20) would yield) that self-defense is prima facie forbidden in cases of murder, but rather that self-defense was excluded from the assumptions of the defeated norm (i.e., that when we say that it is prima facie obligatory for judges to impose sanctions on murderers, we tacitly assume that the normal cases referred to are those in which there was no self-defense).

With this theoretical framework, Alchourrón suggested that a set of statements as the one in Chisholm's paradox could be represented as:

(1') $O_d(p)$
(2') $O_d(q/p)$
(3') $O(\sim q/\sim p)$
(4) $\sim p$

From (3') and (4) it follows:

(22) $O\sim q$

and from (1') and (2') it follows:

(23) $O_d(q)$

This norm is not incompatible with (22), because it expresses a prima facie or defeasible duty, whereas (22) expresses an actual duty: it may well be the case that Jones has a prima facie duty to tell his neighbors he is coming if he is going to their aid, but that, as a matter of fact, he should not tell them he is coming if he is not going to their aid, even if that was his duty.

All this sounds quite elegant and convincing. However, as we try to show, Alchourrón's thesis on the advantages of the bridge conception of conditional norms over the insular conception, as well as the associated thesis that from

---

[33] Defeasibility applied in the normative domain may be taken as a way to represent Ross's idea of *prima facie* obligations (see Ross 1930). See Makinson 1993; Alchourrón 1993.

the bridge conception all relevant intuitions that are captured by the insular conception can also be accounted for, are highly controversial.

3.4. FACTUAL AND DEONTIC DETACHMENT

Alchourrón's main justification for embracing the bridge conception is based on the need to preserve, at least for certain norms, the validity of deontic *modus ponens*, an inference pattern that cannot be accepted as valid within the insular conception, because under the latter representation the scope of the deontic operator encompasses both the antecedent and the consequent of a conditional expression.

But in fact, within the normative domain *modus ponens* may assume two distinct forms (the same two that originate the difficulty exposed by Chisholm's paradox). Following Patricia Greenspan,[34] they may be referred to as *factual detachment* and *deontic detachment*, respectively

(1) $O(q/p) \rightarrow (p \rightarrow Oq)$
(2) $O(q/p) \rightarrow (Op \rightarrow Oq)$

We deliberately preserve here the ambiguity of $O(q/p)$ as representing both $O(p \rightarrow q)$ and $p \rightarrow Oq$. What Alchourrón calls deontic *modus ponens* corresponds to factual detachment, and it is correct to claim that, on the insular conception, it seems unreasonable to admit this form of inference. As in the insular conception, both the antecedent and the consequent of the conditional are under the scope of the deontic operator, from the *truth* of the antecedent no conclusion can be derived as regards the consequent. Moreover, Alchourrón points out that if we add (1) to the standard system of representation of conditional norms, which assumes the insular conception, such a system would collapse because, as the following version of the identity principle holds in it:

(3) $O(p/p)$

by substituting q by p in (1) we obtain:

(4) $O(p/p) \rightarrow (p \rightarrow Op)$

Consequently, as the antecedent of this conditional is an axiom, we would obtain the absurd consequence that all that is in fact the case is obligatory.

However, along the same line of reasoning, it seems at first sight that on the bridge conception of conditional norms, deontic detachment is unacceptable.

---

[34] See Greenspan 1975.

The reason is that if under the bridge conception only the consequent of the conditional is within the scope of the deontic operator, from the *obligation* to perform the antecedent, no conclusion can be derived in regard to the consequent. Moreover, if (2) were valid for the bridge conception of conditional norms, this would have the consequence that $Op{\rightarrow}p$ (i.e., that all that is obligatory is in fact the case), a consequence as absurd as claiming that all that is in fact the case is obligatory. The proof is simple. Substituting q by $p \wedge {\sim}p$ in (2), we obtain:

(5) $(p \rightarrow O(p \wedge {\sim}p)) \rightarrow (Op \rightarrow O(p \wedge {\sim}p))$

which is propositionally equivalent to:

(6) $((p \rightarrow O(p \wedge {\sim}p)) \wedge Op) \rightarrow O(p \wedge {\sim}p))$

and by transposition:

(7) ${\sim}O(p \wedge {\sim}p)) \rightarrow {\sim}((p \rightarrow O(p \wedge {\sim}p)) \wedge Op)$

Because within any reasonable system of deontic logic no contradictory state of affairs should be obligatory, ${\sim}O(p \wedge {\sim}p)$ has to be accepted as a theorem. And because ${\sim}O(p \wedge {\sim}p)$ is the antecedent of the conditional in (7), we get by *modus ponens*:

(8) ${\sim}((p \rightarrow O(p \wedge {\sim}p)) \wedge Op)$

Now, assuming the truth of Op, for (8) to be true the other conjunct should be false:

(9) ${\sim}(p \rightarrow O(p \wedge {\sim}p))$

By definition of the conditional in terms of conjunction this is equivalent to:

(10) $p \wedge {\sim}O(p \wedge {\sim}p)$

Were (10) true, p would be true, and thus we prove that assuming Op we obtain the truth of p:

(11) $Op \rightarrow p$[35]

Therefore, there is a strong connection between factual and deontic detachment, on the one hand, and the two alternative formal representations we have been calling insular and bridge conception of conditional norms, on the other. On the bridge conception, and with the aid of tools similar to those suggested

---

[35] For a similar proof, see Hintikka 1971: 81.

by Alchourrón (i.e., strict conditionals and defeasible conditionals), it is possible to represent norms for which factual detachment holds without restrictions, as well as norms for which factual detachment is only valid under certain conditions. By contrast, from the insular conception and the aid of similar tools, it is possible to represent norms for which deontic detachment holds without restrictions, as well as norms for which deontic detachment is only valid under certain conditions. But deontic detachment is not admissible within the bridge conception, nor is factual detachment within the insular conception. And as each of these two approaches validates different inferences, it makes no sense to compare them to assess which is superior to the other, because they cannot be taken as two different ways to represent a unique idea.

If we assume, just for the sake of simplicity, using the material conditional in schemas such as $p \rightarrow Oq$ and $O(p \rightarrow q)$, the differences between them may be presented more clearly in the language of possible-world semantics. According to the first schema, if in a given world p is true (a p-world), then all deontically ideal worlds regarding it are q-worlds (i.e., worlds in which q is true). Thus, if the actual world is a p-world, there is a categorical duty to bring it about that q, and this means that if the actual world is also a $\sim q$-world, we ought to transform it into a q-world (i.e., we ought to transform the world $p \wedge \sim q$ in a world $p \wedge q$), whereas if the actual world is already a q-world, we ought to prevent it from turning into a $\sim q$-world (i.e., we should "preserve" the world $p \wedge q$). In case the actual world is not a p-world, the norm under consideration imposes no duty whatsoever.

By contrast, according to the second schema (i.e., $O(p \rightarrow q)$), if in the actual world we are subject to this norm, then all deontically ideal worlds related to it will be worlds in which $p \rightarrow q$ is true. In other words, the worlds selected as deontically ideal by this norm are $(p \wedge q)$-worlds, $(\sim p \wedge q)$-worlds, and $(\sim p \wedge \sim q)$-worlds, and that is so regardless of the actual world being a p-world or not. The actual world may be $p \wedge q$, $\sim p \wedge q$, $p \wedge \sim q$, or $\sim p \wedge \sim q$, and for any of these four cases what the norm prescribes is the same; it is obligatory $p \rightarrow q$ (i.e., it ought to be either $\sim p$ or q). Therefore, if the actual world is $p \wedge q$, the duty imposed by this norm is to prevent the world from turning into a $(p \wedge \sim q)$-world, and this can be achieved either preserving the world as $p \wedge q$, or turning it into a $(\sim p \wedge q)$-world or into a $(\sim p \wedge \sim q)$-world (these two last options were not open in the case of a norm such as $p \rightarrow Oq$). If the actual world is $p \wedge \sim q$, the duty the norm imposes is to transform it into a $(p \wedge q)$-world, a $(\sim p \wedge q)$-world, or into a $(\sim p \wedge \sim q)$-world (the last two options were not open in the case of $p \rightarrow Oq$).[36]

---

[36] See Zuleta 2008: 139; also, Rönnedal 2010: 180–188.

Because the difference between $p \to Oq$ and $O(p \to q)$ lies in the scope of the deontic operator, conditional norms adequately represented by $O(p \to q)$ should be such that its addressee is in a position to influence with her actions either the occurrence or non-occurrence of both the antecedent and the consequent of the conditional; whereas in the case of $p \to Oq$, this requirement only verifies regarding the consequent. Hence, it makes no sense to represent a norm such as "You ought to close the window if it is cold" as $O(p \to q)$, being p that it is cold and q that the window is closed, because you cannot control the weather. This is a clear example of a norm that should be represented as $p \to Oq$. Moreover, from this norm and the fact that it rains, it should possible to derive the duty to close the window.[37]

Converse examples (i.e., of conditional norms that should be represented as $O(p \to q)$) are less clear. But suppose a norm such as "If you are going to the aid of your neighbors, you should tell them you are coming." At least it does not strike us as odd to represent it as $O(p \to q)$, because going to the aid of your neighbors and telling them you are coming are both actions prima facie under your control. Moreover, interpreted in this way, and from the duty to go to the aid of your neighbors it should be possible to derive the obligation to tell them you are coming. Now, suppose that the actual world is a p-world (i.e., a world in which you go to the aid of your neighbors). What does this norm, interpreted as $O(p \to q)$ demand? If you are going to the aid of your neighbors, the norm demands that you either tell them you are coming or return home. The norm will be satisfied in each of these two cases, and even someone who does both will have obeyed it.

All these remarks suggest that there are conditional norms in the natural language that seem better represented by one or the other of these two different structures, an idea that is plainly in conflict with Alchourrón's analysis, because he compares both structures as two competing candidates for the formalization of conditional norms, and favors the bridge conception over the insular conception.

The main difference with our view and the one defended by Alchourrón is reflected in the admission in system *AD* of what Alchourrón calls the *distribution principle* (identified as *AD*.9 in his paper):

(12) $O_d(q/p) \to (O_d p \to O_d q)$

---

[37] For reasons that will be made clear in the second part of this book, legal norms – at least most of them – are more appropriately represented through the so-called bridge conception of conditional norms.

According to the definitions offered by the author, $O_d(q/p)$ is equivalent to $p>Oq$, and O_dp is an abbreviation of $T>Op$. Thus (12) is equivalent to:

(13) $(p > Oq) \rightarrow ((T > Op) \rightarrow (T > Oq))$

which is but an application of deontic detachment. As we have shown, because deontic detachment cannot be valid within what Alchourrón calls the bridge conception of conditional norms, Alchourrón's admission of this principle in his system is rather surprising. In our view, Alchourrón has not been entirely consistent with his own ideas, for if he had followed reasoning similar to what he used to reject the interpretation of rational monotonicity in *HL*-systems, he should have noticed that the distribution principle had to take a different form in *AD* than the one he claims. In fact, consider the following inference-schema for defeasible conditionals, which we shall call the *principle of distribution for defeasible conditionals*:

(14) $(p > q) \rightarrow ((T > p) \rightarrow (T > q))$

Intuitively, what this formula expresses seems perfectly acceptable: if q is true in the most normal p-worlds, then if p is true in the most normal of all worlds, then q has to be true in those most normal worlds as well. As we saw, Alchourrón observes that the dyadic operator $O(q/p)$ of *HL*-systems works as a normative reading of the defeasible conditional, and thus it can be interpreted as equivalent to $p>q$. If this is so, the correlate of (14) in *HL*-systems would be:

(15) $O(q/p) \rightarrow (O(p/T) \rightarrow O(q/T))$

But if we use the monadic O-operator as a basis for representing an actual obligation, and defeasible conditional obligations are represented as $p >Oq$, as Alchourrón suggests, replacing q by Oq in (14) will not give as (13) in AD but:

(16) $(p > Oq) \rightarrow ((T > p) \rightarrow (T > Oq))$

There is a clear difference between both derivations: in *HL*-systems the principle of distribution of defeasible conditionals in its deontic interpretation renders valid deontic detachment. Here things are as they should be, because *HL*-systems assume the so-called insular conception of conditional norms. But, instead, (16) expresses that if q is obligatory in the most normal p-worlds, then if p is *true* in the most normal of all worlds, then q is obligatory in those most normal worlds. That should be the appropriate translation of the principle of distribution of defeasible conditionals in AD.

In fact, in the clearest examples of conditional norms of natural language that should be represented as $p \rightarrow Oq$, (16) seems justified, but (13) is not. To see this, notice that (13) is propositionally equivalent to:

(17) $(p > Oq) \rightarrow (\sim(T > Oq) \rightarrow \sim(T > Op))$

and (16) is propositionally equivalent to:

(18) $(p > Oq) \rightarrow (\sim(T > Oq) \rightarrow \sim(T > p))$

As explained previously, the representation $p \rightarrow Oq$ is especially apt for those conditional norms in which the antecedent is not a state of affairs under the control of the agent. For instance, a norm such as "prima facie you ought to close the window if it is cold" satisfies that condition, because its addressee will probably not be in a position to control the weather. In an example such as this, Alchourrón's theorem (13) is unacceptable, whereas (16) gives the right outcome: From the conditional norm "prima facie you ought to close the window if it is cold," and from the fact that in normal circumstances you do not have the obligation of closing the window (e.g., because you live in Ecuador), the absurd consequence that it is not the case that being cold is prima facie obligatory does not follow, but instead that when we say that in normal circumstances it is not obligatory to close the window we implicitly assume that it is not the case that in those normal circumstances it is cold. To illustrate this, see the following diagrams:

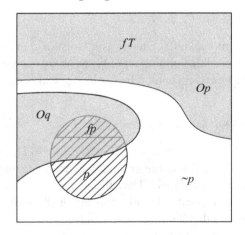

$(p>Oq) \wedge (T>Op)$

But $\sim(T>Oq)$

DIAGRAM 3.1

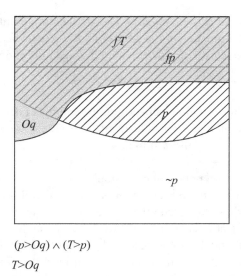

$(p{>}Oq) \wedge (T{>}p)$

$T{>}Oq$

DIAGRAM 3.2

In both cases, the squares represent sets of possible worlds, where in each case those worlds are distributed from the "most normal" (upper zone) to the "less normal" ones (lower zone). The sector above the superior line represents the set of "most normal worlds among all" (fT). In each square, there is a crossed sector representing the set of worlds in which p is true (whose upper sector represents the set fp) and a non-crossed zone representing the complement set ($\sim p$). In Diagram 3.1, $p{>}Oq$ holds, because the most normal p-worlds are included in the set of worlds were Oq. Additionally, it is also the case that $T{>}Op$, because the most normal worlds among all are included in the shadowed sector that stands for the set of worlds in which it is the case that Op. Nevertheless, contrary to Alchourrón's principle AD.9, in those most normal worlds it is not the case that Oq, therefore $T{>}Oq$ does not hold. Were AD.9 valid, the information provided by the premises should be enough to guarantee that the most normal worlds are included in the shadowed sector that represents the worlds in which Oq holds.

Diagram 3.2 represents our suggested alternative reading of the distribution principle in substitution of Alchourrón's AD.9 principle. Here, $p{>}Oq$ holds, because the most normal p-worlds are included in the shadowed sector representing those worlds in which Oq holds. Moreover, $T{>}p$ is also true, because the most normal worlds among all are p-worlds. Given these two premises, $T{>}Oq$ is derivable, because the most normal worlds are included in the shadowed sector that represents the worlds in which Oq holds.

In the same spirit of these remarks, David Makinson pointed out that there is an important limitation in Alchourrón's *AD*-system because it does not validate the *principle of transitivity* for conditional obligations – that is,

(19) $(O(q/p) \land O(r/q)) \rightarrow O(r/p)$[38]

The validity of this principle depends on the validity of deontic detachment. Thus, this principle does not hold in Alchourrón's system because deontic detachment cannot be valid within it.

The idea that $p \rightarrow Oq$ and $O(p \rightarrow q)$ should not be seen as two candidates to represent a unique notion of conditional norms, but instead as formalizations of two different notions of conditional norms, is also shared by Jackson and Pargetter when they argue that there are two ways in which an obligation may be subject to conditions.[39] First, what the authors call *hypothetical obligation*: a statement expressing an obligation of this kind has the form "if it were the case that p, then subject S would have the obligation to do q," and validates factual detachment. Second, what the authors call *restrictive obligation*[40]: a statement expressing an obligation of this kind has the form "Given that p, S has the obligation to do q," and validates deontic detachment instead of factual detachment. Analogously, Rönnedal distinguishes *wide* and *narrow* conditional obligation sentences to refer, respectively, to $O(p \rightarrow q)$ and $p \rightarrow Oq$, and remarks that deontic but not factual detachment is valid for wide conditional obligations, whereas factual but not deontic detachment is valid for narrow conditional obligations.[41]

It is important to observe that Zuleta has claimed that if $O(p \rightarrow q)$ and $p \rightarrow Oq$ were combined in the same system of deontic logic, paradoxical consequences would result. His argument is based on a similar set of statements to the one in Chisholm's paradox:

(20) Op
(21) $O(p \rightarrow q)$
(22) $\sim p \rightarrow O \sim q$
(23) $\sim p$

As we have seen, this set allows to derive Oq (from (20) and (21)) and $O \sim q$ (from (22) and (23)), and consequently $Oq \land O \sim q$ (i.e., an inconsistency). Therefore,

---

[38] See Makinson 1999: 35.
[39] See Jakson and Pargetter 1986.
[40] Zimmerman uses for this notion the expression "conditional obligation proper" (see Zimmerman 1996: 117).
[41] See Rönnedal 2010: 180–188. See also Schroeder 2004: 337–364.

in a world where norms (20), (21), and (22) were valid, $\sim p$ would be impossible, which Zuleta thinks is absurd.[42]

But clearly the set of norms (20), (21), and (22) is *not* inconsistent. Consider a model such as $W = \{w_1, w_2\}$, where the relation of deontic accessibility is $S = \{<w_1, w_2>\}$, and where $v(w_1, p) = v(w_2, p) = v(w_2, q) = V$. Here both Op and $O(p \rightarrow q)$ hold at w_1 because p and q are true in every accessible world (w_2), and $\sim p \rightarrow O \sim q$ also holds at w_1 because p is true at w_1. Hence, the three norms are jointly satisfiable, at least in a p-world, and that is enough to show that they are compatible. Were p false, the set of norms would be no longer satisfiable, but this is no proof of the incompatibility between $O(p \rightarrow q)$ and $\sim p \rightarrow O \sim q$. If we accepted this kind of reasoning, we should also have to accept that, because the set of propositions p, $p \rightarrow q$, and $p \rightarrow \sim q$ is inconsistent, then $p \rightarrow q$ and $p \rightarrow \sim q$ are themselves incompatible, which is plainly wrong as the conjunction of both propositions is consistent.

Zuleta is right to point out that the considered set of norms has factual consequences, namely, that p is true, but that is not because of the joint acceptance of $O(p \rightarrow q)$ and $\sim p \rightarrow O \sim q$. The reason is that a set such as $\sim p \rightarrow O \sim q$ and Pq also implies the factual consequence that p is true, and here we have no "insular" conditional norm. The acceptance of $p \rightarrow Oq$ as a well-formed formula is sufficient to derive factual consequences from normative expressions, given that the material conditional allows transposition (i.e., $\sim Op \rightarrow \sim p$). Therefore, if there is a problem here, that problem is neither the possibility of combining $O(p \rightarrow q)$ and $p \rightarrow Oq$, nor the acceptance of $p \rightarrow Oq$. Instead, the problem concerns the use of the material conditional as an adequate tool to represent conditional norms, a question we have to face now.

3.5. DEFEASIBILITY AND DEONTIC LOGIC

In 1964, von Wright proposed a system of logic for conditional norms.[43] In that system, conditional obligations are formalized through a dyadic deontic operator $O(p/q)$, which may be read as "if it is the case that q, then it is obligatory that p." Von Wright's system contains the following axioms:

(A$_1$) $\sim(O(\alpha/\beta) \land O(\sim\alpha/\beta))$
(A$_2$) $O((\alpha \land \beta)/\gamma) \leftrightarrow O(\alpha/\gamma) \land O(\beta/\gamma)$
(A$_3$) $O(\alpha/(\beta \lor \gamma)) \leftrightarrow O(\alpha/\beta) \land O(\alpha/\gamma)$

---

[42] See Zuleta 2008: 106.
[43] Von Wright 1964: 173–182.

The rules of inference of the system are substitution, *modus ponens*, the extensionality rule, and a rule according to which O-expressions obtained from PC tautologies, replacing their propositional variables by O-expressions, are theorems.

This system, however, presents the following difficulty.[44] Suppose

(1) $O(p/q)$

In that case, because q is propositionally equivalent to $(q \wedge r) \vee (q \wedge {\sim} r)$, we have:

(2) $O(p/((q \wedge r) \vee (q \wedge {\sim} r)))$

Applying (A_3) from left to right we obtain:

(3) $O(p/(q \wedge r)) \wedge O(p/(q \wedge {\sim} r))$

And eliminating the conjunction, we get:

(4) $O(p/(q \wedge r))$

Hence, by introduction of the conditional from (1) to (4), it is possible to conclude:

(5) $O(p/q) \rightarrow O(p/(q \wedge r))$

The formula (5) is the law of strengthening of the antecedent. Suppose now that besides (1) we have:

(6) $O({\sim} p/r)$

As we saw, in virtue of the law of strengthening of the antecedent, from (1) it follows (4). By the same principle, from (6) we obtain:

(7) $O({\sim} p/(q \wedge r))$

And now, by introduction of the conjunction, from (4) and (7) it follows:

(8) $O(p/(q \wedge r)) \wedge O({\sim} p/(q \wedge r))$.

But, this contradicts (A_1), because replacing in it α by p and β by $(q \wedge r)$ we get:

(9) ${\sim} (O(p/(q \wedge r)) \wedge O({\sim} p/(q \wedge r))$

In light of this, in von Wright's 1964 system, two logically independent conditions cannot lead to contradictory normative consequences. This appears, at

---

44 See Soeteman 1989: 185–186.

least at first sight, rather counterintuitive, because there is nothing contradictory in saying, for instance, that thieves ought to be punished, but thieves acting under duress ought not to be punished. In fact, having taken due notice of this consequence, von Wright himself observed that from the duty to do something under certain circumstances nothing can logically follow concerning our duties under different and logically unrelated circumstances.[45]

Two alternatives are open to avoid this consequence; either we have to weaken or abandon (A_1), or weaken or abandon (A_3). In 1965, von Wright chose the first road,[46] and proposed to replace (A_1) by

$$(A_1') \sim(O(\alpha/T) \wedge O(\sim\alpha/T))$$

where T represents any tautology. According to the resulting system, a certain circumstance may lead to a conflict of duties, but that seems rather odd from the point of view of a rational system of logic for conditional norms. If that is seen as unsatisfactory, we should focus on (A_3). Here the difficulty derives, among other things, from the application of the left to right implication. Thus, some scholars opted to reject this implication, replacing (A_3) with:

$$(A_3') \ (O(\alpha/\beta) \wedge O(\alpha/\gamma)) \rightarrow O(\alpha/\beta \vee \gamma)$$

According to the resulting system, conditional norms do not validate the rule of strengthening the antecedent, which as was shown follows from the converse implication.

This line of work gave rise to the development of the so-called *defeasible* deontic logics, a very popular field of research in recent years.[47] The general idea of defeasibility is connected with the notion of "normality." When formulating a conditional assertion, we assume that the circumstances are normal, but admit that under abnormal circumstances the assertion may become false. The use of defeasible deontic logics (or *non-monotonic* deontic logics[48]) has undoubtedly led to profitable results for the analysis of normative discourse. What defeasible deontic logics seek to elucidate is the question: Under what restrictive conditions can the principle of strengthening of the antecedent be admitted?

---

[45] See Von Wright 1964: 116.
[46] See von Wright 1965.
[47] See, for example, Nute 1997.
[48] For an excellent presentation of non-monotonic logic in general, see Makinson 2005.

But the use of defeasible tools in the normative domain has to be clearly distinguished from a substantive thesis that different authors have tried to defend – namely, that for some reason or a set of reasons, general norms (particularly legal rules) *are* defeasible, in the sense that all of them are subject to a list of exceptions incapable of exhaustive statement.[49]

The substantive thesis of the defeasible character of general norms was first introduced by H. L. A. Hart in an early paper that the author declined to reprint later.[50] Referring to legal rules, Hart claimed that all of them should be read as including a clause "unless circumstances demand otherwise," and so the conditions for their application cannot be specified in advance. Thus, the distinctive sign of normative defeasibility would rest not so much on the existence of overriding conditions restricting the scope of rules, but on the impossibility of specifying such defeating conditions.

It is interesting to examine closely the analysis offered by Frederick Schauer of this substantive thesis of normative defeasibility. Schauer considers – with reasons with which we fully agree – that the thesis that prescriptive rules (i.e., general norms) are in this sense necessarily defeasible appears partly confused, partly superfluous, and partly wrong.[51] After examining and rejecting four previous alternatives, he suggests the following reading of the defeasibility thesis:

> (D5) A rule is defeasible when its application is contingent not only on the non-occurrence of events specifiable in advance by particular or type, but also by the non-occurrence of conditions specifiable in advance neither by particular nor by type.[52]

There is a plain connection between this strong reading of the defeasibility thesis and the *over-inclusive character* of prescriptive rules (i.e., that they may encompass cases beyond the scope of their background justification), which is also stressed by Schauer.[53] But this connection is not one of identity. Over-inclusiveness leaves open the question of how a case of discrepancy between the solution indicated by the rule and the one derivable from its underlying justification should be decided. Instead, the defeasibility thesis, under the reconstruction offered by D5, entails that in any of those cases the

---

[49] Of course, this is not the only way to understand the claim of the defeasible character of general norms. Rodríguez and Sucar 1998 offer a conceptual map of the different possible alternatives of interpretation of this thesis.

[50] See Hart 1948.

[51] See Schauer 1998: 223–240.

[52] Schauer 1998: 232.

[53] See Schauer 1991: 31 ff.

priority shall be in favor of the outcome contemplated in the justification that underlies the rule.[54] However, as Schauer correctly observes, rules should be capable of serving as reasons for action *qua* rules (i.e., with a certain degree of independence from the reasons supplied by their background justifications). Thus, by assuming this strong defeasibility thesis, one is forced to pay the cost of implying the impossibility of assigning normative force to rules as such. From this point of view, Schauer argues that if the decision-maker's belief about how a case that falls under the scope of the rule ought to be decided trumps the force of the rule in every case of conflict between the two, then the rule exists only as a rule-of-thumb.[55]

On Schauer's view, defeasibility is not a necessary feature of rules but a contingent aspect of certain systems of decision-making. We fundamentally agree with Schauer on this point. To say that a rule is over-inclusive regarding its background justification merely indicates that it encompasses cases that might not produce the consequence triggered by the rule's justification.[56] However, it is compatible with postulating that in all these cases of discrepancy between the rule and its underlying justification, the normative solution provided by the rule should prevail. On the contrary, claiming that a rule is defeasible in the sense under consideration is tantamount to saying that the rule's normative consequence might be overridden even though a certain case falls within its factual predicate. Consequently, a rule may be deemed defeasible on account of its over-inclusive character. This happens when we treat the rule as completely transparent with respect to its background justification in all cases of over-inclusion. However, it might also be the case that a rule is over-inclusive without being defeasible.

The only point in which we do not fully agree with Schauer is the following. Schauer regards the definition of strong defeasibility expressed by D5 as equivalent to:

(D6) A rule is defeasible when its application is dependent not only on the occurrence of an event lying within the rule's linguistic reach, but on that event lying within the rule's purposes as well.[57]

---

[54] "D5, therefore, by denying the possibility that the occurrence of an unforeseen event within a rule's linguistic reach but outside its purpose can justify application of the rule, appears to justify necessary defeasibility only by rejecting the possibility that the rule qua rule can be a reason for action independent of the reasons for action supplied by its background justification" (Schauer 1998: 233).

[55] See Schauer 1991: 84, note 13.

[56] See Schauer 1991: 32.

[57] Schauer 1998: 236.

Schauer argues that if a rule were only applied when its application is consistent with its background purpose, but subject to defeat when its application does not serve such underlying purpose, there would be no case in which the rule *qua* rule generates an outcome which is not generated by the underlying justification. Accordingly, the normative force of the rule would simply dissolve.[58]

We believe there is at least one reason to reject the identification between D5 and D6, and to distinguish over-inclusiveness and defeasibility in a much broader sense than the one proposed by Schauer. Were D5 and D6 equivalent, the only grounds to introduce an exception into a rule would be its underlying justification. But exceptions to rules can derive from sources different from the rule's underlying justification. In fact, Schauer himself writes that, although a rule cannot be conceived of as completely defeasible, for it has to present some degree of resistance to being overruled, we should take care to distinguish two different phenomena. A rule would be inapplicable in virtue of what Schauer calls an *internal failure* when it is not applicable to those cases in which the justification does not apply. A rule would be inapplicable in virtue of what Schauer calls *external defeasibility* when it is overridden by particularly exigent factors external both to the rule and to its justification. Schauer claims that a rule with no resistance to internal failure whatsoever will not deserve, in an important sense, the name of "rule." However, being partially opaque regarding its underlying justification and thus having the necessary status to be a rule would be compatible with being overridden by external factors.[59]

When we focus our attention on isolated rules, this distinction between internal and external defeasibility appears to be quite clear. However, rules do not present themselves in isolation but as part of complex and interconnected systems. And in the face of normative systems, it is not easy to distinguish the two different situations (i.e., those in which a rule is inapplicable in virtue of the justification *which underlies that rule* and those in which the reason for not applying the rule rests on factors which are external both to the rule and its justification, and stems from other rules of the same system or their underlying justifications). The borderline between both situations will depend on – and vary with – the presupposed criteria of identification of rules. Schauer admits that any case of override can always be reformulated as being outside the scope

---

[58] See Schauer 1998: 237.

[59] See Schauer 1991: 117–118. Schauer's distinction between internal and external defeasibility is not conceptual but merely contingent, as he observes that it would collapse in a single-valued justificatory system, because in such a system the supporting distinction between the justification behind the rule and any other reason cannot be drawn (see Schauer 1991: 118, note 8).

of the rule.[60] But let us imagine a normative system containing two rules, one stating "Murderers should be punished" and the other providing that "Acting in self-defense should not be punished." It is not clear what difference it would make to say that the rule about murderers is externally defeasible in cases of self-defense, instead of saying that the rule about murderers includes an implicit exception restricting its scope to non-self-defense murders.

Regarding normative systems, the distinction between internal and external defeasibility is of some interest only if the qualifications "internal" and "external" are taken as predicates of the system as a whole, and not of isolated rules. Along these lines, a rule, which is a member of a certain normative system, will be internally defeasible when the reason for not applying it stems from that very system, whereas it will be externally defeasible when the reason for not applying it stems from extra-systemic considerations (i.e., when it is overridden by rules or justifications belonging to other normative systems). Needless to say, under this understanding the distinction does not justify the assessment of an isolated rule as a germane prescriptive rule or as a mere rule-of-thumb.[61]

Because the distinction between internal and external defeasibility seems to feature no qualitative aspect, the partisan of the necessary defeasible character of rules could reply to Schauer by means of the following line of argument. If a rule may be internally defeasible and still be a rule, it could also be externally defeasible without losing its normative force *qua* rule. Yet this kind of reply – and the defeasibility thesis in general – has to face a deeper predicament in line with Schauer's remarks, although exceeding the realm of exceptions generated by the underlying justifications of rules. Genuinely defeasible rules, in the sense examined here (i.e., those which are subject to an open list of exceptions), are incapable of justifying decisions or actions in any particular case.

To derive the normative solution contained in a rule regarding a particular case, two conditions must be met. First, the case must be an instance of the factual predicate of the rule. Second, the factual predicate must operate as a sufficient condition of the normative solution supplied by the consequent of the rule. The connection between the factual predicate and the normative solution of the rule shall be strong enough to allow a form of inference, such as factual detachment. But if rules are defeasible in this strong sense (i.e., subject to an open list of exceptions), they cannot validate the form of inference known

---

[60] See Schauer 1991: 90.

[61] This is something Schauer himself seems to acknowledge when he observes that there is little to distinguish the rule that is vulnerable to the inapplicability of its own justification from the rule that is vulnerable to being overridden in virtue of reasons which are external to that rule (see Schauer 1991: 110–111).

as strengthening of the antecedent. For, in such a case, the occurrence of the factual predicate of the rule, together with any of the exceptions limiting its scope, will prevent one from deriving the normative consequence of the rule. But if the law of strengthening of the antecedent is to be rejected, the same shall occur with *modus ponens,* for the latter implies the former.[62]

The proof is simple. Suppose, in general terms, a conditional connective > that validates *modus ponens* – that is,

(10) $((p > q) \land p) \to q$

Because by PC this formula is equivalent to:

(11) $(p > q) \to (p \to q)$

it would be the case that our conditional connective implies the material conditional. And because the rule of strengthening of the antecedent is satisfied by material conditional:

(12) $(p \to q) \to ((p \land r) \to q)$

By transitivity from (11) and (12) we obtain:

(13) $(p > q) \to ((p \land r) \to q)$

This means that the consequent of the conditional connective will be derivable from its antecedent in conjunction with any proposition whatsoever, which precisely constitutes the rule of strengthening the antecedent.[63] Therefore, if we abandon the rule of strengthening the antecedent, we also have to renounce *modus ponens.*

Yet, as already seen in the normative realm, the failure of *modus ponens* can assume two different forms according to the structure of conditional norms; the failure of factual detachment or of deontic detachment, what generates two different notions of defeasibility. The first is the notion of defeasibility related to what may be called "factual normality." A conditional norm is defeasible in this sense whenever the duty imposed in its consequent cannot be derived in spite of the *truth* of its antecedent, in virtue of the occurrence of an exceptional or abnormal fact that blocks the inference. Of course, mere facts do not defeat norms; the fact in question has to trigger the applicability of another norm, incompatible with the former that defeats it.

---

[62] See Alchourrón 1986.
[63] See Alchourrón 1991.

Defeasibility owing to failure of factual detachment:

$p>Oq$ is a defeasible norm if and only if, where r is an exceptional or abnormal fact, the joint occurrence of p and r does not allow inferring Oq.

The second notion of defeasibility is related to what may be called "deontic normality." A conditional norm is defeasible in this sense whenever the duty imposed in its consequent cannot be derivable in spite of the *obligatoriness* of the antecedent, in virtue of the existence of an exceptional or abnormal norm that blocks the inference. In this case it is directly a norm, and not a fact, which defeats the first norm.

Defeasibility owing to failure of deontic detachment:

$O(p>q)$ is a defeasible norm if and only if, where Or is an exceptional or abnormal norm, the joint occurrence of Op and Or does not allow inferring Oq.

This connection between the strengthening of the antecedent and factual/deontic detachment has a serious consequence for the substantive thesis of defeasibility of prescriptive rules: If a rule is understood as subject to an open list of exceptions incapable of exhaustive statement, no inferences whatsoever will be derivable with respect to any particular instance of its factual predicate, because the possibility of exceptions restricting the scope of the rule cannot be excluded.

The choice between interpreting rules as indefeasible, with the difficulties involved in identifying all their exceptions, and interpreting them as defeasible, and so deprived of almost any inferential power regarding individual cases, has been presented by Soeteman with admirable clarity as follows:

> [E]ither we accept ... that there are exceptions to norms (unconditional as well as conditional) which are not already included in the formulation of the norm, with the consequence that it will no longer be possible to deduce from a norm what we have to do under the concrete circumstance we find ourselves in, or we do not accept this possibility of exceptions (in other words: we only accept exceptions which are already included in the formulation of the norm); the question then is, however, whether we are indeed capable of formulating valid norms.[64]

In the second part of the book we argue that the second horn of this dilemma does not represent any genuine complication concerning legal rules. So far, we have just intended to establish that taking general norms as standards that are

---

[64] Soeteman 1989: 196.

subject to exceptions which cannot be exhaustively listed makes them useless tools for practical reasoning. This is so regardless of the source – internal or external – that defeasibility may have. And this problem affects even the weak version of defeasibility that Schauer takes into account, according to which rules are defeasible when their application is contingent upon the non-occurrence of an unspecifiable list of very good reasons for not applying them, such reasons having strength greater than would have been sufficient for those reasons to determine the outcome in the absence of the rules.[65] For if rules had only this presumptive force, an assessment of every member of such an unspecifiable list would be needed in each case of application, and that would inevitably block any possible inference.

---

[65] See Schauer 1998: 238.

PART II

Logic and Legal Systems

4

Legal Systems and Legal Validity

4.1. NORMATIVE SYSTEMS AND THE EXISTENCE OF NORMS

In the preceding chapter we pointed out the importance of distinguishing norms from norm-propositions. Although there are notable difficulties regarding the possibility of a genuine logic of norms, it is relatively uncontroversial that logic can be applied to norm-propositions, understood as propositions about the membership of a certain norm in a normative system. Concerning this last question, the problems are not so much about the very possibility of applying logic to norm-propositions, but rather about whether the logic of norm-propositions is something different from a genuine logic of norms, or whether the logic of norm-propositions is a special kind of logic or, by contrast, is no more than a fragment of classical logic.

One way to show the relevance of the logic of norm-propositions as something different from a logic of norms is through the analysis of the logical consequences of normative systems, particularly their logical properties, such as coherence and completeness. In what follows, we apply this analysis to a particular kind of normative systems: *legal systems*.

The concept of a legal system is one of the most important basic concepts in legal theory.[1] Its main contribution to our understanding of law lies in the relationship between legal systems, validity, and the truth conditions of legal statements. This is so because the descriptions of legal positions – such as rights, obligations, and responsibilities – seem to depend on the membership of certain norms in some particular legal system, and in this sense the truth-values of propositions describing the deontic status attributed by the law to certain actions depend on the truth-values of statements concerning the validity of legal norms.

---

[1] See Fletcher 1996: 28–75.

In spite of the crucial role that legal systems play in our contemporary societies, the study of such systems was rather a neglected topic in legal theory.[2] Legal systems are mainly sets of norms specifically related by certain criteria. A systematic reconstruction of the law needs to identify a set of properties that a norm must exhibit to be part of a certain legal system. In contemporary legal systems these properties of norms refer to a highly heterogeneous family of facts, such as promulgation, judicial recognition, ratification by supra-national institutions, specific commercial customs, and so on.[3] These properties are often called "criteria of validity" and, in this sense, a criterion of validity refers to a legal source as a justification of the membership of a certain norm in a legal system.[4] "Validity" here is a descriptive predicate; it only means that a certain norm satisfies a specific criterion of membership in a legal system.

Unfortunately, in legal theory this concept of validity is often confused with a couple of different ideas, such as the *existence* of norms and the *legality* in the creation of norms. One of the legal philosophers that most emphatically remarked a conceptual connection between validity and existence of norms was Hans Kelsen, and some brief remarks on the *Pure Theory of Law* will be useful to illustrate some recurrent problems in legal theory.

Kelsen regarded norms as ideal entities that belong to the realm of *ought*; their existence cannot be reduced to a matter of social or psychological facts, even though certain facts such as the "creation" of norms by authorities, or the observance of norms, are necessary for the existence of legal norms. In the Pure Theory, legal norms exist to the extent that they are *valid* or *binding*; validity is the *specific existence* of legal norms and, consequently, "invalid" norms are not norms at all.[5] Although this view on the "ontological problem" of legal norms is similar to positions endorsed by Natural Law theories, two crucial differences must be emphasized. On the one hand, legal validity is not an absolute notion. On the contrary, legal norms are not *intrinsically* valid; their validity is relative to a higher legal norm. On the other hand, the validity of the

---

2 For this reason, Raz observes: "It seems that the study of the theory of legal systems is still in its infancy, because the nature of the problems involved in it has not been fully understood nor has their importance been clearly apprehended" (Raz 1970: 121).

3 It is worth noting that even moral criteria are sometimes regarded by many philosophers as validating properties. See Waluchow 1994: 142–165.

4 Hart observes that even the most simple rule of recognition introduces, "although in an embryonic form, the idea of a legal system: for the rules are now not just a discrete unconnected set but are, in a simple way, unified. Further, in the simple operation of identifying a given rule as possessing the required feature of being an item on an authoritative list of rules we have the germ of the idea of legal validity" (Hart 1961: 118).

5 See Kelsen 1960: 267–271 and 1979: 28.

highest positive norm (i.e., the first historical constitution) is only hypothetical; its validity has to be presupposed, and it only makes sense for legal theorists to presuppose it if that highest norm is by and large effective.

One of the most important conclusions that can be drawn from Kelsen's analysis of legal validity is the systematic nature of law. Legal norms cannot exist in isolation because their validity always presupposes the validity of another norm, and these relations of validity confer systematic unity to a certain set of norms (i.e., they transform a normative *set* into a normative *system*). Therefore, legal norms are inevitably part of systems of norms, which are hierarchically *ordered* by chains of validity. Legal validity is, thus, *systematic* validity.

However, Kelsen's identification between validity of legal norms, their existence, their binding force, and the membership in a legal system, runs the peril of bringing about more confusion than illumination. An example of the perplexities that arise from this identification is the difficulty for the *Pure Theory of Law* in dealing with the problem of "invalid" norms, such as unconstitutional norms. According to Kelsen, a certain norm N_1 is valid if and only if it has been enacted by a competent authority, following the procedure and respecting the content fixed by a higher norm N_2. In this case, N_2 is the ground of the validity of N_1 and, consequently, N_1 cannot conflict with N_2, because were such the case, N_1 would be invalid, and for Kelsen this means that it would not exist as a norm. For this reason, Kelsen claims that no conflict is possible between a higher and a lower norm, because the reason of the validity of the lower norm is the higher norm.[6]

However, it is a well-known fact of our legal systems that they have special institutional organs, such as the Supreme Court in the United States or the Spanish Constitutional Court, with the legal power to solve conflicts between norms of different levels (e.g., a conflict between norms enacted by the Congress and constitutional provisions). As Justice Marshall puts it:

> If an act of the legislature, repugnant to the constitution, is void, does it, notwithstanding its invalidity, bind the courts, and oblige them to give it effect? Or, in other words, though it be not law, does it institute a rule as operative as if it was law? This would be to overthrow in fact what was established in theory; and would seem, at first view, an absurdity too gross to be insisted on.[7]

When a given norm is authoritatively declared to be unconstitutional, it is undeniable that it ceases to produce certain legal effects. But this does not

---

[6] See Kelsen 1960: 208.
[7] *Marbury v. Madison*, 5 U.S. 137 (1803).

necessarily mean that invalid norms do not "exist." In fact, if they did not exist, there would be no need for specific organs to repeal them. It is precisely because they have some sort of existence that they pose a serious problem for legal theory.

Kelsen cannot accept this conclusion on account of his identification between validity, existence, and membership in the legal order. In his view, the assertion that a valid norm is "unconstitutional" is self-contradictory, because the constitution is the ultimate positive reason of validity in a legal system.[8] However, he recognizes that unconstitutional norms can produce legal effects until the authority empowered by the legal system to evaluate the compatibility with higher norms declares them unconstitutional. This seems to lead to a paradox, because if a certain statute, for instance, does not fall within the scope of a constitutional empowering norm, according to Kelsen it would not even deserve to be called a "norm"; however, the legal order qualifies the opinions of certain organs to evaluate the compatibility of certain norms with higher norms in the legal hierarchy, and thus, in as much as the empowered organ does not declare it unconstitutional, the statute would be valid and binding over courts.

To solve this problem, Kelsen claims that whenever the legal order empowers the same institutional organ to enact norms in accordance with the constitution, and to pronounce final decisions regarding the conformity of its own norms with the constitution, every power-conferring norm should be read as including a *tacit alternative clause* authorizing the lawmaker to enact norms in accordance with the constitution *or* disregarding the content and procedures expressly established by the constitution. Kelsen thinks that the regulation of legislation by the constitution does not mean that valid statutes should only have the content stipulated by the constitution, but that they may be created "also in a way determined by the legislative organ itself."[9]

Hence, the so-called unconstitutional statutes are valid statues that may be repealed through a special procedure. The legislative organ has an open choice between two paths; the one explicitly prescribed by the constitution and the one to be decided by the legislative organ itself.[10] The same solution is presented by Kelsen for cases of "unlawful" judicial decisions.[11]

From this tacit alternative clause it follows that legislators have the power to enact general norms according to constitutional provisions, *or any other*; and judges have the power to apply general valid norms to justify their

---

[8] See Kelsen 1960: 271.
[9] Kelsen 1960: 273.
[10] See Kelsen 1960: 274.
[11] See Kelsen 1960: 267.

decisions, *or any other*. General norms created by legislative organs, and particular norms created by judicial decisions, would always be valid in the light of this alternative clause, irrespective of their content. This conceptual strategy allows Kelsen to support two related ideas. On the one hand, invalid norms do not exist; on the other hand, law is a *system* of norms, because there cannot be conflicts between norms of different hierarchical levels. The unity of the system is thus secured.

But this doctrine of the alternative clause succeeds in preserving the identity between validity, existence, binding force and membership in a legal system at a very high cost, because it forces Kelsen to give up other central theses of the *Pure Theory*:

1. Regarding the creation and application of norms, the doctrine of the alternative clause deprives the idea of the hierarchical structure of legal systems of its import. The very concept of a hierarchy loses its meaning if we accept the notion that lower norms can be valid in spite of their incompatibility with norms of a higher rank, because this higher rank is precisely shown by the fact that they prevail in case of conflicts with lower norms. It makes no sense to claim that the constitution is the highest positive norm within a legal system if the explicit and implicit constitutional content does not limit the enactment of lower norms.

2. Regarding their normativity, legal norms may be said to guide behavior in different ways, but one essential feature of law – as Hart stresses – is that the existence of a legal norm means that certain actions are no longer optional.[12] However, the addition of a tacit alternative to the explicit content of constitutional and general power-conferring norms turns them into something like a tautology. A norm with a structure such as "Do A or not" cannot be disobeyed and thus fixes no limits to our practical options. Therefore, if judicial decisions were always in accordance with the explicit or implicit content of general norms, judges would have absolute discretion; and if general norms were always in accordance with the explicit or implicit content of constitutional provisions, legislators would have absolute discretion, which is tantamount to saying that no norm in a legal system would have the slightest normative force.

3. The legal powers of authorities are conferred by the content of higher norms; this content is determined not only by explicit provisions, but also by their tacit meaning. Thus, if we accepted the doctrine of the tacit alternative clause, there would be no reason for restricting its scope to substantial norms and not extending tacit authorizations to norm-creating organs

---

[12] See Hart 1961: 6.

as well. An extremely strange consequence follows from such an extension: general power-conferring norms would *tacitly authorize* anyone to enact norms.

The moral of this analysis may be put in the following terms. The identification of the notions of validity, existence, binding force, and membership in a legal system, forces Kelsen to give up some crucial ideas, such as the hierarchical structure of legal systems, the normativity of legal norms, and the specificity of legal authorities. To avoid those consequences, the doctrine of the tacit alternative clause must be abandoned and, consequently, the chain of identification between validity/existence/binding force/membership must be broken at some point.

One possible way to do so is to preserve the identity between validity and membership in a legal system, while rejecting the identification (1) between validity and existence, and (2) between validity and binding force. In other words, even if invalid norms, such as unconstitutional statutes, are not regarded as members in a legal system, this fact does not imply that they cannot exist in other senses or possess binding force.

Under this approach, statements of validity are relative to a given normative system and to a certain historical moment, because any norm N may belong to system S_1 and not belong to system S_2, and may be valid in S_1 at time T_1 and invalid in S_1 at time T_2. Moreover, statements of validity have a purely descriptive character, in as much as they merely report that certain norms are members in a specified legal system.[13] In this reconstruction, statements of validity are simply *factual* statements, and no normative conclusion can be drawn from a mere statement of facts. Consequently, a possible objection that should be addressed is that validity statements so conceived cannot be offered as a plausible reconstruction of legal statements, because as many legal philosophers have stressed – Kelsen, Hart, and Raz among them – a fundamental feature of legal statements that legal theory should be capable of explaining is their normative force.

Kelsen states that, although legal statements are true or false, they are ought-statements, not only because they refer to legal norms, but also because they identify a norm as valid and, as we have seen, in the Kelsenian framework validity is a normative concept. To say that a certain norm is valid is tantamount to saying that one ought to do what that norm prescribes.[14] This is the reason why Kelsen thinks that legal statements not only ascertain empirical facts but also have a normative dimension: they are ought-statements, but *descriptive* ought-statements.

[13] See Raz 1970: 47.
[14] See Kelsen 1960: 10.

However, the idea that legal statements are ought-statements, which do not express prescriptive but descriptive obligations, seems nothing but the product of a confusion derived from the ambiguity that systematically affects deontic terms, which are liable to be read both descriptively and prescriptively. Alf Ross and Herbert Hart, among others, have vigorously criticized this idea. According to Ross, legal statements cannot be ought-statements if they have truth-values. Kelsen's use of the concept of validity as binding force, similar to the one we find in natural law theories, entails that the propositions of legal science have a normative character not compatible with a positivistic theory of law, for they refer to the validity of legal norms.[15]

Hart has explicated the Kelsenian idea of "descriptive" ought-statements with the aid of the distinction between *use* and *mention* of words.[16] He says that when the lawgiver enacts a law she *uses* certain words, whereas when the legal theorist tells us what the law means she *mentions* the very same words, and thus the word "ought" would be mentioned but not used in the statements of legal science. However, Kelsen's explicit rejection of this reading pushed Hart into reconsidering the point. He proposed an analogy with the relationship between a speaker of a foreign language and his interpreter. Suppose a foreign commander in a prisoner camp issues an order, translated by the interpreter as "Stand up!" The interpreter's statement is neither an order, because she is not an authority, nor a second-order statement that mentions the original words and correlates them with a certain meaning. The interpreter's statement tries to *reproduce* the order: it is a special use of language, and we could say with Kelsen that here the use of the grammatical imperative was "descriptive" and not "prescriptive." Nevertheless, Hart points out that logic has been substantially developed in the past centuries – particularly in the realm of the logical analysis of normative discourse, and thus one cannot be satisfied with this problematic category of "descriptive ought."

Hart's distinction between statements formulated from an *internal* and from an *external point of view*, as well as Raz's category of *detached legal statements*, may also be seen as an attempt to elucidate the normative character of legal statements. Hart distinguishes legal statements formulated by those who accept the rules and use them to evaluate their own and other people's conduct, from those formulated by an external observer, who does not need to accept the rules, and may limit herself to registering mere regularities of conduct of those who follow such rules, or may also take into consideration the attitudes of acceptance of those who follow the rules.[17] Only this latter kind of external

[15] See Ross 1958: 9–10; 1998: 159–161.
[16] See Hart 1962. Hart cites on this point Golding 1961: 355–364.
[17] See Hart 1961: 89 ff, and note at p. 291.

statements (i.e., those taking account of the internal point of view of the people who accept the rules) would constitute an adequate tool for a proper description of a legal system. Now, the simple fact that these statements register attitudes of acceptance of rules does not give them any "normative" character, and thus they may be considered apt to truth-values.[18]

The status of Raz's detached legal statements is somewhat more problematic. According to Raz, legal scholars can use normative language to describe the law and make legal statements without endorsing law's moral authority.[19] This kind of statement makes use of normative terms, and the speaker formulates them from the point of view of those who accept the rules, but this point of view is not necessarily shared by her. Those statements can be exemplified by advice given by an expert on a certain system of rules, who does not endorse such rules, to someone that accepts them and has doubts about what they require regarding certain situations. As has been pointed out, the possibility of formulating detached legal statements, or statements formulated from a point of view, makes it possible to account for the way in which normative language can be used to describe a legal system without assuming any normative commitment to it.[20]

Discussing statements of this kind, Raz claims that they are "normative,"[21] although he also states that they can be true or false.[22] Similarly, Hart maintains that they are normative statements but can be used to describe the law.[23] According to this, it seems that we have not gone far beyond Kelsen's "descriptive ought." And so it could be argued that the "normativity" of detached statements, or statements from a legal point of view, is no more than the result of using deontic expressions in them, such as "ought," "duty," or "obligation." However, as we have already seen, deontic expressions can be used to express either genuine norms or norm-propositions. Thus, if detached legal statements are deemed true or false, they will express norm-propositions.[24]

---

[18] This point was nicely stressed by Ross in the following terms: "I want to add that internal statements are not of a descriptive nature. . . . To me it is astonishing that Hart does not see, or at any rate does not mention, the most obvious use of external language in the mouth of an observer who as such neither accepts nor rejects the rules but solely makes a report about them: The legal writer in so far as his job is to give a true statement of the law actually in force" (Ross 1962: 1185). In the introduction of his *Essays in Jurisprudence and Philosophy*, Hart recognizes this external use of normative vocabulary (see Hart 1983: 14).

[19] See Raz 1979: 156–157.

[20] See Bayón 1991: 28.

[21] See Raz 1979: 202.

[22] See Raz 1975: 177.

[23] See Hart 1982: 154.

[24] See Bayón 1991: 28. Raz's detached legal statements have been extensively analyzed in contemporary legal philosophy. See, for example, Shiner 1992: 137–159; for a comprehensive

Be that as it may, this discussion shows that there is a grain of truth in the idea that legal statements have some kind of normative force. The tasks of legal science are complex, and thus many statements formulated by legal scholars are not purely descriptive and apt to truth-values. Some of them may be interpreted in the way Raz suggests. Others are undoubtedly normative in a stronger sense, for they are intended to predicate the binding force of legal norms (whether prima facie or conclusive). Of course, such a stronger notion of normativity is more a part of a moral program than an analysis of the formal aspects of law.

In the forthcoming discussion, we try to explore another notion – *applicability* of legal norms – that at least partially captures the practical dimension of law. However, if our main interest is centered on the truth-conditions of propositions about the content of law, the idea of validity understood as membership in a legal system is of paramount importance. And even if what we have in mind is a suitable account of the normativity of law, a systematic reconstruction is a necessary starting point for identifying the set of norms that makes a practical difference in legal contexts.[25]

4.2. SCOPE AND FORCE OF LEGAL NORMS

Legal norms may be viewed as a conditional relation between certain cases and the normative consequences attached to them. But what is the connection between norms and cases? This is a fundamental problem for a theory of norms, and legal philosophers have endorsed several different positions concerning it, which range from skepticism to formalism. For example, Hart has sometimes conceded that "in applying legal rules, someone must take the responsibility of deciding that words do or do not cover some case in hand, with all the practical consequences."[26] However, the interpretative activity regarding legal rules is not limited to the solution of hard cases; it seems to play a more important role, for Hart has also stressed that norms "cannot provide for their own application, and even in the clearest case a human being must apply them."[27]

---

analysis, see Duarte d'Almeida 2011: 167–199; for an alternative understanding of detached legal statements, see Rodríguez 2013: 127–146.

[25] As Raz points out: "One may say that a normative statement has the general form that p ought to be the case, and that it is true if, and only if, there is, in a certain normative system, a norm to the effect that p ought to be the case" (Raz 1970: 47).

[26] Hart 1983: 63–64.

[27] Hart 1983: 106.

This idea seems to suggest that there is a conceptual gap between general norms and individual cases, a gap that only interpretation can help to bridge. Neither in hard, nor in easy cases do facts await us labelled with the applicable norm. And this seems to make interpretation unavoidable in connecting legal norms with particular cases. As Hart says, "laws require interpretation if they are to be applied to concrete cases."[28]

However, radical skeptics also deny that interpretation can solve the indeterminacy of legal norms; the application of general norms would be, as Kripke said, a "leap in the dark."[29] In his *Philosophical Investigations*, Wittgenstein analyzes the connection between a rule such as "add 2" and its applications. Although we may agree on some examples (e.g., that after 1.000 we must put 1.002), we cannot take it for granted that the agreement on such cases suffices to guide future applications of the rule. On a skeptical interpretation,[30] it could be claimed that because there is nothing additional connecting the rule with its instances of application, there is an unbridgeable gap between them.

Although many interesting philosophical problems concerning the existence and nature of rules are connected to the discussions on rule-following, there is no need here to revisit the entire debate; instead, we *assume* that there are good answers to the skeptical challenge.[31]

As we have said, norms correlate abstract circumstances or properties with deontic consequences. These properties are often called "cases," but they are *generic* cases, which must not be confused with *individual* cases.[32] An individual case is a particular event, such as when we speak of "the case of the murder of John F. Kennedy"; a generic case is a class of circumstances, and may be exemplified by "the case of political murder."

All individual cases regulated by a certain norm are the *immediate range* of such a norm, and in this sense norms *internally apply* to individual cases.[33] Using terminology borrowed from Kelsen, we may define internal applicability in the following terms: a norm N is *internally applicable* at a certain time *t*

---

[28] Hart 1961: 204.

[29] Kripke 1982: 55.

[30] This is Kripke's skeptical reading of Wittgenstein. However, it should be noted that most readings of Wittgenstein on the rule-following problem are not skeptical.

[31] See Wittgenstein 1953: paragraphs 201 and ff.; Kripke 1982. For a careful analysis of the problem of rule-following, see Baker and Hacker 1984. This line of reply to radical skepticism has deeply influenced legal theory. See for example Schauer 1991: 64–68; Marmor 1992: 146–154; Bix 1993: 36–62; Coleman and Leiter 1993: 219–223; Endicott 2000: 22–29; Alexander and Sherwin 2008: 19–24.

[32] See Alchourrón and Bulygin 1971: 28.

[33] See Raz 1970: 123.

regarding a certain individual case *c* if and only if *c* is an instance of a generic case C, and C is defined by the spatial, temporal, personal, and material spheres of validity of N.[34]

The relation between norms and individual cases is *internal* or *conceptual*, and this means that, like the truth of a proposition, it does not depend on the beliefs, attitudes, or decisions of judges. Under this interpretation, the connection between general norms and individual cases is no more mysterious than the relation between descriptive predicates and individuals. As Weinberger points out, someone can believe in the truth of the proposition "All men are mortal" without being conscious of the consequence "The man Socrates is mortal," but the logical validity of the inference is completely independent from those relations between psychic acts.[35]

The analysis of the logical consequences of general norms is necessary to determine their scope (i.e., the individual cases regulated by them). Logical consequences of norms are part of their conceptual content; they project the normative solution of a generic case to every individual case that belongs to it.[36] Consequently, it may be said that individual cases are connected with individual norms that provide them with corresponding individual solutions, and even if such individual norms have not been anticipated by authorities, they are implicit in the regulation of generic cases.[37] This fact is implicit in the previous characterization of internal applicability as a *conceptual* relation between individual cases and general norms. But this conceptual connection should not be confused with the *institutional* relation between particular controversies litigated in courts and general norms. Judicial decisions are often invoked as a proof that the validity of individual norms cannot be drawn from the validity of some general norms and the truth about certain facts. On the contrary, it seems that the validity of these individual norms depends on the fact that they are actually posited by judicial decisions. For example, Kelsen claims that judicial decisions cannot be regarded as "normative syllogisms," and that the connection between general legal norms and individual norms is always mediated by normative acts rather than logical consequences.

---

34 See Kelsen 1960: 10–15; Moreso and Navarro 1997: 206. It is important to notice that general norms regulate classes of situations, and that such classes can be empty because no individual case falls within their immediate range. In this case it would still make sense to say that the norm internally *applies* to this (temporarily empty) set of circumstances.

35 See Weinberger 1995: 264.

36 On the distinction between generic and individual acts, see von Wright 1963a: 36–37; Alchourrón and Bulygin 1971: 27–31.

37 See Hart 1961: 125–126.

Legal theorists usually refer to those disputes in courts as "cases," such as the "Riggs v. Palmer case." To avoid misunderstandings, we use the expression *judicial cases* to refer to them. Judicial cases resemble individual cases in that they refer to the concrete legal situation of specifically determined individuals or groups of individuals. However, an adjudicative process – a judicial case – ordinarily requires solving many different normative problems. Each of those problems can be analyzed in terms of generic cases and individual cases, but the judicial case, globally considered, cannot be identified with either of them. Thus, *general* norms do not resolve judicial cases, because such cases need a final institutional decision. However, this does not mean that individual decisions cannot be deduced from general norms, because *individual* cases are decided as logical consequences obtained from general norms plus certain empirical premises.[38]

In other words, both individual and judicial cases are *particular* cases, but an individual case is an instantiation of a generic case. By contrast, judicial cases are practical problems that call for an institutional solution. A judicial case is resolved only when an appropriate authority (i.e., a judge) puts an end to the controversy. Therefore, the question "What is the connection between general norms and particular cases?" has different answers according to different concepts of particular cases; whereas the connection between general norms and individual cases is *conceptual* or *internal*, the connection between general norms and judicial cases is an *institutional* relation.

Sometimes the skepticism concerning the connection between general and individual norms rests on an ambiguous use of the expression "individual norm."[39] Suppose, on the one hand, a general norm that punishes murderers with death penalty and, on the other hand, the truth of the factual statement "Brutus killed Caesar." The individual norm (N_1) – "Brutus must be punished with the death penalty" – follows logically from the conjunction of the indicated general norm *and* the fact that Brutus killed Caesar. This individual norm can be regarded as a directive addressed to judges. Thus, if judges do not impose the death penalty on Brutus, they would commit a judicial mistake. N_1, insofar as it specifies a duty of judges, does not depend on any adjudicative decision; moreover, it is prior to adjudication and has an implicit existence as part of the conceptual content of certain general norms and relevant facts.

Now, a judge might convict Brutus and sentence him to the death penalty by pronouncing the following prescription (N_2): "Brutus must be punished with

---

[38] See MacCormick 1978: 37.
[39] See Bulygin 1994: 33–35.

the death penalty." This individual norm is not addressed to a judge; instead, it is *formulated* by a judge and addressed to other law-enforcing officials. N_2 does not merely exist as part of the implicit content of the general norm that punishes murderers with the death penalty; it exists as the actual content of an explicit decision made by a judge. Therefore, although a judicial decision is necessary for the existence of N_2, such a normative act is irrelevant for the existence of N_1. To sum up: if an individual case is an instance of a generic case regulated by a general norm, the application of this norm is logically derivable regarding the individual case, and this is completely independent from the fact that an adequate institutional answer to any individual case may require a new decision from legal officials.[40]

In contrast to the internal relation between a certain norm and its scope, the connection between a given norm and its institutional force to regulate a certain case is *external*. This means that the practical relevance of a certain norm to justify institutional decisions regarding certain cases is dependent on a range of factors, such as the relation of that norm with higher norms and legal principles, or the place of the judge that has to make that decision within the hierarchy of norm-applying organs. Hence, we shall call this sense of applicability *external applicability* of legal norms, a notion that may be defined in the following terms: norm N_1 is *externally applicable* at a certain time t regarding a certain individual case c, which is an instance of a generic case C, if and only if another norm N_2 that belongs to the legal system at t allows or imposes the duty on judges to use N_1 to justify their decisions in all individual cases that are instances of C.

It has often been pointed out that only applicable norms are apt to justify legal decisions.[41] Although this seems perfectly reasonable, one may wonder whether the reference is made here to external or internal applicability. It is tempting to claim that, in so far as the ultimate reason for an adequate set of criteria of individuation of legal norms rests on our interest in the solution of legal controversies, the application of such principles will result in the identification of norms that judges and other officials have the duty to apply.

According to Munzer, legal norms must be applied (are externally applicable) to all the cases and only to the cases they regulate (those in which they are internally applicable), and only valid norms that regulate a case (those that

---

[40] Things are more complicated in the case of common law decision-making, because judges often have the authority to modify legal norms in the process of their application to the case before the court.

[41] For example, MacCallum 1993: 68–69.

are internally applicable) should be applied to it (are externally applicable to it).[42] This is tantamount to identifying external applicability with internal applicability plus validity, an idea that seems to capture an important number of ordinary intuitions related to the task of applying the law. In fact, a radical change in our understanding of the law would be needed if, in normal cases, valid internally applicable norms were not applied.

In fact, it would be superfluous to enact a legal norm imposing on judges the duty to apply another *specific* legal norm. Hence, in ordinary circumstances there is no need for a higher-order norm to prescribe that other norms should be applied to those cases they regulate; legal authorities just enact certain norms regulating certain cases, and judges and other officials are supposed to use those norms to justify their decisions in those cases that fall within their scope.

However, there are certain circumstances in which it would be perfectly reasonable, and even required, to enact a norm imposing on judges the duty to apply a certain *class of norms* to a certain *class of cases*. Consider the problems raised by normative conflicts. For any given case there may be more than one internally applicable norm in a legal system.[43] Normative conflicts arise whenever two or more internally applicable norms provide incompatible solutions to a certain case, and so another norm may be needed to provide norm-applying organs with certain criteria to select which norm should be applied. As a result of such a process, some internally applicable norms will be discarded.

Many legal philosophers – notoriously Kelsen among them[44] – have defended the thesis that a proper interpretation of the raw legal materials should avoid conflicts between norms. In other words, in as much as the conceptual task of individuating norms is clearly different from, and logically subsequent to, the identification of raw legal materials, it is possible to defend the position that the former leads to consistent normative sets, at least as an ideal. But to obtain a consistent normative set, a necessary prerequisite is to specify the scope of norms (their internal range of applicability) in such detail

---

[42] See Munzer 1973: 1149–1150.

[43] MacCallum points out that, "[t]he supposition that judges have a duty to apply all applicable rules leads to difficulties in any reasonably complex systems. Briefly, the difficulties concern conflicts of rules. It may appear that of the various rules applicable to a set of circumstances, the application of some will lead to end results in the case different from the results led to by application of the other(s). The question then arises as to how we would describe the duty of judges in such cases" (MacCallum 1993: 69, note 3).

[44] See Kelsen 1960: 71–75. In his latest writings, he abandoned this idea (see Kelsen 1979: 123–127).

as to introduce all possible exceptions, to guarantee the dissolution of any putative conflict. Therefore, principles of individuation of great complexity should be privileged, favoring the *autonomy* of norms.

There is no single or univocal correlation between legal norms and authoritative texts. Such texts are the necessary bricks for the identification of legal norms (i.e., the basic units of the law of a certain political community). Consequently, the identification of norms always requires the application of principles of individuation and, as Raz has clearly shown,[45] the prevalence of *autonomy* entails the sacrifice of *simplicity*, and so the identified norms will depart dramatically from our ordinary intuitions. An example could shed some light on this problem. Let us suppose that in Ireland the criminal code includes a norm N_1, which prescribes "Everyone who commits abortion shall be punished by imprisonment," and norm N_2, which prescribes "N_1 shall be applied when abortion is committed within Ireland, but not otherwise." Suppose further that Jones performs an abortion in England. Does N_1 regulate abortion in Jones's case or is the spatial sphere of validity of N_1 restricted to Ireland by N_2?

The identification of the spheres of validity of a certain norm depends on some accepted principles of individuation of norms. Thus, the applicability of N_1 and N_2 can be reconstructed in two different ways:

(1) N_1 regulates Jones's case, but N_2 prescribes that judges in Ireland must not apply N_1 to Jones's case, and for this reason N_1, although internally applicable, is not externally applicable to it.
(2) N_1 does not regulate Jones's case owing to a restriction on its spatial sphere of validity imposed by N_2, so N_1 is not externally applicable because it is not internally applicable to it.

According to (2), N_2 introduces an exception to N_1, and for this reason neither N_1 nor N_2 can be regarded as complete norms. In fact, they should be interpreted as jointly saying: "Judges must convict those persons who perform abortions in Ireland." Should all legal norms be reformulated by introducing all the exceptions and conditional clauses required by solution (2)?

The answer depends on the functions we assign to the principles of individuation of norms. Principles of individuation promote our understanding of the law by classifying norms into different types and by showing how norms are related to other norms and principles. In this sense, (2) has the disadvantage pointed out by Raz: under this reconstruction we will have fewer

---

[45] See Raz 1970: 114–120.

but much more complex norms.[46] In fact, Raz claims that legal scholars and philosophers should adopt principles of individuation which (i) keep norms to a manageable size; (ii) avoid repetition; (iii) minimize the need to refer to a great variety of statutes and cases as the sources of a single norm; and (iv) do not deviate unnecessarily from the common-sense notion of a norm. According to these principles, any legal system will include a great number of norms interacting with one another, modifying and qualifying their conditions of applicability.

It is impossible to discuss whether a norm such as N_1 actually applies to Jones's case without specifying which principles of individuation are explicitly endorsed. We only assume here that legal raw materials can be arranged in several ways, and that there is not a canonical and accepted test to decide how legal norms must be reconstructed and individuated. However, even if, facing an example similar to Jones's case, the second reconstruction were preferred, according to which the criteria of identification of norms are sufficiently rich to guarantee the incorporation of all possible exceptions within the range of any norm, there would still remain cases where the notion of external applicability does have a decisive role. In what follows, we concentrate our attention on external applicability, and – unless stated otherwise – the expression "applicability" is understood in this sense.

4.3. APPLICABILITY AND VALIDITY

A thorough understanding of the applicability of legal norms is threatened by a possible misunderstanding regarding the relations between validity and applicability. Applicability, like validity, is a function of other norms in the system, but both are independent properties of legal norms. However, legal philosophers often overlook such conceptual independence. For instance, Schauer explicitly claims that validity is a necessary condition for applicability.[47] He rightly emphasizes that the connection between cases and externally applicable norms actually requires something more than internal applicability. According to him, validity is the additional ingredient required for external applicability.[48]

But the relations between validity and applicability are rather more complex. If "validity" means "binding force" and applicable norms are those norms accepted as binding, then the assertion "validity is a necessary condition for

---

[46] See Raz 1972: 831.
[47] See Schauer 1991: 119.
[48] See Schauer 1991: 118.

applicability" is analytically true. However, if "validity" means membership of a given norm in a legal system, then the assertion "validity is a necessary condition for applicability" is *false*, because invalid norms can be, and often are, legally binding.

There is no necessary connection between the applicability of a legal norm and its membership in a legal system at a certain time. Of course, as has already been pointed out, in ordinary circumstances judges will have the duty to apply those valid norms that regulate a certain case.[49] Nevertheless, there are norms that do not belong to a legal system but cannot be ignored by judges in justifying their decisions in certain cases. For example, according to private international law, a certain norm N of state S_1 may be applicable in another state S_2, even if N does not belong to the legal system of state S_2.

In fact, the distinction between validity and applicability is necessary to grasp a crucial feature of legal systems: their *open* nature.[50] One important function of law is to give support to other forms of social grouping; legal norms contribute to this process in several ways, but one of the most important of them is by means of conferring binding force to non-legal norms.[51] Thus, the institutional force of social norms does not stem from their validity but from the fact that the law *adopted* them. Consequently, as Raz points out, in a systematic reconstruction of law, it is necessary to distinguish between norms that are regarded as binding because they are part of the legal system, and other adopted norms that are regarded as binding (although they are not part of the legal system), such as foreign norms, contracts, regulations of commercial companies, and so on.[52]

The *criteria* for identifying adopted norms in a legal system must be distinguished from the *reasons* offered to justify the adoption of such norms. A norm N_1 may be said to be adopted in a legal system LS if and only if N_1 does not

---

[49] It could be argued that, although a certain norm N_1 regulates case c and belongs to the legal system at time t, it may be inapplicable to c at t if another norm N_2 forbids judges to apply N_1 to c. Possible examples of this might be norms in *vacatio legis*, or the temporal inapplicability of certain constitutional rights and guarantees owing to the exercise of exceptional powers (e.g., emergency parliamentary powers). However, any conceivable example of this kind is open to an alternative reconstruction according to which N_1 is inapplicable to c because it does not regulate the case.

[50] See Raz 1979: 119–120; 1975: 152–154.

[51] See Raz 1979: 119.

[52] See Raz 1979: 120. Illuminating as they may be, Raz's arguments on the open nature of legal systems need to be refined to avoid possible misunderstandings. For example, Raz claims that foreign norms are adopted by an open legal system if and only if they are still in force. Nevertheless, it clearly makes sense to say that judges are sometimes bound to apply norms of an extinct state (e.g., USSR). Moreover, as it often occurs in cases of private international law, judges may be bound to apply foreign norms that have been derogated a long time ago.

belong to LS, but another norm N_2, which is a member in LS, imposes the duty to apply N_1 to certain cases. There are several reasons that may be used to justify the adoption of norms: to give necessary support to social groups, private institutions, and individual arrangements are only some of these justifying reasons. Others may be to preserve peace and social order, or to prevent legal uncertainty. Now, suppose that the following norm is present in a certain criminal code:

> CN: If the law in force at the time the crime was committed is different from the law in force at the time of sentence or service thereof, the law more favorable to the accused shall be applied.

According to CN, judges must apply the least severe criminal norm of those that were members in LS between the time an offence is committed and the time of adjudication. Even a repealed norm may be the one selected by CN, provided that it prescribes the least severe sanction. Because that norm has already been derogated, it does not belong to LS at the time of adjudication, and so it may be regarded as adopted by judges at the time of decision-making. A judge's reasons for applying the least severe norm are overtly different from the reasons which legislators relied on when they enacted the criminal norm CN. The former are usually related to the fidelity to law in the decisions of legal cases, but the latter are normally principles which provide moral justification of punishment.

The so-called unconstitutional norms are another interesting example. An unconstitutional norm is an invalid norm, because it does not meet the appropriate systematic relations with other norms of a legal system. Nevertheless, it may happen that the competent authorities empowered to control their constitutional validity, such as a constitutional court, wrongly declare them valid. To deal with these invalid norms, we must bear in mind the distinction between final and infallible judicial decisions, because the constitutionality of a legal norm does not depend on what the constitutional court decides.[53] Norms enacted by incompetent authorities are invalid even if the constitutional court embraces the opposite stance. However, the final decision of the constitutional court determines the applicability of those norms. If the court wrongly says that a certain norm is constitutional, that norm will be applicable, although invalid in the system.[54] A judge's reasons for deferring to applicable unconstitutional norms can be the fidelity to binding

---

[53] See Hart 1961: 141–147.
[54] See Bulygin 1991: 267. In some systems, the final decisions of the Supreme Court are regarded as a criterion of validity. We shall not analyze here this possibility.

precedents or the necessity of meeting formal requirements of justice (i.e., to treat similar cases similarly). Therefore, unconstitutional norms can be regarded as adopted by a legal system, and the reason for such an adoption is an important feature of the law: it necessarily provides a mechanism to solve conflicts. But rules of adjudication can satisfy their function only to the extent that they can settle legal disputes authoritatively.[55] Thus, to obtain the social advantages of the legal process requires accepting the possibility of mistakes in adjudication, and definite decisions must not be confused with infallible decisions.

These examples show that invalid norms may be applicable norms, which is tantamount to recognize that the intuitive idea of a legal system as a set of valid norms must be distinguished from *systems of applicable norms*, or *applicable systems*. Neither legal systems, as the sets of all valid legal norms in different times, nor *momentary legal systems*, which contain – in Raz words – "all valid norms of a municipal law at a certain time," although obviously related to applicable systems, are identical with them. A pair of norms N_1 (enacted in 1906 and repealed in 1927) and N_2 (enacted in 1948) cannot belong to the same momentary system if "they were never valid at one and the same moment."[56] However, both norms may belong to the same *applicable* system regarding a certain case. Moreover, a given norm N_1 of the Argentinean Civil Code and a certain norm N_2 of the Argentinean Criminal Code may belong to the same momentary system even if no applicable system would contain them both (i.e., if they never apply to the same cases).

Unlike internal applicability of legal norms, the connection between the externally applicable norms and a certain case depends on *another* norm or set of norms containing a certain criterion of applicability. This is the reason why we said that the connection between externally applicable norms and cases is *extrinsic* or *institutional*. External applicability is a triadic relation between two norms N_1 and N_2 and a case c. Norms N_1 and N_2 form a "chain of applicability." N_2 belongs to the legal system and imposes the obligation that N_1 be applied to certain cases. For example, N_2 may prescribe that the less severe norm must be applied in criminal cases. In this account, norm N_1 can be applicable at time t to a certain case c without belonging to the legal system at t. Similarly, another norm N_3 may belong to the legal system at t without being applicable to a certain case at t. Thus, the conceptual independence between membership and applicability of norms is preserved while emphasizing the importance of a systematic reconstruction of the law to identify the applicable

---

[55] See Raz 1979: 172–176.
[56] See Raz 1970: 34.

norms: applicability can only be predicated of norms in accordance to certain criteria of applicability that belong to the legal system.

4.4. APPLICABLE SYSTEMS AND HIERARCHICAL ORDERINGS

Statements of external applicability (e.g., "Norm N is applicable to the case c") – seem to assign a specific property to a certain norm. Nevertheless, the logical structure of this kind of statement is more complex and reveals a commitment to a systematic reconstruction of law by tacitly requiring the existence of a higher level norm that imposes on judges the obligation to apply another norm to certain cases. And, more interestingly, it is impossible to grasp a clear understanding of the meaning of the negation of any statement of applicability without identifying all the elements involved in the relation of applicability.

A statement of applicability and its negation must be mutually exclusive and jointly exhaustive. In this sense, the negation of a statement that asserts the existence of a certain norm N_2 that imposes on judges the obligation to apply norm N_1 in case c is another statement that denies the existence of a norm imposing such a duty. Therefore, it may be said that norm N_1 is *non-applicable* to a case c if there is no other norm N_2 in the system imposing on judges an obligation to use N_1 in c. By contrast, it may be said that a norm N_1 is *inapplicable* to a case c when a higher-level norm N_2 forbids judges to apply N_1 to c. From these definitions, it follows that, whereas one and the same norm cannot be *applicable* and *non-applicable* at the same time with respect to the same case, the same norm may be *applicable* and *inapplicable* to the same case if there is a conflict between different criteria of applicability. Thus, applicability and *inapplicability* are neither mutually exclusive nor jointly exhaustive. Moreover, a norm may be non-applicable and yet not inapplicable to a certain case.

Usually, not one but a number of different norms are applicable to a certain case c. For example, in criminal law, the concurrence of legal descriptions of different offences in the same case is a highly debated issue –and very common in practice. All such norms are applicable (i.e., are selected using certain applicability criteria of the system as possible solutions to the instant case). Although they are, prima facie, adequate to solve the case, an ordering relation must be imposed on this set of norms to single out the decision judges are bound to make. Hence, and to avoid possible confusions, if N is an applicable norm and judges have the conclusive legal obligation to apply it to justify their decision in the instant case, N will be called a *strictly applicable norm*. The distinction between applicable norms *simpliciter* and strictly applicable norms shows that an inapplicable norm can be analyzed as a situation in which that norm, although a member of the set of applicable norms, was not selected as the one judges were bound to apply.

It should be noticed that membership in the applicable system may depend on the legal powers of the decision-making officials. A certain judge may have the obligation to apply norm N to case c, whereas another judge within the same system might lack authority to apply norm N to c. For a simple example, consider a judge adjudicating a dispute concerning compensation for emotional injuries caused by adultery. She has no legal power to apply norms of the criminal code regulating adultery as an offence, even if such criminal norms regulate the same individual case. Analogously, in a system with a rigid constitution, where the control of legal validity of the rest of the norms in the system lays in the hands of higher-ranked norm-applying organs, lower-court judges normally have the duty to apply any legal norm that satisfies a set of formal conditions of validity. They cannot refuse to apply hierarchically lower norms on the grounds of their incompatibility with the constitution. On the contrary, higher-ranked norm-applying organs empowered to exert the control of compatibility with constitutional provisions may disregard those incompatible norms that other judges have the duty to apply. Therefore, if applicable norms are those that certain judges may or ought to apply, then the applicable system is partially determined by the jurisdiction in which the dispute has to be settled, and this means that the same case, when discussed by different courts, admits the incorporation of different norms to the set of applicable norms.

If the criteria of applicability are expressed by norms, then nothing prevents those criteria from rendering incompatible solutions to the same case, or even offering no solution at all. In other words, the applicable system may be inconsistent or incomplete. In cases of inconsistencies within the applicable system, there will usually be norms or legal practices determining preferences between the applicable norms. Certain standards (*lex superior, lex posterior*) may be used to select one strictly applicable norm to a certain case. If norms N_1 and N_2 both belong to the applicable system regarding case c, but there is within the system a rule fixing a preference for the latter over the former — and thus solving the conflict between them — N_2 will be selected as the strictly applicable norm in case c. Only when this pair of norms is ordered according to a meta-criterion of applicability, is it possible to identify the strictly applicable norm and disregard the overruled norm as inapplicable.

Legal theorists usually order inconsistent sets of norms by assigning preference to one of them following certain implicit or explicit criteria. As a result,
the conflicting situation is commonly re-described as an apparent or prima
facie inconsistency. Hence, the importance of conceiving the legal system
as a hierarchical set of norms stems primarily from the fact that it supplies
criteria to solve normative conflicts. This means that whenever the hierarchical order varies, the criteria to solve inconsistencies will vary accordingly,
and this ultimately implies that a different set of applicable norms will be
selected.

Frequently, there will be several hierarchical ordering criteria for legal
norms, and it will not be easy to justify a certain choice.[57] Hence, the ordering
relations between the different norms which belong to the set of norms applicable to a certain case are not always fixed, so as to allow the selection of a
single norm as the strictly applicable one. In other words, the existence of one
strictly applicable norm is a special case of the set of applicable norms, where
certain meta-criteria provide a unique result. Nevertheless, even in those cases
in which one strictly applicable norm is in fact selected, it should not be overlooked that the weaker norms were also members of the applicable set and,
consequently, cannot be ignored by decision-making organs.

It can be accepted — with the qualifications already mentioned — that
internal applicability and membership in the legal system jointly count as
an ordinarily sufficient condition for a certain norm to belong to the set of
applicable norms with respect to case c. In this sense, judges cannot arbitrarily
ignore those valid norms regulating a certain case; and if it is the judge's
ultimate decision that they be disregarded, she has to offer a justification for
so doing. What surely cannot be accepted is that internal applicability and
membership in the legal system are sufficient to warrant that a certain norm
will defeat all other competing applicable norms regarding case c (i.e., to
warrant the claim that such norm is the strictly applicable one).

Neither external applicability nor strict applicability is a quality of degree.
A norm is externally applicable to a certain case or not, depending on its
membership in the set of applicable norms fixed by the applicability criteria
of the system. Similarly, a norm is the only strictly applicable norm in a certain case or not, depending on its being selected from among the rest of the
externally applicable norms by some meta-criteria of applicability. What varies
in degree is the force or weight of a certain applicable norm with respect to
the rest of the applicable norms in light of the admitted preference criteria,

57 See Guastini 1995: 257–270; Alchourrón and Bulygin 1981: 95–124.

which occasionally may allow the selection of that norm as the strictly applicable one.

It seems clear that a certain norm may belong to different systems: the applicable system for a case c and the legal system (i.e., the set of valid norms). However, this possibility is frequently overlooked as a consequence of the confusion of applicability and membership in the legal system. If a judge imposes a certain order to solve a conflict between two norms equally applicable to a certain case, the weaker norm will be disregarded for the decision she has to make. But this does not mean that such a norm will be eliminated from all the systems to which it belongs. It can survive as a member in the legal system and contribute to the solution of other cases in the future. Similarly, the normal way to eliminate a norm from the legal system is through an act of derogation, but even if a norm is suppressed in this way, this does not mean that such a norm cannot survive as a member in the applicable system with respect to certain cases.

In short, to impose a hierarchical order and to derogate,[58] both have the effect of eliminating certain norms from a system of norms. Yet, it should be noticed that the word "system" is dangerously ambiguous here. On the one hand, it may refer to the set of norms which is *applicable* to a certain case c at time t; on the other hand, it may refer to the set of *legal* norms in a certain community at time t. This ambiguity often passes unnoticed because normally there is some overlap between both sets, and this gives the misleading impression that the two classes are coextensive.[59]

Although applicable systems are not a subclass of the set of valid norms, applicable norms are, ultimately, *selected* by norms that are valid in the legal system at a certain time. This connection also shows that the reconstruction of the legal system (or a systematic reconstruction of law at a particular time) enjoys conceptual priority over the identification of applicable norms, even if it is true that the solution to particular controversies depends on applicable norms rather than on valid norms.

---

[58] It should be noticed that "derogation" encompasses here both repealing (a legislative power) and invalidating (a judicial power).

[59] It seems that Dworkin missed this point in his arguments against Legal Positivism. In Dworkin's view, valid rules offer conclusive solutions to legal disputes, and thus he attributes to Legal Positivism the bizarre doctrine that whenever a conflict between rules arises — in contradistinction with what happens in conflicts between principles — one of the rules cannot be valid (see Dworkin 1977: 27). In a similar line as the one suggested in the text, Hart replied that there is no reason to deny that a valid rule may also survive conflicts with other rules to determine the outcome in other cases (see Hart 1961: 261–262).

Analyzing the logic of applying normative rules, Hansson and Makinson have drawn a distinction between *unrestrained* application, that is, one which is carried through even when it gives rise to contradiction, and *restrained* application, defined as one which is carried through as fully as compatible with the avoidance of contradictions or other undesirable consequences.[60]

Restrained application is reconstructed as different from *revision* of a normative set, because revision eliminates some normative rules so as to make consistent place for the incorporation of new rules, whereas restrained application leaves the normative set intact, even though it ignores some of its elements in a specific situation. The idea of restrained application rests on instantiation and closure under logical consequence, together with maximization-and-choice up to the limit of consistency. The peculiarity of this operation is shown through the following example. A doctor works according to these two norms:

N_1: "If a person is reported as having a heart attack, the doctor should visit her immediately."

N_2: "If a person is reported as having a severed hand, the doctor should visit him immediately."

The potential patients are 1, 1', 2, and 3. Patients 1 and 1' live next door to each other, and so they can be visited by the doctor almost at the same time. However, they both live far from 2 and 3, who also live far from each other, so that it is impossible to visit more than one of them immediately. On one occasion the following situation is reported: 1 has a heart attack; 1' has a severed hand; 2 has a heart attack, and 3 a severed hand. Hansson and Makinson observe that the rules considered are not in themselves inconsistent, although they do produce a conflict.[61] Unrestrained application in a situation of conflict such as this, with classical logic, would render everything and its opposite obligatory for the doctor. Intuitively, however, a restrained application of these rules would require the doctor to visit 1 and 1' immediately, with the second priority being to visit 2, and the third to visit 3.[62] The authors' proposal is not to block the derivation of contradictions by replacing classical logic, but to moderate the process of application while respecting classical logic.[63]

---

[60] See Hansson and Makinson 1997: 313.

[61] We shall call this kind of situation *conflicts of instantiation*, for the conflict arises from a factual impossibility of complying with all the consequences logically derivable from general norms within the legal system (see Chapter 5, Section 5.4).

[62] See Hansson and Makinson 1997: 313–314.

[63] They represent unrestrained application of N (a normative code) to D (a domain of individuals) in the light of S (a given situation) as $a(N, D, S)$ or, simply, $a(N, S)$, with domain D implicit and constant, as the set $Cn(I(N) \cup S) \cap A_N$, where I is the set of all instantiations into D, and

Now, beyond the details of their formal analysis, the important point for our discussion is that Hansson and Makinson show the pragmatic differences between the process of restrained application and the operations of contraction and revision, which as we shall later see may be used to reconstruct the dynamics of legal systems.[64] In their view, the process of application of rules – restrained or not – is always relative to the resolution of a particular case; whereas contraction and revision – which in the legal domain may be identified with derogation (or abrogation) and amendment – refer to rules themselves and are not directly related to individual cases. One of the manifestations of this difference is that when a rule is derogated (contracted from a normative system), it ceases to be a member of the system and cannot be used in the future unless it is reenacted. By contrast, when restrained application is performed, we merely set aside certain rules by not using them in the particular case at hand, but return to the whole set of rules when we face another case. Another manifestation of the basic difference is that derogation and amendment are actions performed by a legislature, for which judges usually have no authority,[65] whereas restrained application is a task of judges, not usually the concern of a legislature, for its business is to operate on general rules and apply them to individual cases.[66]

The idea that whenever judges decide an individual case, eliminating possible inconsistencies by a restrained application of legal norms, this procedure does not alter the legal system, and in the face of a new case judges may return to "the full set of rules," is in line with the thesis defended previously that imposing a hierarchical ordering within the set of applicable norms does not imply by itself a modification in the legal system. Although in such a case the judge will have altered the applicable system through the incorporation of a preference relation over its norms, this operation has no necessary impact on the identity of the legal system.[67] The same is true in the case of legal gaps: whenever judges "fill legal gaps" to justify their decisions in particular

---

A_N the set of all normative assertions without variables, all of whose individual constants are drawn from D (see Hansson and Makinson 1997: 316). Restrained application, in its turn, is represented as $c(N, S)$. Some of the formal properties that Hansson and Makinson regard as desirable of restrained application are: (1) restriction: $c(N, S) \subseteq a(N, S)$); (2) consistency: $\perp \notin Cn(c(N, S))$; (3) non-complaisance: If $\perp \notin Cn(a(N, S))$ then $c(N, S) = a(N, S)$; and (4) right equivalence: If $Cn(S) = Cn(S')$ then $c(N, S) = c(N, S')$ (see Hansson and Makinson 1997: 318–319).

[64] See Chapter 6.

[65] With the qualifications already mentioned regarding common law decision-making.

[66] See Hansson and Makinson 1997: 320.

[67] A contingent impact cannot be ruled out, but it will be dependent on the specific configuration of the rule of recognition of the legal system taken into account.

cases, the norms they integrate to fill the gap, although necessary members of the applicable system that constitutes part of the premises of their reasoning, are not necessarily new elements incorporated in the legal system as a consequence of the decision judges make.[68]

There is another important consequence of Hansson and Makinson's analysis. Among the different levels in which maximization-and-choice may be performed,[69] the level of instantiation or application of rules would be preferable for logical reasons. Hansson and Makinson offer here another medical example, but with a domain of patients 1, 2, 3, and 4 geographically located so that the doctor can visit two of them immediately, but not more. The rules are here, as before, N_1 (heart attack (h), obligatory to visit immediately) and N_2 (severed hand (s), obligatory to visit immediately), plus a third: N_3: "If a person is reported as having a persistent cough (c), the doctor should visit him immediately." Now the situation is: h(1), s(2), s(3), and c(4) – that is, 1 has suffered a heart attack; 2 and 3 have suffered a severed hand, and 4 has a persistent cough. Here the only maximal subsets of norms which render a consistent unrestrained application are $\{N_1,N_3\}$ and $\{N_2\}$. The result of the first subset is that the doctor should visit 1 and 4, whereas the result of the second is that the doctor should visit 2 and 3. But taking into account the relative seriousness of the three medical conditions, our intuitions tell us that the only acceptable results are that the doctor should visit either 1 and 2 or else 1 and 3. The example shows that maximization-and-choice at the level of rules produces wrong outputs that cannot be corrected by additional maximization-and-choice at a later stage. In case maximization-and-choice takes place at the level of instantiation or application of norms, those counterintuitive outcomes can be avoided.[70]

There is a close connection between this reconstruction of the idea of application – restrained or unrestrained – and our distinction between applicable systems and the legal system. The selection of applicable systems, and the correlative difference between applicability and validity, is necessarily a prior step

---

[68] Of course, it may be the case that in certain systems (e.g., as the effect of a rule of *stare decisis*), the applicable norm is incorporated into the set of valid norms. However, this is just a contingent characteristic of certain institutional designs.

[69] Those different levels would be the level of derived normative assertions, the level of normative rules, and the level of instantiation or application of normative rules (see Hansson and Makinson 1997: 322–323).

[70] Hansson and Makinson's proposal consists of maximizing at the level of instantiation, where maximization-and-choice consists of choosing a maximal subset K of $I(N)$ such that $Cn(K \cup S) \cap A_N$ is consistent and $c(N, S) = Cn(K \cup S) \cap A_N$, but through a procedure broken up into steps according to a ranking of the rules, so as to avoid excessive arbitrariness (see Hansson and Makinson 1997: 324).

in analyzing the operation of application in Hansson and Makinson's terms. The reason is that the idea of a normative code assumed in the former analysis is not that of the entire set of valid norms in a certain jurisdiction, but of those norms that are relevant for a certain case or situation. And, as we have shown, this selection of relevant norms is not necessarily a subset of those norms that are valid at the time of application. The set with which norm-applying organs operate is not the same as the set with which norm-creating organs operate, and even if applicable norms and valid norms are obviously related, this relation is not one of identity, but a far more complex one.

Moreover, the arguments used by Hansson and Makinson to privilege maximization-and-choice at the level of instantiation have another important consequence for our purposes. When faced with an individual case to solve, norm-applying organs are not solely concerned with a certain set of expressly enacted legal norms: they have to take into account the entire set of logical consequences of those norms. The acceptance of certain norms as relevant for a particular case forces the decision-maker to evaluate, compare, and rank all their consequences.[71] Hence, even if both legal systems and applicable systems can be regarded as the result of conceptual activities performed by legal theorists, for the reasons just mentioned, the reconstruction of the systematic structure of the set of externally applicable norms is intrinsically tied to the derivation of their logical consequences, in a way that legal systems are not. Thus, the set of externally applicable norms can be regarded as a system structured by means of deductive relations, among others. Our criteria of applicability are the criteria for identifying the normative basis of an applicable system, but the conceptual content of such a system depends on their logical consequences.

4.5. TWO CONCEPTS OF LEGAL SYSTEMS

Many legal philosophers have remarked that the law is not merely a collection of norms. Legal norms are grouped in complex systems (i.e., organized sets with a certain internal structure). However, it remains contested which are the relevant relations that give such systematic structure to the law.[72] It seems rather paradoxical that Kelsen, who always defended the idea that what

---

[71] As we see in Chapter 6, operations such as revision or application can be reconstructed either through finite normative bases or through normative sets closed under logical consequence. In fact, Hansson and Makinson do not postulate logical closure of the normative code in their reconstruction. However, for the reasons and with the qualifications to be made later, we will assume logical closure of the system of applicable norms.

[72] For an excellent overview of such discussions, see Ratti 2008.

distinguishes law from other normative systems, such as morality, was a distinctive characteristic of each of its norms – their coercive nature – has been one of the leading philosophers to develop the notion of legal system. Kelsen's ideas concerning the relations of derivation between legal norms, and regarding the formal aspects of legal systems, such as their hierarchical structure, are among the fundamental contributions to the theory of legal systems. The fact that Kelsen's ideas have been decisive for the development of the theory of legal systems does not mean that they are free from complex difficulties and shortcomings, some of which have already been pointed out. One of the most controversial aspects of Kelsen's theory has been his aspiration to reduce the structure of all legal norms to a single common pattern: the imputation of coercive sanctions to certain acts.

Since the time Hart's criticism was directed toward any such reductionist view,[73] it is commonplace in contemporary legal theory to accept that every legal system is composed of many different kinds of norms, with distinct functions and structures. Thus, the terms of Kelsen's equation should be reversed: given that there is no common characteristic to all legal norms which could be used to distinguish them from other kinds of norms, a sound characterization of law should focus not on norms, but on the distinctive features of a legal system as a whole. This idea, implicit in Hart's work, was improved by Joseph Raz, who also proposed to distinguish the problem of identity and the problem of structure of legal systems, as well as two different approaches for their analysis: the static dimension (momentary legal systems) and the dynamic dimension (non-momentary legal systems),[74] something that was also outlined by Kelsen.

An interpretation of law as a system of norms demands selecting a certain relation among their components. Two major candidates have been explored: deductive relations among norms (*deducibility*) and genetic relations of legal creation of norms (*legality*). These two relations may be taken as the grounds for two different criteria of membership of norms to legal systems. Under such view, it could be claimed that a certain norm N belongs to a legal system S according to the criterion of deducibility if and only if N belongs to the logical consequences of S; whereas a certain norm N belongs to a legal system S according to the criterion of legality if and only if N has been created in accordance with another norm N_1, being N_1 a power conferring norm that is also a member of S. That N has been created in accordance with N_1 depends here at least on the joint satisfaction of two conditions: first,

---

[73] See Hart 1961: chapter 3.
[74] See Raz 1970.

that N_1 empowers x to create N; second, that x has created N. A bit more formally:

Criterion of deducibility: $(N\ D{\in}\ S)$ iff $(N \in Cn(S))$

(where "$D{\in}$" means "membership according to the criterion of deducibilty" and "$Cn(S)$" means "closure of system S under logical consequence.")

Criterion of legality:
$(N\ L{\in}\ S)$ iff $(N\ LC\ N_1 {\in}\ S)$ and $(N\ LC\ N_1)$ iff
1. $N_1\ Ex\ C(N)$, and
2. $x\ C(N)$

(where "$L{\in}$" means "membership according to the criterion of legality"; "$N\ LC\ N_1 {\in}\ S$" means that N has been created according to N_1 that belongs to S; "$N_1\ Ex\ C(N)$" means that N_1 empowers x to create N; and "$x\ C(N)$" means that x has created N).[75]

Four analytical models of membership in a legal system may be developed on the basis of these two criteria:[76]

M_1: $(N \in S)$ iff $(N\ D{\in}S)$

M_2: $(N \in S)$ iff $(N\ L{\in}S)$

M_3: $(N \in S)$ iff $(N\ D{\in}S) \wedge (N\ L{\in}S)$

M_4: $(N \in S)$ iff $(N\ D{\in}S) \vee (N\ L{\in}S)$

According to M_1, all the norms in a legal system would be those satisfying the criterion of deducibility; according to M_2, all the norms in a legal system would be those satisfying the criterion of legality; according to M_3, all the norms in a legal system would be those jointly meeting the criteria of legality and deducibility; and according to M_4, all the norms in a legal system would be those meeting either the criterion of legality or the criterion of deducibility.

Of these four models, M_1 and M_2 both seem to be inadequate as a proper reconstruction of the criteria of membership of norms to a legal system, because each one overlooks at least one relevant relation between norms. Moreover, M_3 also seems inadequate, for it imposes an excessively strong requirement: jointly meeting of both criteria for the membership of each norm in the system. Consequently, M_4 seems preferable over the

---

[75] Another criterion would be necessary to explain the validity of customary norms. We shall not analyze such norms here.
[76] See Caracciolo 1988: 59–60.

other three as a thorough reconstruction of membership criteria in a legal system.[77]

However, things are not so simple. First, both legality and deducibility justify the membership of a certain norm in a legal system by virtue of a certain relation existing between that norm and other norms of the system. Therefore, both criteria presuppose the previous existence of at least one norm in the system and, for this reason, neither M_4 nor any of the three other models can be accepted as an adequate reconstruction of the criteria of membership of *every* norm in a legal system. Thus, if systematic relations among norms are not circular, then in every legal system there must be at least one norm whose membership does not depend on the satisfaction of any relations with other norms in the system (i.e., there must be at least one *independent* norm). Of course, this does not mean that M_4 cannot be read as a model for membership to a certain subset of legal norms: the subset of *dependent* norms, taking for granted that in every legal system there coexist dependent norms (the membership of which is a function of their relation with other norms) with independent norms (the membership of which is not a function of their relation with other norms). Consequently, both legality and deducibility are criteria of membership of dependent norms, at least in the sense that their application actually assumes that other norms are valid.

Second – and more important – in as much as deducibility takes as relevant the relation of logical consequence it can only be taken as a criterion of membership in a set, and by virtue of the extensionality principle, the identity of a set depends on the identity of its members. By contrast, legality is presented as a way of taking into account the dynamic nature of law (i.e., the idea that the content of law may change without losing its identity). Unlike morality, that cannot be deliberately changed, legal systems contain norms which regulate normative powers, which confer the ability to introduce or eliminate any normative content. These norm-conferring powers define authorities and regulate the exercise of legal competence.

Now, if legal systems are conceived of as sets of norms – a static notion – deducibility may be taken as a criterion of membership in such sets, but not legality. On the contrary, if legal systems are conceived of as dynamic systems, which requires reconstructing them as sequences of sets of norms over time, then – as is shown later – legality may be taken as a criterion of membership of sets of norms belonging to those sequences, but not deducibility. The reason for this is that, under this interpretation, the identity that persists despite changes of

---

[77] See Caracciolo 1988: 66.

norms over time has to be seen as that of a succession of sets that are replaced by other sets with each and every valid act of promulgation, amendment or derogation. Therefore, under this approach, norms do not belong to the sequence, but to the different sets that belong to the sequence, and the legality of the normative acts of promulgation, amendment, or derogation is a reason to substitute one set for another in the same sequence. Being so, the two considered criteria cannot determine the membership of the same kind of elements in a unique entity: deducibility may determine the membership of norms to a static set; legality, in turn, can only determine the membership of sets of norms in a dynamic sequence.

But in that case, two notions of legal system should be distinguished: one of them related to the tasks of lawyers and judges (whose concerns are fundamentally centered on normative solutions to concrete legal problems), and the other related to legal theory and legal philosophy (a point of view that demands a satisfactory reconstruction of legal dynamics). The first notion coincides with the idea, already presented, of the set of applicable norms – that is, those that are relevant to give an answer to a particular legal problem. In general, lawyers mainly deal with legal problems at a particular moment; they need to determine the deontic status of certain actions in a specific context.[78] For example, someone asks her lawyer about some complexities of taxation and, unlike a historian or a philosopher, her interest is mainly a practical one: it refers to the identification of legal norms that are actually relevant "here and now" for the solution of her problem. These legal norms are norms that judges and individuals have to take into consideration for the solution of a concrete legal issue. The second notion of legal system, in its turn, cannot be adequately explained in terms of a static set, because the law of a political community has a dynamic character; its content changes in different times as a result of the introduction or elimination of legal norms by means of specific normative acts.

When the notion of legal system is used in relation to the identification of those norms that are relevant to find a legal solution to a certain case, the importance of the distinction between external applicability and membership to the legal order – understood as something that persists over time – can be fully appreciated. This distinction forces us to conclude that the system of relevant or applicable norms to solve a certain case is not necessarily a subset of any of the sets of norms that belong to the same historical sequence that constitutes the law in a certain political community. Thus, a generalization of the idea of the system of relevant norms for a certain case does not necessarily

[78] See, for example, Harris 1979: 20.

have to coincide with the idea of the global set of norms that represents a temporal moment in the sequence of the same legal order.[79]

The law at a certain time may be understood as a *macrosystem*, whereas the set of norms that judges have to take into account to decide a particular problem may be understood as a *microsystem*. Those microsystems can be integrated by norms that are valid in different temporal moments of the legal order, or even by norms that do not belong to any system in the sequence that forms the legal order in which judges perform their functions. Of course, this does not deny the existence of complex relations between the two systems.[80] In fact, both concepts of legal system are deeply intertwined and no complete picture of the systematic structure of law can be provided without a proper explanation of the conceptual relations between them.

Dworkin has recently distinguished different concepts of law to investigate their relations with morality. First, he suggests that a *doctrinal* concept of law is used to express legal propositions (i.e., claims concerning what the law requires or permits or prohibits). The use of such propositions about the law implies that certain assumptions and beliefs are shared about the kind of arguments that are relevant to decide whether such propositions are true, as well as the consequences that follow when they are true. Second, a *sociological* concept of law is used when reference is made to a particular type of social structure, institution or standard of conduct. Using this concept we might ask when law appeared for the first time in a primitive tribal society, or whether commerce is possible without law. Third, a *taxonomic* concept of law is used when we classify a certain rule or principle as legal and not of another kind. According to Dworkin, a few legal theorists use this concept when they assume that every political community that has law in the sociological sense also has a set of rules and other kind of standards that are legal, as opposed to moral or customary or some other kind of standards. Finally, an *aspirational* concept of law is used when reference is made to the ideal of legality or to the rule of law.[81]

The two notions of legal system, which have been suggested here and are explored more deeply later, have proximate affinities with Dworkin's distinctions: on the one hand, the idea of the set of relevant norms to solve a particular case seems very close to Dworkin's doctrinal concept of law, whereas the idea of

---

[79] See Bulygin 1982. A detailed exploration of this idea was presented in Navarro, Orunesu, Rodríguez and Sucar 2004.

[80] Rodríguez 2002: 147–158 offers a preliminary analysis of those relations.

[81] See Dworkin 2006: 2–5.

an institutional notion of a historical legal order seems very close to Dworkin's sociological and taxonomic concepts of law.

In the following chapters, we show that logic is not only essential for explaining the relation among norms in applicable systems, but also necessary in the reconstruction of legal dynamics. Therefore, static and dynamic aspects of law are necessarily connected and a complete explanation of the nature of legal systems cannot ignore logical relations.

5

Legal Indeterminacy: Normative Gaps and Conflicts of Norms

5.1. FORMAL PROPERTIES OF APPLICABLE SYSTEMS

The main task performed by lawyers and legal scholars is the identification of the applicable systems of norms used to develop solutions to legal cases. In the previous chapter, we claimed that the set of externally applicable norms has to be distinguished from the set of valid norms. In virtue of the "open nature" of law, applicable norms need not belong to the same system that provides the criteria of applicability. However, what is the relation that confers systematic structure to the set of externally applicable norms? As applicable norms are not necessarily valid norms, the criterion of legality seems to be inappropriate for determining the structure of such systems. On the contrary, the criterion of deducibility plays a crucial role here, because the logical consequences of general applicable norms are essential for the solution of legal problems.

In *Normative Systems*, Alchourrón and Bulygin developed a methodology for the analysis of legal problems that seems particularly suitable for applicable systems.[1] In their view, legal problems are questions regarding the normative status of a certain action or set of actions. They illustrate their analysis with an example borrowed from Argentinean Law: the recovery of real estate from a third-party holder that obtained it from someone who was not its owner. Such an action may take place under a certain set of situations or states of affairs, which will be called universe of discourse (UD). The elements of a certain UD are the states of affairs that share a certain property, which is the defining property of that UD. The relevant normative question in this example is whether – and if so, in what circumstances – the third-party holder has the obligation to restore it to its owner, and in what circumstances (if any) is she allowed to retain it. The answers to these questions are dependent on

---

[1] See Alchourrón and Bulygin 1971.

the contents of the legal system under consideration: both legal problems and solutions are always relative to a certain legal system (here, Argentinean Law) that provides the starting point for identifying the applicable norms. However, legal scholars do not need to consider the whole set of valid legal norms at a certain time to find the answer to a problem such as this.

The abstract circumstances explicitly anticipated by applicable general norms are a finite set of properties – that is, a finite universe of properties (UP). As we have seen in the previous chapter, the presence or absence of these properties defines generic cases, which should be distinguished from particular situations or controversies that occur in a certain place and at a certain time that instantiate such properties (individual cases). Generic cases divide the individual cases of UD into mutually exclusive and jointly exhaustive classes. A certain property may be instantiated in an unlimited number of individual cases, and normative authorities do not need to consider explicitly an infinite number of individual cases because the solution of all generic cases also solves all individual cases of a certain UD.[2] Such norms internally apply to all individual cases that are within the scope of general norms.

The solution of an infinite number of individual cases by means of a finite number of general norms implies that a potentially infinite number of characteristics of individual cases are normatively irrelevant. Particular events present many characteristics,[3] and it would be clearly mistaken to claim that there is only one correct description of them. However, legal norms regard such additional characteristics as irrelevant. If all the properties of individual cases were relevant for legal adjudication, general norms would only be useful as "rules of thumb," and rule-based decision making would be impossible. Therefore, it seems necessary to conclude that the enactment of general norms is tantamount to rendering some properties irrelevant.

Any relevant property p selected by normative authorities determines two classes within the UD: (1) the class of elements possessing the property p, and (2) the complementary class $\sim p$.[4] For example, the property "self-defense" divides the universe of homicides in two complementary classes of cases: the cases of homicides committed in self-defense and the cases of homicides

---

[2] See Alchourrón and Bulygin 1971: 29.

[3] Remember Llewellyn's famous reference, when he explains the strict doctrine of precedent according to which rules are confined to particular facts, of a doctrine such as "[t]his rule holds only of redheaded Walpoles in pale Buick cars" (Llewellyn 1930: 71).

[4] Properties are usually represented – and in fact we ourselves have represented them in the first part of the book – using upper-case letters, and because legal norms are general norms (in relation to subjects and circumstances), an adequate formalization of them would require a recourse to predicate logic. However, for the sake of simplicity we will stick here to propositional calculus, and thus properties and classes of cases will be represented simply by propositional variables.

committed not in self-defense. Because each property of UP determines two generic cases (classes of UD), the conjunction of each property of UP (or their negations) define an *elementary* generic case. For example, if both p and q are relevant properties of a certain UP, then $(p \wedge q)$; $(\sim p \wedge q)$; $(p \wedge \sim q)$, and $(\sim p \wedge \sim q)$ are the elementary cases that divide the universe of discourse. Thus, a UP of n properties determines 2^n elementary cases. Generic cases that are not elementary cases may be called *complex cases*, and they are equivalent to disjunctions of elementary cases. For example, in UP $= \{p, q\}$, as q is equivalent to $((p \wedge q) \vee (\sim p \wedge q))$, q is a complex case of the universe of elementary cases (UC) determined by UP.

A normative problem, such as the recovery of real estate, may be regarded as a question concerning whether certain actions are obligatory, permitted, or prohibited. Let r represent the action of restoration. Some actions are *basic*, in the sense that all other actions (*complex* actions) are truth-functional compounds of them.[5] A finite set of basic actions will be called the universe of actions (UA). Alchourrón and Bulygin take permitted (P) as the basic deontic operator, and the rest of them (also called *solutions*) are defined in terms of it. Suppose there is only one basic action in UA (action r); insofar as the elements of UA can be permitted or not permitted, the following combinations are possible:

r	$\sim r$	Solutions
P	P	Fr (Facultative)
$\sim P$	P	PHr (Prohibited)
P	$\sim P$	Or (Obligatory)

The combination of $\sim Pr$ and $\sim P \sim r$ is excluded as a deontic solution because it is contradictory. The three other possible combinations – Fr, permitting both r and $\sim r$; PHr, permitting $\sim r$ but not r; and Or, permitting r, but not $\sim r$ – are *maximal solutions* for action r in this particular UA, in the sense that each one of them qualifies every element of UA (in our example, r and $\sim r$) as permitted or not permitted.[6] A particular set of legal norms offers a *complete* solution to a normative problem if and only if it solves all elementary cases

---

[5] For the sake of simplicity, we only deal with a basic action r.

[6] Solutions which are not maximal are called *partial* solutions, because they only solve certain elements, but not others, of UA. For example, Pr is a partial solution because it says nothing about the element $\sim r$ of UA. However, as $\sim r$ can only be either permitted or not permitted, from Pr it follows $Pr \wedge (P \sim r \vee \sim P \sim r)$. After distribution we obtain the disjunction $(Pr \wedge P \sim r) \vee (Pr \wedge \sim P \sim r)$. The first member of this disjunction is equivalent to Fr and the second to Or. Therefore, a partial solution is equivalent to a non-tautological disjunction of maximal solutions.

defined by the relevant properties, but complete legal answers also require those solutions to be maximal in the sense here defined.

Action r in conjunction with UD defines the normative problem. Action r determines two elements of UA: r and $\sim r$. In Argentina, this normative problem was regulated following a proposal made by the Brazilian legal scholar Augusto Texeira da Freitas, who wrote a draft of the Brazilian Civil Code. Freitas introduced three properties as relevant to solving the problem; the good faith of the former possessor or transferor (f); the good faith of the present holder or transferee (g), and the onerous character of the act of assignment – that is, the so-called consideration (h). The combination of these three properties determines the UC, which Freitas proposed to regulate with the following set of norms (S_1):[7]

$$N_1: \sim f \to Or; \qquad N_2: \sim g \to Or;$$
$$N_3: \sim h \to Or; \qquad N_4: (f \wedge g \wedge h) \to Fr$$

A sentence such as $\sim f \to Or$ is the symbolic expression of a norm that correlates the deontic consequence Or to the case $\sim f$. N_1 says that it is obligatory to restore the state if the transferor acted in bad faith; N_2 says that it is obligatory to restore the state if the present holder acted in bad faith, and so on. The solutions offered by S_1 can be presented in a matrix like this:

				S_1			
UC	f	g	h	N_1	N_2	N_3	N_4
1	+	+	+				Fr
2	–	+	+	Or			
3	+	–	+		Or		
4	–	–	+	Or	Or		
5	+	+	–			Or	
6	–	+	–	Or		Or	
7	+	–	–		Or	Or	
8	–	–	–	Or	Or	Or	

For any similar table, we may give the following definitions of the formal properties of normative systems. A case to which no maximal solution is correlated is a *normative gap*.[8] A normative gap can be either complete or

---

[7] Alchourrón and Bulygin favor the "bridge conception" in the representation of conditional norms. Henceforth, we also represent such norms by formulations such as $p \to Oq$.

[8] This is only one of several possible concepts of legal gaps examined in this chapter.

partial; there is a complete normative gap if no (maximal or partial) solution is correlated to a certain case; there is a partial normative gap when there is a partial solution in a certain case. An applicable system is *incomplete* if and only if it has at least one normative gap; it is *complete* if and only if there are no gaps.

An applicable system is *inconsistent* if and only if two or more different and incompatible solutions are correlated at least to one case; it is *consistent* if and only if none of the cases of the UC is inconsistently regulated.

An applicable system is *redundant* if and only if the same solution occurs more than once in the line corresponding to at least one case. The norms of the system will be called *independent* if and only if there is no case redundantly regulated.

As it is easy to see, the eight elementary cases of the UC determined by S_1 are correlated to a certain maximal solution. However, if any of the norms of S_1 were eliminated, the system would become incomplete. For example, the elimination of N_1 would produce a normative gap in case 2; the elimination of N_4 would produce a normative gap in case 1, and so on. Moreover, to the extent that there are no incompatible solutions correlated to any of the eight cases, S_1 is also *consistent*. Nevertheless, as in cases 4, 6, 7, and 8 the same solution is derivable from different norms, S_1 is a *redundant* normative system.

The Argentinean Civil Code was written by Dalmacio Vélez Sársfield following Freitas' proposal. Vélez Sársfield attempted to eliminate the redundant character of S_1, replacing Freitas' norms by the following system (S_2):

$$N_3: \sim h \rightarrow Or$$
$$N_5: (\sim f \wedge g \wedge h) \rightarrow Or$$

				S_2	
UC	f	g	h	N_3	N_5
1	+	+	+		
2	−	+	+		Or
3	+	−	+		
4	−	−	+		
5	+	+	−	Or	
6	−	+	−	Or	
7	+	−	−	Or	
8	−	−	−	Or	

According to this matrix, S_2 has been successful in eliminating all redundancies. But now the system does not give a complete answer to the problem, because considering the properties taken as relevant by Vélez Sársfield, cases 1, 3, and 4 are correlated with no solution whatsoever. As the comparison between S_1 and S_2 makes clear, the completeness of a legal system is a contingent property that depends on the norms enacted by normative authorities. Moreover, normative gaps are relative to a certain universe of actions, a universe of cases and a universe of maximal solutions. Thus, from the truth or falsity of a statement such as "there are three normative gaps in system S_2," nothing can be inferred regarding the completeness or not of a different system S_n.

To claim that a certain legal system S has a gap is tantamount to saying that no complete legal solution for a certain case can be derived from the normative basis (i.e., the set of applicable norms). However, the diagnosis of this defect is almost always followed by a proposal concerning the way in which the legal system should be completed. This latter step is usually grounded on *normative* claims regarding the best solution for a certain problem. For example, let us assume that in the case of the Argentinean Law concerning the recovery of real estate, a legal scholar claims that the relevant system of norms S_2 consists in norms N_3 and N_5, and not in a larger set that includes another valid relevant norm N_6. Another scholar may argue that S_2 is a defective systematization for our problem, because it does not take into account the consequences of another relevant norm. And it would also be tempting to claim – as some legal philosophers actually do – the strong thesis that the law always provides a complete answer to any legal problem. These philosophers invite us to accept that legal gaps would only be the result of a defective identification of the relevant legal standards. However, as Brian Bix stresses, this suggestion begs the question, because "what is or is not part of law is as contested as whether law is or is not a closed system."[9]

In fact, even if the discovery of a legal gap were only the first step of a more complex process concerning the correct identification of the relevant legal materials, the subsequent stages of this process would be needed precisely because *there was a legal gap* in the first reconstruction of the system. And, at least in as much as the strong thesis of the necessary completeness of all legal systems is not conclusively proven, the indeterminacy generated by legal gaps may be either the product of a *defective identification* of the relevant legal norms, or the consequence of *a defective legal system*.

---

[9] Bix 1993: 27. See also Soeteman 1997: 324–326.

Legal gaps can only be solved by the introduction of *new* norms. For example, in the case of the Argentinean Law concerning the recovery of real estate, the logical consequences of N_3 and N_5 do not regulate case 4. Cases 4 and 2 are complementary regarding the property g (i.e., the good faith of the actual possessor), because the only difference between both cases is the presence or absence of such a property. Consequently, a possible suggestion to avoid the normative gap in case 4 is to correlate it with the solution *Or*, in analogy with the solution correlated to case 2. The justification seems to be apparent: if the actual possessor is under an obligation to restore the real estate even though she obtained it in good faith (case 2), then *a fortiori* she should be obligated to restore in case she received it in bad faith (case 4). However, cases 4 and 8 are also complementary if we take into account property h. This fact also renders intuitive proposing a different solution to case 4, based on an *argumentum a contrario*: if the actual possessor has the obligation to restore the real estate in case she had obtained it gratuitously, then *contrario sensu* it follows that if the acquisition had been sufficiently costly she should be allowed to retain it. Although additional reasons can be offered to justify each of these arguments and to show that one should be preferred over the other, neither of them seems conclusive. Thus, the possibility of indeterminacies generated by normative gaps in the sense previously defined should not be conceptually excluded.

Legal scholars are mainly interested in the UCs that stem from the relevant properties. The *relevance* of a certain property p means that the presence or absence of p is correlated by the system to different solutions. It could be said that a property p is relevant in a certain case C of a UC if and only if the case C and its complementary case regarding the property p have a different normative status in relation to a certain set of actions and solutions.[10] As it can be easily proven, properties f, g, and h in our example of the Argentinean Law are relevant properties in UC because there is *at least* one case where the presence or absence of such properties makes a deontic difference.

If we compare two different UCs, we may say that UC_1 is *finer* than UC_2 if and only if every element of UC_1 logically entails some element of UC_2, and at least one element of UC_1 is not entailed by any element of UC_2. Of course, two universes of cases UC_1 and UC_2 may be incomparable regarding

---

[10] Two cases of a certain UC are complementary regarding a property p if and only if the two cases differ from each other in that p is present in one of them and absent in the other, and all the other defining properties remain constant (see Alchourrón and Bulygin 1971: 100–103).

the relation of fineness. These ideas can be used as a starting point in the analysis of some interesting conceptual relations between completeness and coherence:[11]

1. If a normative system NS is complete in relation to the UC, it is also complete in relation to all UCs which are finer than UC.[12]

Let the system NS be formed by the norms:

$$N_1: p \rightarrow Or$$
$$N_2: \sim p \rightarrow PHr$$

In this example, the UP is formed by the property p, so the corresponding universe of cases $UC_1 = \{p, \sim p\}$. The system NS assigns a normative solution to all elementary cases of this universe of cases, and it is complete and coherent. Now, under the assumption that in a norm such as $p \rightarrow Or$, p operates as a sufficient condition for qualifying action r as obligatory, in virtue of the *law of the strengthening of the antecedent*, from $p \rightarrow Or$ it follows, for example, that $(p \wedge q) \rightarrow Or$ and $(p \wedge \sim q) \rightarrow Or$. In other words, the addition of other properties to the antecedent p does not change the normative consequence Or. Under this assumption, the solutions that NS offers to a finer universe UC_2, formed by the combination of properties p and q, is the following:

$p \wedge q$	Or
$p \wedge \sim q$	Or
$\sim p \wedge q$	PHr
$\sim p \wedge \sim q$	PHr

Thus, the system has preserved its completeness as far as both p and $\sim p$ are regarded as sufficient conditions of their corresponding normative consequences. However:

2. The fact that a normative system is complete in relation to a certain UC does not imply its completeness in relation to any UCs less fine than UC.

[11] Alchourrón-Bulygin 1971: 99–101.
[12] But those properties that characterize UC but do not characterize the finer UCs will be irrelevant for the solutions of the system, provided the system is consistent in UC (see Alchourrón and Bulygin 1971: 100).

In contradistinction, consistency seems to operate the other way round:

3. If a normative system is consistent in a UC, then it is also consistent in any UCs less fine than UC.

4. If a normative system is inconsistent in UC, then it is also inconsistent in any UCs finer than UC (although it may be consistent in relation to UCs less fine than UC).

Under this model of analysis, both consistency and completeness are *ideal* properties of legal systems. They define standards of excellence for a normative order, at least in the sense that inconsistent or incomplete legal systems cannot guide behavior in an appropriate way. Moreover, they are *contingent* formal properties of legal systems. But because this latter thesis has always been a controversial topic in legal theory, it deserves a more exhaustive discussion.

5.2. THE PROBLEM OF LEGAL GAPS

Many legal philosophers assume as an evident truth that law is always complete because it regulates either explicitly or implicitly every possible action. Therefore, non-prohibited actions are considered as implicitly regulated; they are often regarded as permitted actions.[13] According to Raz, this thesis is a consequence entailed by our understanding of law as a tool for regulating behavior. Legal norms guide human actions qualifying them as obligatory or prohibited, and therefore, "to say that an act is permitted is to say that is not guided in a certain way, it is not prohibited."[14] However, is this assumption indeed reasonable (i.e., that every action is deontically qualified in some way by the norms of any legal system)? Is it true that there is always a complete set of applicable norms for any legal controversy?

The problem of legal gaps is a classic topic of analytical legal philosophy. Its consideration involves a great variety of issues that must be carefully distinguished. For example, legal philosophers sometimes analyze the problem of legal gaps as a necessary step to elucidate the relations between the application of norms and judicial discretion.[15] On other occasions, legal scholars disagree about the connections between semantic indeterminacies and legal gaps.[16] However, perhaps the most important reason that explains the persistence of controversies on legal gaps is the relation of this topic with other more

---

[13] See Kelsen 1979: 131–132; Raz 1970: 170.
[14] Raz 1970: 171.
[15] See Atria 2001: 63–86.
[16] See Coleman and Leiter 1993.

general philosophical problems, such as the truth-values of legal propositions. For example, Dworkin has claimed that the Social Sources Thesis, a defining tenet of Legal Positivism, implies the counterintuitive consequence that legal systems are necessarily complete. Dworkin's argument can be formalized as follows:

(1) $p \leftrightarrow Sp$ Social Sources Thesis
(2) $\sim p \leftrightarrow \sim Sp$ by transposition from (1)
(3) $\sim p \leftrightarrow S\sim p$ by substitution of p by $\sim p$ in (1)
(4) $\sim Sp \leftrightarrow S\sim p$ by transitivity of biconditional in (2) and (3).[17]

Let us rephrase the point in clearer terms: if from a positivistic point of view the truth of a legal proposition such as "Murder is forbidden" is – at least – materially equivalent to the existence of a social source for such a proposition, this would logically imply that the falsehood of the proposition "Murder is forbidden" is materially equivalent to the absence of a social source for such a proposition, but also that the falsehood of the same proposition is materially equivalent to the existence of a social source for the proposition "Murder is not forbidden" ("Murder is permitted"). By transitivity, this allows one to conclude that the absence of a social source for the proposition "Murder is forbidden" is materially equivalent to the existence of a social source for the proposition "Murder is permitted." In brief, what is not legally prohibited is legally permitted.

At first sight, the rejection of this consequence seems to force legal positivists to abandon the principle of bivalence regarding legal propositions. Let us introduce the following slight variation on the reconstruction of the preceding argument. Instead of representing the truth of a legal proposition simply as p, we will use the expression Tp, where T stands for the operator "true."[18]

(1') $Tp \leftrightarrow Sp$ Social Sources Thesis
(2') $\sim Tp \leftrightarrow \sim Sp$ by transposition in (1')
(3') $T\sim p \leftrightarrow S\sim p$ by substitution of p by $\sim p$ in (1')

Following a traditional point of view, a proposition p is false if and only if its negation is true. Thus, $T\sim p$ represents the *falsehood* of p. Classical logic not only assumes the principle of excluded middle (i.e., that a certain proposition is either true or not true $(Tp \vee \sim Tp)$), but also the principle of bivalence (i.e., that either a certain proposition is true or false $(Tp \vee T\sim p)$). Therefore, under the

---

[17] See Dworkin 1985: 133; also Dworkin 1986: 8–9, 37–39.
[18] Here we follow von Wright 1984: 26–41 and 1996. See also Moreso, Navarro and Redondo 2001: 47–73.

assumption of these two principles, the claim that a certain proposition is not true and the claim that its negation is true – that is, that the proposition is false – are equivalent ($\sim Tp \leftrightarrow T\sim p$). Of course, if the principle of bivalence is rejected, this equivalence does not hold any longer.

From the rejection of the principle of bivalence, it follows that a certain proposition may be (a) true, (b) false, or (c) neither true nor false ($Tp \vee T\sim p \vee (\sim Tp \wedge \sim T\sim p)$); and so not true ($\sim Tp$) cannot be taken now as equivalent to false ($T\sim p$), as the former formula now comprises not only cases of (b), but cases of (c) as well.[19] Therefore, if we reject the principle of bivalence regarding legal propositions, the analogy to the step (4) in the former reconstruction of the argument would not be admissible, and Dworkin's conclusion can be avoided because the first terms of (2') and (3') will not be equivalent.

This seems to be the path followed by different scholars, under the idea that a *realist* thesis regarding legal statements, implying that every legal statement is true or false according to a certain objective reality whose existence and constitution is independent of our knowledge, is incompatible with the basic thesis of legal positivism.[20] From this perspective, the truth of legal propositions under a positivistic approach is dependent on the conditions for the recognition of such truth.[21] If the Social Sources Thesis claims that a proposition such as "In Argentina murder is forbidden" is true if there exists a social convention supporting that proposition, then Legal Positivism would be committed to the rejection of the principle of bivalence regarding the truth conditions of legal propositions. This is so because it seems plain that either there is a convention in Argentina that murder is forbidden, or there is a convention in Argentina that murder is not forbidden, or there is not a convention on either of those things.[22]

But there is an alternative way of avoiding the undesirable conclusion of the argument that has the advantage of being more deferential to Quine's *minimal*

---

[19] See von Wright 1963a: 106.

[20] On anti-realism in general, see Dummett 1991: 1–19; Engel 1989: 135–141. On the implications for legal theory, see, for instance, Marmor 1992: 90. However, see also Marmor 2001: 142–143.

[21] The same idea is explicitly defended in Moreso 1998: chapter 2.

[22] The argument has already been suggested by Dworkin as a possible way out for Legal Positivism (see Dworkin 1985: 133). Dworkin examines two versions of the rejection of logical bivalence concerning legal propositions. According to the first, two propositions such as "The contract signed by x and y is valid" and "The contract signed by x and y is not valid" may both be false because the latter would not be the negation of the former, as there could be intermediary categories. According to the second, we would assume that one of the two propositions is the negation of the other, but reject that one of them necessarily holds as a consequence of the rejection of the principle of bivalence.

mutilation maxim.[23] According to this view, the Social Sources Thesis does not hold that the truth of the proposition "In Argentina murder is forbidden" requires the existence of a social convention for the truth of such proposition. Instead, it says that the truth of such a proposition depends on a social convention for *the existence of a rule* in Argentina forbidding murder or, better, a social convention for *the criteria of identification of a rule* forbidding murder as belonging to the Argentine legal system.[24] Thus, what is needed to avoid the conclusion Dworkin attributes to Legal Positivism is not the rejection of the principle of bivalence, but a clear distinction between legal norms and propositions about them, something that is impossible in the previous reconstructions of the argument because the symbol *p* was being ambiguously used to represent both norms and norm-propositions.[25]

By taking seriously this distinction, and replacing *p* as a means to represent a legal proposition such as "In Argentina murder is forbidden" by *PHm* $\in$ *LS* (the rule "Murder is prohibited" belongs to legal system *LS*), it is possible to reconstruct the premises of the argument as follows:

(1") $(PHm \in LS) \leftrightarrow S_{LS}PHm$ Social Sources Thesis
(2") $(PHm \notin LS) \leftrightarrow {\sim}S_{LS}PHm$ by transposition in (1")
(3") $({\sim}PHm \in LS) \leftrightarrow S_{LS}{\sim}PHm$ by substitution of *PHm*
                                          by ${\sim}PHm$ in (1").

According to this reading of the Social Sources Thesis, the proposition that in the legal system LS murder is forbidden is equivalent to the existence of a social source in *LS* for the rule "murder is forbidden." The claim that there is no rule in *LS* forbidding murder is equivalent to the absence of a social source in *LS* for the rule "murder is forbidden." And to say that there is a rule in *LS* not forbidding (permitting) murder is equivalent to asserting the existence of a social source in *LS* for the rule "murder is not forbidden." As we have already stressed, when we distinguish norms from norm-propositions it is possible to see there are two different senses in which an action may be said to be permitted: a mere negative sense (there is no forbidding norm) and a positive sense (there is a permissive norm). The absence of a social convention for the

---

[23] See Quine 1990: 13–17.
[24] For simplicity, in what follows we will assume the former understanding of the social sources thesis.
[25] Dworkin clearly commits this mistake when he states that the structure of positivism as a type of legal theory may be presented this way "if 'p' represents a proposition of law, and 'L(p)' expresses the fact that someone or some group has acted in a way that makes (p) true, then positivism holds that (p) cannot be true unless L(p) is true" (Dworkin 1985: 131).

identification of the norm "murder is forbidden" as belonging to legal system *LS* (as in (2")) is not equivalent to the existence of a social convention for the identification of the norm "murder is not forbidden" as belonging to *LS* (as in (3")). Hence, Legal Positivism can avoid the counterintuitive consequence that its basic thesis implies the necessary completeness of legal systems without any commitment to the antirealist thesis that rejects the principle of bivalence regarding the truth-conditions of legal propositions.[26]

A very similar confusion between norms and norm-propositions obscures Raz's views on legal gaps. Raz claims that "a legal system is complete if and only if it provides a complete answer to all the legal questions over which the court have jurisdiction."[27] Still, Raz makes a considerable effort to examine to what extent legal systems may contain gaps. In his view, some gaps arise from simple indeterminacy (e.g., vagueness of legal concepts, or from unresolved conflicts). In these cases, when "law speaks with uncertain voice or speaks with many voices," both the claim that there is a conclusive legal reason to perform a certain action and its negation are neither true nor false. Nevertheless, when "law is silent," Raz claims, closure rules ensure the absence of gaps.

On Raz's view, there are two possible complete answers concerning the conclusive legal status of an action:[28] on the one hand, the law conclusively requires p (LRp); on the other hand, the law conclusively permits not p $(LPer\sim p)$. This latter alternative would be equivalent to saying that according to the law, there is no conclusive reason requiring p $(L\sim Rp)$.[29]

Raz considers that there is a complete legal answer if and only if the following disjunction is true:

(5) $LRp \vee L\sim Rp$

We may call (5) the *thesis of complete legal answers*. It sets an adequacy criterion for any concept of legal gap, because legal gaps arise if and only if (5) is negated. According to this restriction, Raz remarks that there are two possible kinds of legal gaps that emerge in the following cases:[30]

---

[26] As we have already stressed, the importance of the distinction between norms and norm-propositions and, correlatively, of a logic of norms and a logic of norm-propositions, for the analysis of the ambiguity lying behind the principle "what is not legally forbidden is legally permitted" and the postulate of the necessary completeness of law was first stressed by Alchourrón 1969 and developed in detail in Alchourrón and Bulygin 1971: chapter 7.

[27] Raz 1979: 70.

[28] See Raz 1979: 71.

[29] See Raz 1979: 76. $L\sim R_c$ x, ø can be read as "it is the law that it is not the case that one legally ought to ø" (see Raz 1979: 67).

[30] See Raz 1979: 71.

(6) *LRp* is neither true nor false, and *L~Rp* is neither true nor false.
(7) ~*LRp* ∧ ~*L~Rp*

To avoid ambiguities, cases such as (6) will be called *truth-value gaps*, and cases such as (7) will be called *genuine legal gaps*. Although both (6) and (7) seem incompatible with (5), Raz only accepts the existence of truth-value legal gaps, which would arise in situations of semantic indeterminacy or unresolved conflicts. In what follows, we restrict our attention to genuine gaps, and to the argument used by Raz to deny their very possibility.

The thesis presented in (7) is the classical negation of (5). However, Raz claims that it is logically true that:[31]

(8) ~*LRp* ↔ *L~Rp*

and, from (7) and (8), it follows that:

(9) *L~Rp* ∧ ~*L~Rp*

Because (9) is a contradiction, (8) would imply the rejection of (7), and so the rejection of the existence of genuine legal gaps. Thus, the kernel of Raz's argument lies in (8), which will be called *Raz's law*.[32]

The symbolism used by Raz is somewhat puzzling, what poses serious difficulties for a clear understanding of his theses and, consequently, for an adequate critical assessment of them. Raz claims that statements of the form *LRp* mean the same as "Legally it ought to be that *p*" or "It is the law that it ought to be that *p*,"[33] so they can be translated without any loss of meaning into norm-propositions (i.e., propositions concerning the existence of legal norms). However, it is not clear at all what exactly *L* and *R* represent in an expression such as *LRp*. Two different alternatives should be considered, according to the familiar ambiguity between norms and norm-propositions that has already been examined. A first possibility is to read *Rp* as the expression of a genuine norm that requires *p*, and *LRp* as a proposition affirming that the norm *Rp* belongs to the legal system *L*. In such a case, the negation sign preceding *R* shall be read as an internal negation operating over a norm, whereas the negation sign preceding *L* shall be read as the external negation

---

[31] See Raz 1979: 76.
[32] See Raz 1979: 76. Eugenio Bulygin has criticized Raz's proposal in Bulygin 2003: 21–28.
[33] Raz 1979: 65.

of the whole legal proposition. If we accept this, the following definitions are obtained:

$$LRp = (Op \in L)$$
$$L{\sim}Rp = ({\sim}Op \in L)$$
$${\sim}LRp = (Op \notin L)$$
$${\sim}L{\sim}Rp = ({\sim}Op \notin L)$$

The thesis of complete legal answers (5) receives here the following reading:

(5') $LRp \vee L{\sim}Rp = (Op \in L \vee {\sim}Op \in L)$

This is a sound reconstruction of the completeness of a legal system, because if it holds true for any given action p, it means that either there is in the system a norm that requires p, or there is a norm in the system that does not require p, which is tantamount to saying that there is a norm in the system to the effect that ${\sim}p$ is deliberately permitted.

The classical negation of (5'), and thus the definition of genuine gaps, is here:

(7') ${\sim}LRp \wedge {\sim}L{\sim}Rp = (Op \notin L \wedge {\sim}Op \notin L)$

Now, is Raz's argument able to show that (5') is a logical truth? In other words, is it possible to demonstrate that the negation of (5') — that is, (7') — leads to contradiction? We have seen that Raz assumes that (8) is a logical truth. However, under this reconstruction (8) amounts to:

(8') ${\sim}LRp \leftrightarrow L{\sim}Rp = (Op \notin L \leftrightarrow {\sim}Op \in L)$

But this is plainly *not* a logical truth: the mere negative fact that a certain element is not a member of a set is no reason to claim that *another* element is in fact a member of the same set. We have shown in Chapter 3 that accepting this identity without restrictions leads to conflating norms with norm-propositions, and that only in case the system taken into consideration is complete and consistent (two contingent properties) should we assume the (contingent) truth (8'). Hence, even though (7'), together with (8'), leads to the contradiction:

(9') $L{\sim}Rp \wedge {\sim}L{\sim}Rp = ({\sim}Op \in L \wedge {\sim}Op \notin L)$

Far from being a logical truth, (8') is precisely the contingent thesis of the completeness of a legal system. It is no surprise, then, that (8'), together with the expression of a genuine gap, leads to contradiction. Therefore, under this reading, Raz's argument does not demonstrate the logical impossibility of genuine gaps:[34] it just proves that the joint acceptance and rejection of the completeness of a legal system is contradictory.

There is, however, another possible interpretation of Raz's formulas. We may take Rp to mean, not the norm referred to in a legal proposition, but a whole norm-proposition that affirms the existence of the norm Op in a given normative system S:

$$Rp = Op \in S$$

This being so, what would L amount to? One alternative is to read L as a mere specification of system S as a particular legal system L.[35] Although there is nothing objectionable in this understanding, it does not seem to capture the intuition underlying the use in Raz's symbolism of the negation sign as operating either over R or over L. In fact, this renders $\sim L \sim Rp$ a simple case of double negation: $\sim(Op \notin L) = (Op \in L)$, and consequently, indistinguishable from LRp. On account of this fact, we suggest reading "Legally it ought to be that p" as "It is legally true that it ought to be that p"; "it ought to be that p" (Rp) as "$Op \in L$"; and "It is legally true that" as T. Thus, we have:

$$LRp = T(Op \in L)$$
$$L \sim Rp = T(Op \notin L)$$
$$\sim LRp = \sim T(Op \in L)$$
$$\sim L \sim Rp = \sim T(Op \notin L)^{36}$$

With these equivalences, Raz's law means:

(8") $L \sim Rp \leftrightarrow \sim LRp = T(Op \notin L) \leftrightarrow \sim T(Op \in L)$

which – under the assumption of bivalence of legal propositions – is obviously a logical truth, as Raz claims, for it just expresses that "it is true that a certain norm does not belong to L" is equivalent to saying "it is not true that such

---

[34] What about truth-value gaps? Given (5') $LRp \lor L \sim Rp = (Op \in L \lor \sim Op \in L)$, and its classical negation (7') $\sim LRp \land \sim L \sim Rp = (Op \notin L \land \sim Op \notin L)$, the possibility of truth-value gaps requires rejection of the principle of bivalence for legal propositions ($\sim Tp \rightarrow T \sim p$), and thus to assume that any legal proposition may be true, false, or neither true nor false. So the analog here of (6) would be (6') $(Op \in L)$ is neither true nor false, and $(\sim Op \in L)$ is neither true nor false: $(\sim(Op \in L) \land \sim(Op \notin L) \land \sim(\sim Op \in L) \land \sim(\sim Op \notin L))$. Therefore, truth-value gaps, such as genuine gaps, are under this reading logically possible.

[35] This is the interpretation adopted in Bulygin 2003. With the slight difference in formalization pointed in the text, our conclusions under this reading are the same to Bulygin's.

[36] Moreso, Navarro and Redondo 2001 presents an analysis of Raz's theses using the framework of truth-logic developed in von Wright 1984 and 1996. However, the authors apply the operator T directly to Raz symbolism, thus inheriting all the ambiguities exposed here.

norm belongs to L." Under this reconstruction, the implication from right to left $(\sim T(Op \in L) \rightarrow T(Op \notin L))$ is propositionally equivalent to the disjunction $(T(Op \in L) \vee T(Op \notin L))$, which represents here the thesis of complete legal answers:

(5") $LRp \vee L \sim Rp = T(Op \in L) \vee T(Op \notin L)$

This thesis is also a logical truth, for it merely claims that either it is true that a given norm belongs to L or it is true that it does not belong to L. And, therefore, its negation (i.e., the definition of genuine gaps) becomes:

(7") $\sim LRp \wedge \sim L \sim Rp = \sim T(Op \in L) \wedge \sim T(Op \notin L)$

(7"), together with (8"), leads again to contradiction:

(9") $L \sim Rp \wedge \sim L \sim Rp = T(Op \notin L) \wedge \sim T(Op \notin L)$

But the reason here for this conclusion is that (7") itself, as the negation of a logical truth, is a contradiction, in as much as it claims that it is neither true that a certain norm belongs to L, nor true that the same norm does not belong to L.[37] Therefore, under this interpretation, Raz's "demonstration" that genuine gaps are not possible is as impeccable as fruitless, for a "genuine gap" in this sense would be absurd. Of course, this says nothing about the possibility that neither Op nor $\sim Op$ belongs to the legal system, so that p is not regulated by the law. In brief, under the first interpretation, genuine gaps are possible because Raz's law is not logically true; under the second interpretation, Raz's law is logically true, but does not prevent genuine gaps. And the whole problem derives from the absence of the distinction between norms and norm-propositions.

The moral of this discussion is that none of the conceptual arguments examined above is able to justify the strong thesis that all legal systems are necessarily complete (i.e., that there is no logical possibility of legal gaps).

5.3. NORMATIVE RELEVANCE AND AXIOLOGICAL GAPS

Normative gaps are not merely situations not regulated by the law. Otherwise, there would be a huge number of gaps in the law because there are almost

---

[37] Under the acceptance of bivalence $(\sim Tp \rightarrow T \sim p)$, (7") is equivalent to: $T(Op \notin L) \wedge \sim T(Op \notin L)$, a plain contradiction. What about truth-value gaps under this approach? Given (5) $LRp \vee L \sim Rp = T(Op \in L) \vee T(Op \notin L)$, the possibility of truth-value gaps requires the rejection of the principle of bivalence, and thus we obtain: (a) $\sim T(Op \in L)$; (b) $\sim T(Op \notin L)$; (c) $\sim T \sim (Op \in L)$; and (d) $\sim T \sim (Op \notin L)$. But, because c = b and d = a, the definition of a truth-value gap should simply be: (6") $\sim T(Op \in L) \wedge \sim T(Op \notin L)$.

infinite numbers of situations that legal authorities do not even intend to regulate.[38] A normative gap, as has been defined here, is a situation that has been left without regulation, even though the law purported to regulate it. Thus, the identification of a normative gap in a legal system is not a value judgment but a descriptive statement of a *factual* problem, because it is a contingent fact that a normative basis offers a solution to all relevant cases of a certain universe of cases.

This kind of inadequacy must be carefully distinguished from a different problem that may be called *axiological gap*. According to the characterization offered by Alchourrón and Bulygin, the definition of axiological gaps requires a proper distinction between two senses in which the expression *normative relevance* may be understood: a descriptive and a prescriptive sense.[39] To say that a property is *descriptively relevant* – in a case and in relation to a normative system and a universe of actions (UA) – is to say that a certain state of affairs exists; this state of affairs is the fact that the case in question and its complementary case have a different normative status in the system. To say that a property is *prescriptively relevant* is to say that a certain state of affairs *ought to be* or *should be the case* (i.e., that a case and its complementary ought to have a different normative status).

More rigorously, Alchourrón and Bulygin state that a property p is *relevant* in the descriptive sense in a case of a universe of cases (UC) in relation to a normative system S and a universe of actions (UA) if and only if that case and its complementary case relative to p have a different normative status in relation to S and the universe of solutions (US). To say that two cases have a different normative status in relation to a normative system S and a UA means that there is a solution that is correlated by S with one of the cases but not with the other. A property p is *irrelevant* in the descriptive sense in a case of a UC in relation to a normative system S and a UA if and only if p is not relevant in that case (i.e., the case and its complementary case relative to p in the UC have the same normative status in relation to S and the US). To say that two cases have the same normative status means either that both cases are correlated with the same solution or that neither is correlated with any solution.

On the basis of these ideas, Alchourrón and Bulygin define what they call the *thesis of relevance* and the *hypothesis of relevance*. The thesis of relevance of a normative system S for a UA is a proposition that identifies the set of all relevant properties in relation to S and that UA. The hypothesis of relevance for a UA is the proposition that identifies the set of all properties that ought to

---

[38] See Endicott 2003: 109–110.
[39] See Alchourrón and Bulygin 1971: 103.

be relevant for that UA. The thesis of relevance is a criterion for the selection of the universe of properties (UP) and, consequently, for the UC, thus allowing to determine the formal properties of a normative system, such as consistency and completeness. The hypothesis of relevance is a criterion of axiological adequacy for normative systems because it determines the set of properties that ought to be relevant for the UA. The problem of deciding if a property ought to be relevant or not for a certain UA is an axiological problem, and supposes a value judgment.

With these distinctions, Alchourrón and Bulygin define the notion of axiological gap in the following way: a case of a UC is an *axiological gap* of the normative system S in relation to a UA if and only if that case is correlated by S with a solution of the US, and there is a property p such that p ought to be relevant for that case according to a certain hypothesis of relevance, and p is irrelevant for S in relation to the thesis of relevance.[40]

As an example of axiological gap, the authors offer a German case decided in 1927 concerning the termination of pregnancy by medical prescription. The Penal Code in force in Germany at that time punished abortion generally, without making any distinctions. In the case in question, a physician procured an abortion to save the life of a woman who had suicidal tendencies as a consequence of the pregnancy, and was acquitted by the Court on the ground that there was a gap in the Penal Code, which was filled by an extended application of another article of the same Code referring to the state of necessity. In the opinion of Alchourrón and Bulygin, that article was inapplicable to the case because it merely provided that an action should not be punished when there was actual danger for its author or a relative of his. Hence, they consider that in this case there was a clear solution for the case according to the Penal Code, but the Court decided in a different way because it found that solution unjust, and that was so precisely because the Penal Code did not take into account a circumstance that the Court regarded as relevant.

An axiological gap is a property of a case. It is a relative concept; it is relative to a normative system, to a universe of actions and also to a certain hypothesis of relevance. Additionally, the case has to be correlated with some normative solution to allow us to predicate the existence of an axiological gap; otherwise there would be a normative gap, whereas in this characterization, the concepts of axiological gap and normative gap are incompatible by definition.

It is important to notice that not every inadequate solution can qualify as an axiological gap in the sense defined: if the normative authority takes into account every circumstance that ought to be relevant in a case, but correlates

---

[40] See Alchourrón and Bulygin 1971: 107.

the case with an inadequate solution from an axiological point of view, the result will be a defect of the system, but not an axiological gap. A discrepancy between the thesis of relevance of the system and the hypothesis of relevance is a necessary condition for the existence of an axiological gap. But if they both match, that does not assure all solutions established by the normative authority to be satisfactory, for a solution may be considered unfair even though all pertinent distinctions have been taken into account. But when the hypothesis of relevance is wider than the thesis of relevance, there will be at least one property that ought to be relevant, even though it is not relevant in the system. The universe of cases of the hypothesis of relevance will be *finer than* the universe of cases of the thesis of relevance and thus there will be at least one axiological gap.

The definition of axiological gap given here offers many interesting points for analysis. A first issue that deserves special consideration is related to the notion of hypothesis of relevance conceived as a prescriptive statement. Alchourrón and Bulygin say that in the sentence "The property p is relevant, though the legislator did not consider it when he solved the case C (i.e., did not take it into account for the solution of the case C)" the term "relevant" is being used in its prescriptive meaning, because if it were used in its descriptive meaning the sentence would be self-contradictory. However, this seems to be an excessively strong claim: the use of the term "relevant" in the former sentence does not necessarily have to be prescriptive to preserve consistency. In a sentence such as "property p is relevant for this case, though the legal authority has not taken it into account," the expression "relevant" can be understood descriptively without falling into any contradiction *if the reference is made to a different normative system*. When we say that a property "ought to be considered relevant" although in fact in the legal system *LS* it has not been taken as relevant, the hypothesis of relevance may be understood as a norm-proposition saying that the property in question ought to be taken as relevant *according to a certain axiological system A_xS*, rather than a genuine prescriptive sentence. In such case, to say that a property is relevant according to the hypothesis of relevance would be a descriptive sentence as well.

The use of the term "gap" to refer to this axiological problem is not arbitrary; the idea is that the normative authority did not take into account a certain property because *she did not consider it*, and had she considered it, instead of solving the case as she did, she would have given it a different solution. When legal scholars say they are "interpreting the normative authority's intentions," they frequently express their own evaluations in a concealed way. The use of the term "gap" in this sense is a typical instance of this procedure. For although it can actually be true that, had the normative authority taken into account a certain property, the case would have been correlated with a different solution, it is obvious that this counterfactual statement is very difficult to prove, so sometimes legal scholars propose for the case the solution they judge most appropriate, protected by the impossibility of disproof.

By pointing out the existence of an axiological gap, however, they can also be genuinely trying to reconstruct those properties that ought to be relevant according to the axiological system assumed by the normative authority, and not presenting their own value judgments in a concealed way. This seems to be the case, for example, when Pufendorf interpreted a Bolognese Law that prescribed that whoever drew blood in the streets should be punished with the utmost severity as inapplicable to a surgeon who opened the vein of a person who, in a fit, fell down in the street.

The role that intention plays in interpretation is a very controversial topic and we do not discuss it here. Let us only say, following Raz, that "to the extent that the law derives from deliberate law-making, its interpretation should reflect the intentions of its law makers."[41] Legal authorities assume a corpus of values whenever they enact certain norms. If it is true that a property has not been regarded as relevant because it was not considered at the time the norms were enacted, but, had the authority taken it into consideration, the case would have been correlated with a different normative solution, means that, according to the authority's underlying axiological system, that property ought to be regarded as relevant.

Therefore, to assert the existence of an axiological gap in a normative system, at least sometimes, can be interpreted as a statement declaring not only that a certain property ought to be considered relevant in a legal system LS according to an axiological system A_xS, but also that this axiological system is — or coincides with — the axiological system assumed by normative authorities. In that case, the hypothesis of relevance would express a descriptive statement, relative to system A_xS, according to which a certain property *ought to be* (norm-proposition) relevant in a legal system LS. As such, that statement would be true or false.

With this descriptive reading of the hypothesis of relevance, and accepting the additional premise that the axiological system from which the hypothesis of relevance is derived is a reconstruction of the axiological system assumed by normative authorities, it could be argued that the property in question *is* relevant in the normative system, and not merely that it *ought to be* so. After all, legal authorities express certain sentences to let us know their intentions,

---

[41] Raz 2009: 275.

sentences we have to interpret. And if we have to be faithful to their actual intentions when interpreting these words, and if it is true that they had the intention to give relevance to a certain property, then this property *is* in fact relevant in the system.

Our suggestion is that two notions seem to be confused under this concept of axiological gap: axiological gaps as critical statements about a normative system (a prescriptive statement) expressed from the internal point of view of another normative system (the interpreter's axiological system), and axiological gaps as interpretative statements about a certain set of normative formulations that tries to reconstruct the intentions of normative authorities. In this second sense, to predicate the existence of an axiological gap does not necessarily express an evaluative or prescriptive statement, for it can simply be a description of the fact that, although the normative authority has not assigned relevance to a certain property by an explicit sentence, it is implicitly relevant in the normative system according to the axiological system presupposed by the authority, which may be reconstructed by a cautious analysis of other norms enacted by that authority.

Taking into account the two readings of the hypothesis of relevance as a genuine norm or as a norm-proposition, Alchourrón and Bulygin's definition of axiological gap could be expanded in two definitions:

(1) Descriptive hypothesis of relevance: a case C of a UC is an axiological gap of normative system S in relation to a UA if and only if there is a property p such that p ought to be relevant for case C according to a certain descriptive hypothesis of relevance relative to an axiological system $A_x S$, and p is irrelevant for S in relation to the UA.

(2) Prescriptive hypothesis of relevance: a case C of a UC is an axiological gap of normative system S in relation to a UA if and only if there is a property p such that p ought to be relevant for case C according to a certain prescriptive hypothesis of relevance, and p is irrelevant for S in relation to the UA.

If we add to (1) the assumption that system $A_x S$ is a reconstruction of the axiological system presupposed by the normative authority, which has been elucidated through the analysis of other enacted norms, this would yield the idea of an axiological gap as an *interpretative* statement. By contrast, definition (2) expresses the idea of an axiological gap as a *critical* statement.

However, there is a different problem that has to be thoroughly analyzed concerning the elusive notion of normative relevance, for there is an ambiguity in the characterization of descriptive normative irrelevance that has passed unnoticed in the analysis offered up to this point. The use of a prescriptive notion of normative relevance places us in the realm of a logic of norms, which attempts to reconstruct the rationality of the acts of enacting norms, and consequently implies the assumption of consistency and completeness. Prescriptive normative relevance of a circumstance of the kind p for the normative qualification of an action q requires the satisfaction of two conditions. First, that if action q is prohibited in case p, it cannot be also prohibited in case $\sim p$, and if action q is permitted in case p, it cannot be also permitted in case $\sim p$. Second, that p has to be a sufficient condition for the normative qualification of q as permitted or prohibited, or at least a contributory condition, that is to say, a necessary condition of a sufficient condition. Now, more important here is to point out that in this prescriptive sense, the characterization of prescriptive irrelevance is unambiguous: it can be defined as the negation of prescriptive relevance.

Things are quite different when descriptive normative relevance is examined. Here, because what we have in mind is to determine which properties or circumstances are relevant according to a certain normative system, we are in this case in the realm of a logic of norm-propositions, and so we can assume neither consistency nor completeness. This generates two senses in which we can say that a property or circumstance is descriptively irrelevant in a normative system. That a case and its complementary case have in fact the same *normative status* in a certain system (the descriptive meaning of "irrelevance" according to Alchourrón and Bulygin) is an ambiguous statement because this can happen (a) as a consequence of the correlation of both cases with the same solution, or (b) as a consequence that in both cases we can find no difference in the normative status of certain action.

To face this ambiguity, it is necessary to distinguish *positive descriptive irrelevance* from *negative descriptive irrelevance*, in analogy with the distinction between the positive and negative senses of permission in the logic of norm-propositions. The reason for the two distinctions is the same: in the case of the descriptive notion of prohibition, which, as previously shown, is a metalinguistic notion, its negation can be understood in two ways: to say that an action is not prohibited in a certain normative system can mean that a norm prohibiting that action does not exist in the considered system, where the negation acts on the whole metalinguistic statement, and this generates the notion of negative permission, or that a norm not prohibiting that action exists in the considered system, where the negation acts on the norm mentioned in the statement, and this generates the notion of positive permission. In the case of irrelevance, the negation of the metalinguistic statement that predicates the descriptive relevance of a certain property for the normative qualification of an action according to the norms of a system can be understood as acting on the whole statement (the negation of descriptive relevance) or acting on the prescriptive notion of relevance mentioned in the statement.

Therefore, a property p is descriptively relevant in normative system S in relation to case C of a UC for a UA when that case and its complementary case relative to property p have a different *normative status*, in the sense that there is a (minimal) solution in the US corresponding to the UA which is correlated by S with one of the cases and not with the other.[42]

Positive descriptive relevance of p in S for case C:

$$\exists s \in USMin/UA: (s \in S/C \wedge s \notin S/\sim C)$$

This corresponds to the definition of descriptive relevance given by Alchourrón and Bulygin. Of course, a stronger notion of relevance can be conceived of, requiring at least one solution correlated to a case and not to its complementary case, *and, what is more, the reason for this difference in normative status being attributed to the presence in one case and the absence in the other of the property in question.* If the latter condition is not satisfied, the correlation of a normative solution to a certain case could be merely *defeasible* (i.e., subject to implicit exceptions derived from the absence on a certain occasion of the underlying reason whose presence justifies the difference in normative status). We only say here that this problem is related to the identification of certain norms starting from the normative formulations expressed by some authority, a complex process in which the interpreter usually introduces implicit exceptions in norms using this argument. But when the norms of a certain normative system have been identified (those explicitly formulated as well as the ones added to the system by the interpreter, although not expressly formulated by the authority), the definition of descriptive relevance assumed here seems to be satisfactory.

One way to understand the negation of such statement is what we propose to call *positive descriptive irrelevance*. A property p is positively irrelevant for a case C in a normative system S if and only if according to S, the case C and its complementary case have the same *normative status*, in the sense that there is

---

[42] Following Alchourrón and Bulygin, we said that maximal solutions are those that deontically qualify every element of the UA; solutions which are not maximal are partial solutions, in the sense that they only qualify some (but not all) elements of the UA. Minimal solutions are a subset of partial solutions: those that deontically qualify only one element of the UA. For instance, considering a UA formed by only one action, three maximal solutions and three minimal solutions must be distinguished:

Maximal solutions: $(Pp \wedge P\sim p) = Fp$; $(Pp \wedge \sim P\sim p) = Op$ and $(\sim Pp \wedge P\sim p) = PHp$.
Minimal solutions: $(Pp \vee \sim P\sim p) = Pp$; $(\sim Pp \vee P\sim p) = P\sim p$ and $(\sim Pp \vee \sim P\sim p) = \sim Fp$.

a maximal solution in the US corresponding to the UA that is correlated by S both to the case C and its complementary case.

Positive descriptive irrelevance of p in S for case C:

$$\exists s \in \text{USMax/UA: } (s \in \text{S/C} \land s \in \text{S/}{\sim}\text{C})$$

The second way to understand the negation of descriptive relevance is what we propose to call *negative descriptive irrelevance*. A property p is negatively irrelevant for a case C in a normative system S if and only if according to S, the case C and its complementary case have the same *normative status*, in the sense that for every minimal solution in the US corresponding to the UA, if it is correlated by S with case C, then it is also correlated with its complementary case.[43]

Negative descriptive irrelevance of p in S for case C:

$$\forall s \in \text{USMin/UA: } (s \in \text{S/C} \rightarrow s \in \text{S/}{\sim}\text{C})$$

As a result of these definitions, the positive irrelevance of a property in relation to a case depends on the possibility of deriving from the system the same normative status for both the case in question and its complementary case (both are correlated with the same maximal solution), and thus an action of the normative authority assigning the same solution to both cases is needed. For a property to be irrelevant in the negative sense in relation to a case, it is sufficient to say that it is not true that both cases have different normative status.

The relations between these concepts so defined are analogous to those between prohibition, positive permission, and negative permission in the logic of norm-propositions. A property can be relevant and irrelevant in the positive sense (but in that case, the system will be inconsistent); it can also be relevant and irrelevant in the negative sense, although in that case the system will be incomplete. If a normative system is consistent, positive irrelevance of a property implies its negative irrelevance. If it is complete, negative irrelevance of a property implies its positive irrelevance. Therefore, for a complete and consistent normative system both notions are equivalent and there would be no reason to distinguish between them.[44]

With the aid of these two notions of descriptive irrelevance and the two readings of the hypothesis of relevance previously distinguished – as a genuine

---

43 It should be noticed in passing that the notion of descriptive relevance here defined is a positive notion, and although it would be difficult to find a correlate in ordinary language, a negative descriptive notion of relevance could also be defined.

44 We return to these distinctions in connection with the discussion of defeasibility.

prescription or as a norm-proposition – Alchourrón and Bulygin's definition of axiological gap can be expanded to four definitions. But on account of the imposed condition according to which the case should be correlated with at least one solution, we will eliminate negative irrelevance from the thesis of relevance. Therefore, only two possibilities are left:

(1) Descriptive hypothesis of relevance: Case C of a UC is an axiological gap in legal system S for a certain UA if and only if there is a property p such that p is relevant in C according to a certain descriptive hypothesis of relevance relative to axiological system A_xS, and p is positively irrelevant in S for case C.

(2) Prescriptive hypothesis of relevance: Case C of a UC is an axiological gap in legal system S for a certain UA if and only if there is a property p such that p is relevant in C according to a certain prescriptive hypothesis of relevance, and p is positively irrelevant in S for case C.

If we assume in (1) that the axiological system A_xS is the one presupposed by legal authorities, reconstructed through the analysis of the rest of the enacted norms, predicating the existence of an axiological gap in sense (1) would be an interpretative statement. By contrast, predicating the existence of an axiological gap in sense (2) would be a critical statement of the solutions offered by system S from the internal point of view of a certain axiological system.

5.4. LEGAL CONFLICTS AND COHERENCE

The structure of an applicable system is given by the relation of logical consequence between legal norms. The derivation of logical consequences plays a major role in the analysis of normative contradictions, because many conflicts are not explicit, but are "hidden" in the conceptual content of explicitly formulated norms. However, the characterization of normative contradictions is a serious problem in deontic logic.[45]

The paradigm of what deontic logicians understand as a normative contradiction is represented by the deontic pair Op and $O\sim p$ (i.e., the obligation to fulfill an action and to refrain from fulfilling the same action or, what amounts to the same thing, the obligation and prohibition of the same action). However, although it is hard to deny that those norms contradict each other, it is a matter of dispute how to explain the reason why they are incompatible.[46]

---

[45] See von Wright 1963a: 148.
[46] "Contradiction," "inconsistency," and "logical incompatibility" will be taken here as synonyms.

For instance, if norms lack truth-values, it cannot be claimed that they contradict each other because they cannot be both true. Thus, some theorists have suggested the substitution of truth by other bivalent values, such as validity, and proposed that Op and $O\sim p$ are contradictory because they cannot be both valid. Now, the question here is whether something has really been changed with this substitution, or whether with "validity" we are just meaning "truth" with another word.[47] Nor is it possible to justify the incompatibility by the fact that both norms cannot coexist within the same set;[48] the fact is that nothing prevents normative authorities from mandating and forbidding the same action, so they can indeed coexist. What is meant by saying that incompatible norms cannot coexist within the same set of norms is that they cannot *coherently* coexist, but this is tantamount to assuming what has to be explained.

A more promising alternative is to place the analysis at the pragmatic level and, from the perspective of the normative authority, claim that there is a normative contradiction whenever there is a discrepancy between the intention to prescribe and its verbal formulation.[49] The normal thing when we prescribe a certain course of action is to intend that this action be fulfilled. Consequently, two norms would be contradictory for a "normal legislator" if the linguistic formulations frustrate such generic intention.

The problem with this suggestion is that, as nothing prevents an authority from mandating and forbidding the same action, there is nothing impossible in the idea of an authority with the intention that the same action be fulfilled and omitted: any real normative authority can have conflicting interests or volitions. An attempt to escape from this objection is what is meant by the reference to the intention of a "normal legislator," but then with this characterization we are just saying that normative contradictions are in some sense *abnormal*, something that we knew from the very beginning.

Another possibility from the pragmatic point of view is to place ourselves in the perspective of the normative subject, and identify the notion of normative contradiction with the logical impossibility of fulfillment by the same subject at the same time. However, in such a case it seems we are saying that, for logical reasons, the same subject cannot make true at the same time the proposition that p and the proposition that $\sim p$, that is, the normative *contents* of two contradictory norms. This would be a sound criterion to identify contradictions between normative contents (p and $\sim p$ cannot both be true), but it does not seem to explain why *norms* are incompatible. The fact that two permissive

---

[47] See Alchourrón and Martino 1990: 55.

[48] See von Wright 1963a: 48. For criticism, see Alchourrón and Bulygin 1989: 673–678.

[49] See Alchourrón and Bulygin 1984: 458.

norms with incompatible contents (i.e., Pp and $P{\sim}p$) do not contradict each other shows that contradiction between normative contents is a necessary but not a sufficient condition to characterize normative contradictions.[50]

This latter objection, centered on the deontic character of norms, highlights the need to take this component into consideration for an adequate reconstruction of the notion of normative contradiction, at least if permissions are understood as distinct normative acts. In such a case, there will be a contradiction not only whenever a normative authority has commanded and forbidden the same action, but also whenever she has permitted and forbidden it.

Therefore, to obtain a plausible characterization of normative contradictions, we need specific criteria for identifying contradictions regarding sets of commands, sets of permissions, and mixed sets of norms containing both. To this end, Alchourrón has proposed the following criteria of consistency for each of those sets:[51]

1. a set of imperative norms is consistent if, and only if, there is an interpretation that makes true every statement of action that follows the deontic operator O;
2. a set of permissive norms is consistent if, and only if, for each statement of action that follows the deontic operator P, there is an interpretation that makes each one of them true; and
3. a mixed set of imperative and permissive norms is consistent if, and only if, for each permissive statement there is an interpretation that makes true its statement of action, and also makes true every statement of action contained in all the imperative statements of the set.

According to this pragmatic point of view, the notion of contradiction between norms is partially dependent on the authority that enacted them. If we also take into account the possibility of compliance by the normative subject, we find that two norms formulated by the same authority can contradict each other in relation to one subject and not to another, and that two norms formulated by different authorities can be incompatible regarding a certain subject. In the first case, let us suppose that a normative authority x enacts the two following norms:

N_1: '*It is obligatory for y and z to see to it that p*'.
N_2: '*It is obligatory for y not to see to it that p*'.

---

[50] See Weinberger 1984: 469 and Alchourrón and Bulygin 1984: 457.
[51] See Alchourrón 1991: 417–418.

This normative set is inconsistent for y but perfectly consistent for z. In other words, in this case the authority x has consistently regulated the conduct of z but inconsistently regulated the conduct of y.

In the second case, if normative authority x commands subject y to see to it that p, and normative authority z commands her not to see to it that p, although the set of norms enacted by x as well as the set of norms enacted by z, considered independently from one another, may be perfectly consistent, the union of both sets is inconsistent regarding subject y.

In contemporary legal systems, there is not one, but a plurality of individuals and organs empowered to enact norms, even if metaphorically we take them all to be acting as representatives of a unique normative authority (the state). The most frequent case of legal contradiction occurs when a certain authority enacts a norm incompatible with another enacted by a different authority. When those authorities have different hierarchies, legal scholars use the criterion that the one enacted by the hierarchically superior authority trumps the one enacted by the hierarchically inferior authority (*lex superior*). Every legal system – either explicitly or implicitly – fixes certain hierarchies among their norms and authorities, because hierarchy is one of the aspects to be taken into consideration in solving normative conflicts (*lex superior*). Other frequently used criteria focus on the time of enactment of norms (*lex posterior*) or the more local or specific character of the regulation (*lex specialis*).

Still, to resort to such criteria to offer a solution for contradictions or conflicts between legal norms is not a sufficient ground for justifying the thesis of the necessary consistency of every legal system. This is so, on the one hand, because they neither jointly guarantee a complete ordering of all possible conflicting norms, nor are they free from offering incompatible solutions for the same conflict. Moreover, far from being a sound demonstration that all legal systems are necessarily consistent, the use of such criteria strongly suggests not only that legal contradictions exist, but that they are perceived by legal scholars as something intolerable.

Accepting the ideas suggested here, the notion of normative contradiction may be reconstructed as *the logical impossibility for a subject jointly to satisfy the deontic contents of every mandatory norm together with each of the deontic contents of every permissive norm of a system of norms enacted by a certain authority and in relation to a certain occasion.*

Nonetheless, there are a significant number of cases in which seemingly consistent norms generate "normative conflicts."[52] Let S be a normative system

---

[52] The distinction between normative contradictions or inconsistencies and "normative conflicts" was introduced in Hilpinen 1987: 37–49.

in which the following two statements coexist:

NF$_1$: '*Drivers ought to stop in front of red lights*'.
NF$_2$: '*Drivers ought not to stop next to militar zones*'.

Do these statements contradict each other? A possible formalization of the norms expressed by them is:

N$_1$: $p \rightarrow Oq$
N$_2$: $r \rightarrow O{\sim}q$

where p represents the fact of a driver being in front of a red light; r the fact of a driver being next to a military zone, and Oq and $O{\sim}q$ the obligation and prohibition to stop, respectively.

N$_1$ and N$_2$ do not seem to be in contradiction, but this does not prevent them from generating a conflicting situation, indistinguishable from the canonical contradiction between Op and $O{\sim}p$, for those who are subject to their prescriptions. That would be the case were the normative authority to have the hardly brilliant but perfectly conceivable idea of locating a traffic light next to a military zone.

The example shows that two seemingly consistent norms can produce a normative conflict given the occurrence of certain factual circumstances. In our example, the joint verification of conditions p and r — red light and military zone — renders as a result the obligation and prohibition to stop (Oq and $O{\sim}q$). Therefore, here is a new element that has to be taken into consideration for a proper characterization of normative inconsistency: a set of norms can be consistent *via* certain facts – under the occurrence of certain factual circumstances – and inconsistent *via* other facts.[53]

Most systems of deontic logic have been designed to take into account only categorical norms. As we have seen in Part I, one of the fundamental difficulties of deontic logic has been to give adequate representation to conditional norms. This is particularly problematic in the case of legal systems, as most legal duties and rights are not established by authorities in categorical terms, but subject to certain conditions. To the extent that we can find an adequate logical framework to reconstruct conditional norms, it will be easy to give a proper account of categorical norms too, because categorical norms may then be understood as prescriptions for any possible circumstance (i.e., prescriptions *via* an empty set of facts).[54]

---

53 See Alchourrón 1991: 423–425.
54 See Alchourrón 1991: 424.

With legal norms, the problematic issue is not so much that of reconstructing the positive conditions required by norms for the existence of duties and rights, but of reconstructing their negative conditions. A certain action may be required as obligatory under certain factual situations, but cease to be so under other circumstances. Thus, returning to our driver example, the two problematic norms concerned could be interpreted in such a way that the generic obligation to stop before a red light is overruled in the particular case of conflict with the obligation to proceed next to the military zones. Under this interpretation, the relevant normative system would be:

$$N_1': (p \wedge \sim r) \rightarrow Oq$$
$$N_2: r \rightarrow O\sim q$$

According to N_1', if a driver faces a red light, she has to stop, unless it jointly occurs that she is next to a military zone, for according to N_2, in that case, her duty is to go on. This restatement of our norms eliminates the undesired inconsistency, but this is only possible with the additional information that one of the norms prevails over the other. This path, as with any other one used to reconstruct conditional norms, is not free from obstacles. But in spite of such difficulties, it is much more satisfactory to represent legal norms in conditional terms than in categorical terms.

It is beyond dispute that categorical norms are theoretically conceivable and, correlatively, an absolute notion of normative contradiction in relation to circumstances, but that is not the kind of contradictions with which legal scholars have to deal. The closest representation of what legal scholars would intuitively call "contradiction between norms" is a pair of norms of the form $p \rightarrow Oq$ and $r \rightarrow O\sim q$, where the inconsistency results in the case of the joint occurrence of their antecedents. This is another way of saying that a system of norms may be inconsistent regarding certain facts and not others.

Three comments should be added to the preceding remarks:

(i) The identification of normative contradictions within a legal system requires the previous attribution of a certain interpretation to the normative formulations enacted by legal authorities. Texts are not contradictory; therefore, there are no contradictions without interpretation. However, interpretation is a complex task, and it consists in a process continued in time. Suppose the interpreter begins with a certain normative formulation NF_1 and correlates prima facie to it a certain interpretation (i.e., it is assumed that NF_1 expresses the norm N_1). But then the interpreter finds another normative formulation NF_2 which she interprets as expressing norm N_2, the result being that both interpretations generate a normative contradiction (i.e., N_1 and

N_2 are logically incompatible). In such a case, our interpreter will probably retreat and reconsider one of the two interpretations (e.g., assigning NF_1 an interpretation according to which it expresses norm N_1', that is compatible with N_2).

As legal norms are formulated in a technical language that is based on the natural language, a considerable space is always open to assign to any given legal formulation several different interpretations. Yet, what was written in the previous paragraph could mistakenly lead to an incorrect conclusion: that every legal system is a coherent set of norms, for any seemingly normative contradiction would be no more than a mere difficulty in the harmonization of legal texts, which could always be overcome through interpretation.

The reason why this is an unjustified conclusion is that the possibility cannot be ruled out that all available interpretations of a certain normative formulation NF_1 are incompatible with any possible interpretation of another normative formulation NF_2. In other words, there may be no way to assign a plausible interpretation to NF_1 that is consistent with any of the possible interpretations of NF_2.

(ii) Normative contradictions should be distinguished from what may be called *axiological contradictions*, i.e., situations in which the solution offered by the legal system to a certain case indicates, together with a set of axiological standards, that another case should have a different solution from the one derivable from the system.[55] Lars Lindahl, in more precise terms, examines what he calls "incoherence in value implementation", i.e., incoherence in the way a set of background values is implemented by legal norms. This sort of inconsistency appears, according to Lindahl, when the evaluation of regulated actions in terms of requisiteness by a set of background values leads to a legitimate expectation of a set of regulations other than those manifested by the norms actually enacted.[56] What distinguishes axiological incoherence from normative contradictions *stricto sensu* is that in the case of axiological incoherence the norms of the system can be jointly realizable: the conflict is not between norms, but between norms and background values.

Lindahl distinguishes between conditions for *weak* and for *strong* value implementation coherence. According to the former, if in the axiology of the system action p is more intensely requisite than q, then it is not the case that q is prescribed in the legal system, while $\sim p$ is permitted. This is tantamount to saying that there will be an axiological contradiction in legal system S if, and

---

[55] See Nino 1984: 278.
[56] See Lindahl 1992: 60 ff.

only if, $P\sim p$ and Oq belong to the consequences of S and, from the axiological background assumed by the interpreter, p is strongly preferred over q.

Lindahl rightly observes that there is a connection between violations of weak implementation coherence and the use of the *argumentum a fortiori*.[57] However, in his view violation of weak implementation coherence amounts to a "neglect" of that kind of argument. But it seems more appropriate to claim that violations of weak implementation coherence *presuppose* the use of arguments *a fortiori*. Let S be a legal system that permits children to work more than eight hours a day, while it prohibits adults from doing so, and that according to the background values of the system it is more important that children not work more than eight hours than that adults do not so. In that case, to claim that the regulations of S violate weak implementation coherence is tantamount to claiming that, from the norms and background values in S, the use of an argument *a fortiori* allows the derivation of a contradiction; if S prohibits adults from working more than eight hours a day, *a fortiori* it should prohibit children from doing so.

By contrast, strong implementation coherence requires that, if in the axiology of the system, p is as intensely required as q, then it is not the case that q is prescribed in the system while $\sim p$ is permitted. In other words, there will be an axiological contradiction in legal system S if and only if $P\sim p$ and Oq belong to the consequences of S, and – from the axiological background assumed by the interpreter – p is at least as good as q. Here, again, Lindahl remarks that violation of strong implementation coherence amounts to a "neglect" of the *argumentum ex analogia*. Now, let S be a legal system that prescribes compensation in the case of an accident, but gives no claim for compensation in a case of fault, and that according to the background values of S, payment of compensation for harm caused by fault is at least as required as payment of compensation for harms caused by accident. In such a case, we will say that the system violates strong implementation coherence because, from the background values and the norms in S, the use of an argument *ex analogia* – if S prescribes compensation in case of accident, then analogously it should prescribe compensation in case of fault – produces a contradiction.[58]

(iii) Let N be a legal norm with the following structure:

$$N: \forall x, y (Axy \rightarrow O(Pyx))$$

---

[57] See Lindahl 1992: 60.

[58] Lindahl rightly observes that there is a close connection between strong value implementation and the principle of universability of moral judgments: If x and y are relevantly similar, then $R(x)$ iff $R(y)$, being R any deontic predicate (see Lindahl 1992: 61).

This may be read as: For all pairs of individuals x and y, if x is in relation A with y, then it is obligatory for y to perform action P in relation to x. For instance, for any x and y, if x has a credit from y, then it is obligatory for y to pay x. A norm such as this can contradict no other norm in a given normative system and, nevertheless, generate a conflict when applied to particular situations if, for example, both a and c have credits of ten dollars from b, and b has only ten dollars. Our norm produces a conflict for b, because when applied to the considered situation it generates two obligations that b cannot jointly satisfy:

$$N': Aab \rightarrow O(Pba)$$
$$N'': Acb \rightarrow O(Pbc)$$

In this case, there is an empirical impossibility for b to satisfy both consequences of the general norm N. But the fact that b cannot pay both creditors does not mean that she does not have an obligation to do so. In other words, the general norm N exhibits no defect whatsoever, even though it may be the case that a certain subject in a particular situation cannot satisfy all the consequences that follow from it.

Situations such as this may be called *conflicts of instantiation*, because they involve individual norms logically derivable from at least one general norm,[59] or instances of application of the same general norm, that generate a conflict because it is empirically impossible jointly to satisfy them. The fundamental difference between conflicts of instantiation and normative contradictions *stricto sensu*, even in the case in which the latter arise *via* certain facts, is that in the case of normative contradictions the impossibility of satisfaction is logical (e.g., it is logically impossible for the same subject at the same time jointly to satisfy the norms Op and $O{\sim}p$), whereas in the case of conflicts of instantiation the impossibility is factual (e.g., b cannot pay now both creditors, not because such a thing is logically impossible, but merely because she has run out of money to do so).

Although in an example such as this there is no defect at all in the general norm from which the conflict of instantiation derives, such conflicts may deserve the attention of normative authorities. For example, let N' be a norm in a public hospital prescribing that doctors should treat immediately patients having heart attacks, and there is only one doctor available at a certain time to assist in emergency cases.[60] N' will produce a conflict whenever two or more cases of patients with heart attacks are reported at the same time. Our doctor

---

[59] The problematic individual norms may be derivable from different general norms. The case considered in the text is the simplest one.

[60] The example is taken from Hansson and Makinson 1997.

will not know which patient ought to be given priority, and whichever one she treats first, she will be failing to satisfy one of the consequences of N'. Again, N' itself should not be seen here as defective; after all, the best solution to the problem seems to be to assign more doctors to the hospital. However, if such an alternative is in fact unattainable and this limitation is seen as axiologically relevant,[61] then it would appear desirable to modify the normative system.

As shown in Chapter 4, Hansson and Makinson regard situations such as this as cases where the maximization and choice to avoid the undesired result should be performed at the level of application. Hence, conflicts of instantiation do not demand an amendment of the legal system, but only the selection of a hierarchy over the applicable set of norms by norm-applying organs.

The general problem with an inconsistent normative set is that, according to the principle *ex falso sequitur quodlibet,* any norm can be derived from it as a solution to the conflicting case. Therefore, from an inconsistent regulation, no useful information can be obtained for the normative guide to behavior. However, in the legal domain the consequences of deontic conflicts seem to be less troublesome. The reason why this is so is that the idea suggested by Hansson and Makinson regarding conflicts of instantiation can be generalized for any kind of normative conflict in the following sense. Norm-applying organs do not need to take into account the whole set of valid legal norms at a certain time, where deontic conflicts may proliferate, to find a legal answer for a certain particular problem. They select a microsystem of the relevant legal norms (an applicable normative set), and within it the notion of inconsistency seems to work as a *relational* concept; legal norms correlate certain abstract cases or circumstances with deontic solutions, and thus a legal inconsistency arises when the same case is correlated by two or more valid norms with different and logically incompatible deontic solutions. In the context of applicable sets of norms, legal conflicts are often merely *partial,* for two incompatible norms in this sense may preserve an area of univocal application. If norm N_1 contradicts another norm N_2 in a legal system, it may still be possible to derive from each of them some information for those cases not affected by the normative conflict.

An example can cast some light on this idea. Consider the following case involving the principles of bargained-for consideration and estoppel presented by Susan Hurley.[62] The doctrine of consideration demands an element of

---

[61] In the case of the previously considered norm N, we would hardly consider the fact that *b* does not have more than ten dollars as axiologically relevant to excuse her from paying all her debts.

[62] See Hurley 1989: chapter 11.

bargain or exchange for a valid and enforceable contractual relationship to arise. A promise not connected to consideration has no legal consequence in contract law, so that is a reason to hold that the promisor is not legally obligated. The doctrine of estoppel prevents a party from taking unfair advantage of a predicament in which that party's own bad behavior has adversely affected the other party. Suppose that a promise was made gratuitously and the promisee acts in reliance on it, so that she will be injured if the promise is not kept, and that the promisor should reasonably have expected the promise to induce action on the part of the promisee, but has no particular interest in the matter. Under such premises, something of value passes from the promisor to the promisee if the promise is enforceable, but nothing of value passes back to the promisor, and thus the consideration requirement is not met. The promisor is not under a contractual obligation, but has acted irresponsibly in making and then breaking a promise that she should reasonably have expected to induce reliance, and so the principle of estoppel seems to support holding that the promisor should not be permitted to take advantage of his own wrongdoing.

Note that the conflict is here only relative to the gratuitous promise under the premises listed previously, and does not affect other cases of application of the principles of consideration and estoppel. Thus, even if the case considered seems to be inconsistently regulated, this does not eliminate the practical relevance of the principles for other cases. In other words, the normative conflict is *encapsulated* in the gratuitous-promise case.

5.5. RELEVANCE, CONFLICTS, AND DEFEASIBILITY OF LEGAL NORMS

As has already been shown, the defeasibility of legal norms is a thesis that has been defended with a great variety of different arguments.[63] In what follows, we only examine two of those arguments, one of them related to the previous discussion on normative relevance and axiological gaps, and the other related to legal conflicts.

One line of reasoning that has been frequently used to support the idea of the defeasible character of legal norms runs as follows: the process of reformulating and incorporating exceptions in legal norms can never be taken as completed, because in deciding a legal case it is necessary to assess the relevance or irrelevance of each singular feature of it, and thus, it is not possible to invoke a predetermined rule declaring the irrelevance of any feature of the situation different from those found in an already closed list.

---

[63] See Chapter 3, Section 3.5.

In this sense, the defeasibility of legal norms depends on their being subject to implicit exceptions that cannot be exhaustively listed. If defeasibility were the case, legal norms would provide solutions solely for *normal* cases. According to this idea, the acceptance of an indefeasible norm would be rational only if the agent considers every possible situation in which the properties in question could be verified, and judge that one has to act in the same way in all of them because the rest of the possible descriptions are normatively irrelevant. But when enacting norms, legal authorities can only foresee normal cases. It would be impossible to take into consideration every possible characteristic of particular cases to assess their normative relevance or irrelevance. Therefore, legal norms cannot be interpreted as indefeasible, for that would imply a blind exclusion of the possible relevance of properties of the case which are different from those explicitly taken into account by the lawgiver when enacting certain norms.[64] Thus, MacCormick has stressed that there is a view of defeasibility closely linked with a related view about one omnipresent problem concerning the formulation or articulation of the law:

> Notoriously, it would be extremely difficult, perhaps impossible, and for sure the enemy of any kind of clarity or cognoscibility in Law, to attempt a formulation of every conceivable precondition of validity in every statement of every rule. So general formulations of rights are apt to leave many background conditions unstated, especially those that arise only in very exceptional cases. The presence of unstated elements appears to be a general feature of Law, albeit different legal systems take different characteristic lines on the degree to which statutory draftsmanship should tend toward completeness in each statutory formulation, rather than giving broader allowance to a reading of statutes in the light of their whole systemic context.[65]

We have already seen the way in which, with the aid of the distinction between the prescriptive and the descriptive concepts of permission, it is possible to expose an ambiguity in the principle "every action that has not been legally prohibited is legally permitted" and, therefore, to reject the claim of the necessary completeness of all legal systems. Analogously, the argument here presented, which upholds the defeasible character of legal norms on the grounds of the irrationality of taking as irrelevant those properties that have not been legally regarded as relevant, can be examined more carefully with the help of the different notions of normative irrelevance that have been previously presented.

---

[64] See Hart 1961: 129–130.
[65] MacCormick 1995: 103.

Some preliminary clarifications are needed. First, legal authorities formulate certain sentences from which the properties they have expressly contemplated as relevant can be identified. But those normative formulations are subject to interpretation, and it would certainly be a mistake to speak of normative relevance at the level of normative formulations, for this can only be done once they have been interpreted. Now, when assigning meaning to the normative formulations expressed by legal authorities, the interpreter can take as relevant not only those properties expressly regarded as such by legal authorities, but also those other properties that are brought to light from other expressions of the authority or from other sources of law admitted as valid.

This could lead us to suppose that the argument here considered focuses on the possibility of the interpreter's incorporation of implicitly relevant properties in addition to those explicitly regarded as such by legal authorities. However, the problem reappears at the level of the interpreter: according to a certain attribution of meaning to a set of normative formulations, there will be some relevant properties (expressly taken as such by the authority or implicitly derived by the interpreter). The question will now be: What happens to the rest of the conceivable properties? Are they irrelevant? It seems that the possibility of introducing exceptions on the basis of properties that have not been taken into account is still not eliminated.

Second, it is obvious that legal norms are defeasible in the sense that we can always assign *prescriptive* normative relevance to certain properties that have not been taken into account by normative authorities. In those cases we may say that there is an axiological gap in the system, in the sense of a critical statement from the internal point of view of a certain axiological system. However, the point here does not rest on what the system *should say* but in what it actually *says*. The argument under analysis claims that legal norms *are* defeasible, for – because in the evaluation of any legal case it is necessary to assess the relevance or irrelevance of each and every particular characteristic of it – legal norms should be regarded as open to an indeterminate number of possible exceptions. Properties that have not been declared relevant by general norms may still be legally relevant.

Now, apart from these two situations (i.e., the cases of axiological gaps in the two senses distinguished), the apparent persuasiveness of the argument loses much of its force. Normative authorities take into account certain properties, assigning (explicitly or implicitly) normative relevance to some of them and disqualifying others as normatively irrelevant. In a descriptive analysis of the resulting normative system, there will be certain properties descriptively relevant and the rest will be descriptively irrelevant. If there are no logical defects in the system (i.e., if the system is complete and consistent), the positive and negative notions of irrelevance characterized previously will be coextensive. If that is not the case, both properties have to be distinguished, but in any event the categories of descriptive relevance and negative descriptive irrelevance will be jointly exhaustive and mutually exclusive. Therefore, restricting our view to a descriptive analysis of a normative system, all those properties that have not been taken into account (either explicitly or implicitly) by normative authorities will be irrelevant in that sense. Because any given property can only be called descriptively relevant if there is a norm *in the system* that renders it so, from a purely descriptive point of view, once all norms in the system have been properly identified it is certainly the case that all properties that are not descriptively relevant are irrelevant.

Things are quite different when we change the perspective and associate the idea of defeasibility, not with a descriptive analysis of normative systems (i.e., with the *identification* of their norms), but with the *application* of such norms to practical problems. In a prescriptive reading of the notion of irrelevance, the statement "any property which has not been taken as relevant is irrelevant" can be interpreted as a directive to the courts in the sense they should not assign relevance to any other property that has not been explicitly taken as such by legislators. The presence in a legal system of a second level residual rule of closure of this kind is obviously contingent. But in case it exists, the system in question would establish what Schauer calls an "entrenched model" of the application of norms, according to which judges would lack legal powers to introduce exceptions in the application of general norms apart from those explicitly introduced by the legislator through other general norms.[66]

When judges face the problem of having to determine whether a property should be considered relevant for the decision they are supposed to make, and that property is irrelevant in the negative sense according to the system, a rule of closure for relevance may or may not be present. If present, the property in question should be considered irrelevant. And if judges, regardless of this fact, decide to take it as relevant for their decision, they will be leaving aside the normative solution determined by the system. If, on the other hand, such rule of closure is not included in the legal system, judges will have no obligation to consider it irrelevant, but if they decide to take it as relevant, they will not be able to justify its relevance — and their decision — in the norms of the system, being thus forced to use some extrasystematic standard.[67]

---

[66] The rationality or irrationality of such a model could be a matter of dispute, but in any case the different arguments discussed by Schauer for its justification should be considered. See Schauer 1991: 42–52.

[67] For a clear distinction between intrasystematic and extrasystematic defeasibility, and the conceptual priority of the former over the latter, see Belzer and Loewer 1997.

In any case, it must be observed that most legal systems authorize judges to justify their decisions by invoking implicit exceptions in the enacted norms in cases of axiological gaps in the two senses analyzed. However, the singularities of a certain case are not rendered normatively relevant or irrelevant only in virtue of some natural property. Their relevance is dependent on a qualification which can be drawn from certain norms or other normative considerations. To justify the introduction of an exception within a certain norm, another norm with an incompatible solution has to be accepted, as well as a preference selecting the solution provided by the latter in case of conflict. Therefore, the central question is the following: on the basis of what other norms is it possible to justify the legal relevance of properties that have not been rendered relevant by the whole set of norms of a legal system?

Consider the case of two legal norms, both of them identifiable from a certain legally relevant texts (e.g., a provision of the Criminal Code), one of them punishing whoever performs an abortion and the other exempting from punishment abortions in cases of rape. One way to construe these two norms is to claim that the first is defeasible because it does not state explicitly the rape-exception. Yet in this example the exception is clearly identifiable from another legally relevant text. In fact, there is nothing that prevents us from using the idea of defeasibility here, if defeasibility only means that enacted legal norms are liable to those exceptions grounded on other enacted legal norms. However, because the law is the result of a finite set of human normative acts, it cannot be maintained that the exceptions to enacted legal norms are incapable of exhaustive statement on these grounds.

In other words, either those norms that allow introducing exceptions to enacted legal norms are identifiable within the same normative system or they are not. In the first case, legal norms cannot be taken as liable to exceptions *incapable of exhaustive statement*, because a thorough examination of enacted law will suffice to detect such exceptions, potential problems being merely epistemic. Only in the second case (i.e., when those norms justifying the introduction of exceptions to enacted legal norms are not part of the legal system), can the open character of the list of exceptions be defended. Now, whether judges have or lack legal powers — depending on the absence or presence of a rule of closure of relevance, respectively — to incorporate new norms introducing exceptions to other norms of the system to justify their decisions in particular cases is something entirely independent of the question whether those norms used by judges to defeat the existing norms will be considered incorporated into the system. Hence, the fact that in deciding particular cases judges sometimes introduce implicit exceptions to the applicable legal norms on the basis of external normative considerations, can be regarded as cases in which the judge:

a. infringes her legal duty as imposed by the secondary rules of the system;
b. uses a discretionary power conferred by the secondary rules of the system;
c. complies with her legal duty, whenever a secondary rule of the system binds her to take into consideration moral norms for the adequate application of legal norms so as to avoid grossly unjust consequences; or
d. modifies the legal system, whenever the existing rule of recognition takes the fact that judges use certain norms to justify implicit exceptions to enacted legal norms as a reason to incorporate those new norms into the system.[68]

Consequently, the idea that the application of legal norms always requires a discretionary decision by norm-applying organs between open alternatives regarding the relevance or irrelevance of any property of the particular case different from those contemplated in the legal system has to be revised. It only allows maintaining that normative qualifications that follow from enacted legal norms are *defeasible in their application to particular cases*, according to extrasystematic normative considerations that norm-applying organs may take into account in their decisions. But this is entirely compatible with the claim that, restricting the analysis to the identification of legal norms (i.e., without taking into account other possible normative systems that may compete with legal solutions at the time of decision-making in particular cases), any legal system indefeasibly correlates certain normative solutions to certain cases.

A second argument in defense of the strong thesis of the defeasible character of – at least some – legal norms may be sketched as follows. In our previous analysis, it has been assumed that as enacted legal norms constitute a finite set, by way of a revision of the antecedent of each norm taking into account the rest of the enacted norms and the preference relations admitted among them, all possible legal exceptions that should be introduced in each legal norm could be identified.[69] However, this idea might be contested on the ground that the identification of all possible exceptions to the solution correlated to a certain case by a given legal norm requires a complete hierarchical ordering

---

[68] These alternatives are inspired by the various explanations legal positivism may embrace of the way moral norms may figure in adjudication according to Coleman 2000: 174–175.

[69] Note, however, that this thorough reconstruction of every exception along the whole set of all valid legal norms at a certain time is unnecessary for norm-applying organs to find a legal answer for certain particular dispute, because they only need to considerate microsystems of the relevant legal norms (applicable normative sets).

of the whole set of norms, so that for any pair of them correlating incompatible solutions to independent cases there is a predetermined criterion of preference assigning superiority to one of the norms over the other. By contrast, whenever a given norm does not register preference relations with all the rest of enacted legal norms, the normative solution it offers would be merely defeasible. In other words, if regarding a certain norm N_1 within system S there is at least one another norm N_2 in S with an incompatible solution, and there is no fixed preference relation between them, as the possibility of N_2 introducing an exception over N_1 cannot be ruled out, the latter should be considered merely defeasible.

Some authors have used this idea to draw a qualitative distinction between *rules* – understood as indefeasible norms – and *principles* – understood as defeasible norms, and claimed that a legal system is a complex set of both types of elements.[70] On the assumption that hierarchical orderings within legal systems are incomplete, legal rules (those norms with established preference relations with any other one in the legal system) would coexist with principles (those norms that lack a predetermined preference relation with at least another norm in the system).

This argument is no more convincing than the former. Let S be a legal system integrated by the following three norms: N_1 correlates the obligation to perform action *s* to case *p*; N_2 prohibits action *s* in case *q*, and N_3 assigns a facultative (optional) normative character to action *s* in case *r*. Furthermore, suppose that according to S, N_1 is preferred over N_3 for any case of conflict among them and, similarly, N_2 is preferred over N_3 for any case of conflict among them, whereas there is no established preference criterion between N_1 and N_2. In the approach under consideration, N_1 and N_2 would be defeasible norms, whereas the revision of N_3 including the exceptions introduced by N_1 and N_2 would be an indefeasible norm:

$$N_1: p > Os$$
$$N_2: q > PHs$$
$$N_3: (r \wedge \sim p \wedge \sim q) \rightarrow Fs^{71}$$

But this reconstruction is plainly inadequate. A simple analysis of all possible cases defined by properties *p*, *q*, and *r* is sufficient to show that there is no reason here justifying the introduction of the notion of defeasibility:

[70] For the classical distinction between rules and principles, see Dworkin 1977: 24 ff.; for the indicated reading of the distinction, see, for instance, Atienza and Ruiz Manero 1998: 34–36.

[71] The symbol > is commonly used to represent defeasible conditionals. For simplicity, we represent indefeasible conditionals here with material implication.

				N_1	N_2	N_3
1	p	q	r	Os	PHs	
2	$\sim p$	q	r		PHs	
3	p	$\sim q$	r	Os		
4	$\sim p$	$\sim q$	r			Fs
5	p	q	$\sim r$	Os	PHs	
6	$\sim p$	q	$\sim r$		PHs	
7	p	$\sim q$	$\sim r$	Os		
8	$\sim p$	$\sim q$	$\sim r$			

As the table illustrates, this system is actually inconsistent in the cases of joint occurrence of p and q, because both cases are correlated with incompatible normative solutions and there is no generally accepted criterion of preference between N_1 and N_2 to solve this conflict. By contrast, as both N_1 and N_2 are preferred over N_3, the solution Fs is only derivable in case 4, not in the former three cases, even though they are all r cases. Accordingly, a more satisfactory interpretation of this system is:

$$N_1': p \to Os$$
$$N_2': q \to PHs$$
$$N_3: (r \wedge \sim p \wedge \sim q) \to Fs$$

where the three norms are indefeasible. In other words, whenever a normative system is not equipped with a complete hierarchical ordering to solve uniquely any possible normative conflict, it does not follow that it will contain defeasible norms, but that some conflicts will remain unsolved. It makes perfect sense to use the notion of defeasibility *before* considering hierarchical criteria among norms, but once those criteria are taken into account, the fact that they are insufficient to give a unique answer to any possible conflict cannot be used as an argument to justify the conclusion that legal norms have a defeasible character.

A possible objection to this analysis may be that indefeasibility is being here presupposed, because to conclude that there is a genuine normative contradiction between two conditional norms it is necessary to interpret the antecedent of each of them as a sufficient condition for their normative solutions. There is a grain of truth in this remark: one of the assumptions of our analysis is that if a certain rule correlates one normative solution to a generic case, blocking the derivation of such a solution in an instance of that generic case requires additional arguments. Thus, norms may be deemed defeasible to the extent that there is some additional factor that defeats them. General norms may certainly be subject to exceptions for a variety of different circumstances, but each of those exceptions has to be grounded on sufficient reasons, and the justification for introducing exceptions in general norms can only be provided by other general norms. This idea may be reflected in the following definition:

> A rule (for example, "one ought to do A given B") is *defeasible* in a normative system S iff S contains another rule to the effect that one ought not do A given B&C or one is permitted not to do A given B&C. In these cases the latter rule *defeat* the first one.[72]

Incompatibility between normative solutions is a necessary but not a sufficient condition of defeasibility. If there are no reasons to assign priority to one norm over another in cases of conflict, it does not seem sound to claim that the former *defeats* the latter. We may certainly speak in such cases of the *indeterminacy* of the normative system under analysis; nonetheless this indeterminacy is not a matter of defeasibility but a mere consequence of the absence of general criteria for solving the conflict.

There is, however, a way in which the defeasible character of norm N_1 in conflict with another norm N_2 could be argued in spite of there not being general criteria of preference assigning priority to the latter over the former in every case of conflict. It could be claimed that in certain cases of normative conflicts, the solution must be searched in the relative *weight* of the conflicting norms regarding particular cases. Although facing a particular case there may be reasons for one of the norms to prevail, this fact would not mean that in other cases those reasons might not exist or even be reversed.[73] Conflicts between constitutionally entrenched rights are often presented as examples of this mode of conflict-resolution. For instance, it may be said that freedom of press prevails over the right of privacy of public officials or public figures such that one should only find defamation and libel if the actual malice standard is met, which requires that the plaintiff in a defamation or libel case prove that the publisher of the statement in question knew that the statement was false or acted in reckless disregard of its truth or falsity.[74] In such cases, there is no

---

[72] Belzer and Loewer 1997: 45.

[73] This is the way in which Dworkin originally presented the distinctive characteristic of legal principles (see Dworkin 1977: 24–27).

[74] See *N.Y. Times v. Sullivan*, 376 U.S. 254 (1964).

unconditional preference of one right over the other; however, as the example shows, this does not mean that no preference whatsoever is accepted between the two rights. The standard of actual malice acts as a *conditional* preference: *if* there is actual malice, the right of privacy of public officers prevails over freedom of press.

Normative conflicts may be solved through the introduction of unconditional or conditional preferences.[75] For an example of latter procedure, consider the following system: N_1 assigns the normative solution Os to case p and N_2 correlates the solution PHs to case q. From these two norms, a contradiction is derivable for every joint occurrence of their antecedents. If there is an unconditional preference of N_1 over N_2 or vice versa, the normative solution of the preferred norm will overrule the other in every case of conflict between them. But the problem can also be solved by assigning preference to one of the norms over the other *under the condition* that a different circumstance r occurs, reversing the preference in case r does not occur.

				N_1	N_2
1	p	q	r	Os	
2	$\sim p$	q	r		PHs
3	p	$\sim q$	r	Os	
4	$\sim p$	$\sim q$	r		
5	p	q	$\sim r$		PHs
6	$\sim p$	q	$\sim r$		PHs
7	p	$\sim q$	$\sim r$	Os	
8	$\sim p$	$\sim q$	$\sim r$		

Here N_1 is preferred to N_2 in cases r, whereas the inverse preference holds in cases $\sim r$. Alexy perspicuously observed that the dimension of weight, which has been proposed as a distinctive characteristic of legal principles, in contradistinction to legal rules, is just a metaphorical way of referring to the introduction of conditional preferences, and that this mode of conflict-resolution makes it possible to reconcile a proper assessment of the singularities of each case with the requirement of universability.[76] Through this procedure, a certain scope of application is preserved for each of the norms in conflict.

[75] Of course, and contrary to Dworkin, the existence of two ways to solve normative conflicts is no sufficient ground to justify the idea that there are two different kinds of norms – rules and principles, each one with a peculiar mode of dealing with conflicts.

[76] See Alexy 1986: 87 ff. and 167.

Now, in a situation such as that, if – on the one hand – the criterion of conditional preference preexisted in the system, the only thing that could be grounded on that basis is a weak notion of defeasibility, according to which the norms under consideration would be subject to *implicit* exceptions, not the strong thesis that those exceptions are incapable of exhaustive statement. If – on the other hand – the criterion of conditional preference was not part of the system, but introduced by norm-applying organs in the context of the applicable set of norms to justify a particular decision, the use of such a criterion at the level of application does not necessarily imply a modification of the legal system, and so the conflict will persist within it. By contrast, if according to the secondary rules of the system the existence of such an adjudicative practice is contemplated as a valid source of law, the incorporation of this new criterion should be interpreted as a modification in the legal system at the dynamic level. But then, any attempt to justify the defeasible character of legal norms on those grounds would trivialize the very idea of defeasibility, for it is obvious that all legal norms are defeasible in the sense that they are subject to the incorporation of possible exceptions in the future as a consequence of possible changes in the legal system.

6

Legal Dynamics

6.1. MOMENTARY AND NON-MOMENTARY LEGAL SYSTEMS

Raz made a fundamental step forward in the theoretical reconstruction of legal dynamics when he introduced the distinction between momentary and non-momentary legal systems. The former concept refers to all those norms that are valid at a particular time; the latter is a broader concept that refers to something like the legal history of a particular community.[1] The distinction between momentary and non-momentary legal systems is designed to shed light on the interplay between the changing content of law and its continuity over time, because it helps us to understand the reason why a pair of norms which were valid at different times can be regarded as members of the same municipal law even if they never belonged to the same *momentary* system. Non-momentary legal systems – also called "legal systems" *simpliciter* by Raz – show how the legal history of a political community is mainly developed by means of the introduction and elimination of valid norms. In non-momentary legal systems, genetic relations play a fundamental role because they define normative hierarchies and conditions for exercising normative powers. For this reason, Raz stresses that in every legal system there are genetic relations between norms.[2]

In the creation of norms, there is a genetic relation between a power-conferring norm and the new norms created by the exercise of such power. The relevance of such relations among norms seems to be obvious: unlike morality, law often changes by specific normative acts performed by legal authorities. In fact, a person (or organ) is a legal authority only to the extent that she is allowed to modify the deontic status of certain actions. Thus,

[1] See Raz 1970: 34.
[2] See Raz 1970: 164, 184–185.

authority and creation of norms are conceptually related, and any explanation of the nature of law would be defective if this characteristic of legal systems were not taken into consideration.

As has been shown, there is no univocal concept of a legal system in legal discourse. On the contrary, several concepts are actually needed for understanding to what extent the idea of a system is required by different operations, such as the identification of the scope of externally applicable norms or the analysis of the dynamic nature of law. Whereas the structure of applicable systems is based on *deductive* relations, non-momentary legal systems have a different structure, mainly based on genetic relations. It was a great merit of Raz to stress the different structure of momentary and non-momentary systems. However, his analysis of non-momentary systems is defective.

Raz's reconstruction suggests that both momentary and non-momentary legal systems are normative *sets*. In fact, it seems to be a platitude regarding legal systems that they are basically sets of norms. However, there is another platitude, as strong and extended as the former, that cannot be easily reconciled with it: legal systems are subject to changes in virtue of deliberate normative acts of promulgation, amendment or derogation, and those changes affect the content and not the identity of legal systems, because they persist over time even though their content changes. The problem is that it is impossible to take due account of this identity over time in spite of changes in content if legal systems are understood as *sets* of norms. Sets are usually defined extensionally (i.e., the identity of the set is a function of the identity of their members), in the sense that with any modification of their members the set loses its identity.

The same conclusion holds for legal systems. In so far as legal systems are conceived of as normative sets, each valid act of promulgation, amendment or derogation performed over a given set S_1 produces as a result another set S_2. Legal systems understood as sets of norms are *static* entities, or – as Raz observed – *momentary* systems (i.e., relative to a particular temporal moment). Therefore, if we want to preserve the platitude that law is subject to changes over time, the concept of legal system presupposed in that idea has to be different from the one used when we think of law as a set of norms.[3]

Raz's distinction between momentary and non-momentary legal systems may be seen as a way to reconcile the continuous existence of law over time and its varying content. Nonetheless, Bulygin has rightly remarked that Raz's reconstruction of non-momentary legal systems is ambiguous.[4] On the one hand,

3   See Alchourrón and Bulygin 1991: 393–408.
4   See Bulygin 1982: 66–67, note 7.

Raz claims that momentary legal systems are *subclasses* of (non-momentary) legal systems.[5] On the other hand, Raz also says that an expression such as "The English legal system at the beginning of the reign of Elizabeth II" can refer either to the momentary system of that particular time or to the legal system to which this momentary system *belongs*.[6] According to this latter interpretation, momentary legal systems are *members* of a certain non-momentary system; the dynamic unit is not a set of norms, but an ordered set of systems of norms. The non-momentary legal system would then be a *sequence* of all momentary legal systems that result from each valid normative act of promulgation, amendment, or derogation.[7]

Hence, two different interpretations of the logical nature of non-momentary legal systems can be offered in terms of the relations of *inclusion* and *membership* of momentary systems.[8] On the one hand, in what can be referred to as the *model of inclusion*, momentary legal systems can be regarded as subsets included in a non-momentary legal system, understood as a larger set of norms. Under this idea, each momentary legal system is the set of all valid norms at a certain time, whereas the non-momentary legal system is the whole set of all valid norms at any time. A given norm N belongs to a non-momentary legal system S_1 if and only if it satisfies a specific condition of membership (e.g., validity). What distinguishes the members of each subset is the possession of this condition of membership at different moments $t_1, t_2, \ldots, t_n$. For example, if the set of human beings is H, we may say that Kelsen belongs to the subset H_1 of humans living in 1970. Kelsen belongs to H because H_1 is included in H, even if he does not belong to the different subset H_2 of humans living in 1990. Similarly, a certain norm N may belong to the subset S_1 of valid norms at moment t_1 of system S, and not belong to the subset S_2 of valid norms at t_2.

On the other hand, in what can be referred to as the *model of membership*, non-momentary legal systems can be seen as sequences (i.e., ordered sets of momentary legal systems). Under this reconstruction, a legal system S_1 belongs to a non-momentary legal system S if and only if it satisfies a specific condition of membership resulting from the legality of a normative act of promulgation, amendment or derogation.[9] Now, according to this idea, norms do not belong

---

[5] See Raz 1970: 35.
[6] See Raz 1970: 35.
[7] A sequence can be alternatively defined as an ordered set or as a function $f: \text{N+} \rightarrow \text{A}$ for some appropriately chosen set A, with $f(i) = a_i$ for each i belonging to N+. The ith term in the sequence is just the value of the function for argument i (see Makinson 2008: 82).
[8] For a thorough exploration of these two alternatives, see Moreso and Navarro 1993: 48–63.
[9] See Bulygin 1982: 67.

to non-momentary legal systems; norms belong to momentary legal systems which, in turn, are members of a certain non-momentary legal system. The reason for this is that membership is not a transitive relation: although Kelsen is a member of the Viennese school of legal theory, and the Viennese school is a member of the class of schools of legal theory, it is not true that Kelsen belongs to the set of schools of legal theory, for Kelsen is not a school but a *member* of a school.

Although there is nothing conceptually flawed in either of these two conceptions of non-momentary legal systems, it can be demonstrated that the model of inclusion is not able to offer a proper reconstruction of legal dynamics. First, against the model of inclusion it may be objected that it inevitably leads to an unacceptable result: as a matter of fact, non-momentary systems would be inconsistent sets of norms. Normative authorities almost daily introduce changes in the law; they replace norms that are no longer useful or adequate by other norms that regulate the same circumstances in different and incompatible ways. In Argentina, for example, the age required for a valid marriage without authorization is now eighteen years, but some time ago it was twenty-one. Under the model of inclusion, even if these (partially) incompatible norms are members of different momentary systems, they both belong to the unique non-momentary set of all valid norms in Argentina. Therefore, if non-momentary systems are understood as sets of norms, they will contain all derogated norms together with those incompatible norms that replaced them.[10] Be that as it may, this argument does not invalidate by itself this conception of non-momentary legal systems, given that – as discussed in the previous chapter – consistency is a contingent property of normative sets.[11]

There is, however, a much more decisive argument for dismissing this theoretical model of non-momentary legal systems that shows its radical inadequacy where giving a proper account of legal dynamics is concerned.[12] Under the model of membership, whenever a given norm is promulgated, amended or derogated, changes are represented as the incorporation of a new static system into the sequence that forms the non-momentary system. But as the dynamic system is precisely a sequence of static systems, it preserves its identity despite changes. If at time t a given non-momentary system is integrated by a sequence of static systems and a normative act of promulgation, amendment, or derogation is performed, this act will result in the incorporation into the sequence of a new momentary system at t_{+1}, but the non-momentary system

[10] See Bulygin 1991: 260.
[11] See Rodríguez 2002: 120–127.
[12] See Rodríguez 2002: 122–123; also see Caracciolo 1996: 170.

will preserve its identity because the latter depends solely on the criteria used to identify the static systems that are part of it.

By contrast, under the model of inclusion, non-momentary systems are sets of norms, and thus, they are as static as all the subsets of valid norms at a certain time that they include: if the set of all valid norms up to time t according to certain criteria of validity is constituted by certain norms (which can be divided by theorists into the subsets of all valid norms at t, t_{-1}, t_{-2}, and so on), and a competent authority exercises its powers and enacts a new norm at t_{+1}, the resulting set of all valid norms up to t_{+1} will contain – possibly among others – this new norm and, consequently, will be different from the previous set. Hence, in a retrospective view, this model is only apt to reflect legal dynamics as different subsets delimited on a set that includes them, and in a prospective view it proves useless to give due account of the continuous identity despite changes, because the set of all valid norms up to now will have to be replaced by another set if a new norm is promulgated.

It seems clear that there is a difference in the level of abstraction between conceiving the dynamic legal system as a set of norms and interpreting it as an ordered set of sets of norms, the latter perspective being obviously more abstract than the former. It is also clear that if for certain purposes a less abstract reconstruction is sufficient to evaluate a specific problem, it may be preferable to a more elaborate one. But the price we must be willing to pay for this greater economy is the loss of explanatory power. If the image of a dynamic legal system is presented as a set of norms and the static systems as subsets of valid norms at different times, it is impossible to give proper account of certain relations between those sets. By contrast, if the dynamic legal system is interpreted as a sequence (i.e., an ordered set of static systems), relations of temporal succession among static systems can be analyzed within the dynamic system – something that is conceptually impossible in the alternative model.

Eugenio Bulygin has proposed the following criterion of identification for non-momentary legal systems – *legal orders* (O) in his terminology – understood according to the model of membership:

(1) The set of norms $(N_1, N_2, \ldots, N_n)$ is the originating system (first constitution) of O_1.

(2) If a norm N_j is valid in a system S_t that belongs to O_1, and N_j empowers an authority x to enact norm N_k, and x enacts norm N_k at time t, then N_k is valid in the system S_{t+1} that belongs to O_1.

(3) If a norm N_j is valid in a system S_t that belongs to O_1, and N_j empowers an authority x to derogate norm N_k which is valid in S_t, and x derogates N_k at time t, then N_k is not valid in the system S_{t+1} that belongs to O_1.

(4) All valid norms in a system S_t that belongs to O_1 that have not been derogated at time t are valid in the system S_{t+1} of O_1.

(5) All the logical consequences of valid norms in a system S_t which belongs to O_1 are also valid in S_t.[13]

Rule (1) identifies the originating system S_0. Rules (2) through (5) identify the structure of the non-momentary legal system (legal order). Rules (2), (3), and (4) explain the dynamic character of non-momentary legal systems, and rule (5) closes under logical consequence the different momentary systems belonging to the same non-momentary legal system.

Let us briefly remark some interesting aspects of this definitional scheme:

1. *Identification of the originating system.* To avoid circularity, the norms of the originating system (the *first* system) are extensionally identified. The identification of such an independent set of norms is often based on certain assumptions concerning the relations between legal systems and political systems (i.e., the relations between Law and State). As Raz points out, no rigid or formal criteria can provide the key for understanding the problem of the continuity of a particular State.[14] The definitional scheme proposed by Bulygin does not assume that the first system is originated by a revolution, emancipation, or any other specific political factor. However, it explains to what extent the identity of non-momentary legal systems depends on certain relations between norms; in particular, it shows that a change in the sequence of momentary systems is the result of valid normative acts performed by legal authorities. The identity of non-momentary legal systems depends on the legality of changes, and thus any illegal modification of the constitution should give rise to a new non-momentary system.

   This conclusion, however, is controversial. What are the effects of invalid normative acts? Does the enactment of an unconstitutional norm entail the collapse of the legal order and produce a new order? Is a non-momentary legal system O_1 replaced by another system O_2 whenever an invalid normative act is performed? A possible answer, defended by von Wright,[15] is to claim that invalid norms mark a *recession* from the system and do not imply a change of non-momentary legal systems. On the other hand, a "realist" answer would be to admit that in as much as invalid norms are effective, the non-momentary system is modified

---

[13] Bulygin 1991: 263–264.
[14] See Raz 1979: 99–102.
[15] See von Wright 1963a: 203.

and this results in a new originating system (i.e., the first static system in a new non-momentary system). Another possible answer is to select a "basic core" whose illegal modification implies a change of the non-momentary system.[16]

Just as non-momentary systems may be reconstructed as sequences of static systems, political systems may be understood as sequences of non-momentary systems. A political community (e.g., Argentina), contains several non-momentary systems produced by different revolutions and illegal changes in its institutional history. Under this approach, the identity of a particular State would be basically dependent on the relations between law and political factors, but the identity of non-momentary systems understood as sequences of momentary systems would only depend on the legality of normative changes.

In cases of substitution of a certain non-momentary legal system by another, it may occur that some norms of the last static system of the previous non-momentary system persist in the successive systems of the new non-momentary system. This is what Kelsen called *the reception of norms*.[17] A proper account of such cases requires a refinement of the proposed criterion of identification. Perhaps a generalization of the principle of persistence of norms expressed by rule (4) should be incorporated with the following content:[18] *If norm N_i belongs to the system S_i, which is a member of an order O_i, then it belongs to all legal systems successive to S_i of all legal orders successive to O_i until its elimination.*

2. *Criteria of legality.* Rules (2), (3), and (4) determine the genetic structure of non-momentary legal systems; they set the criterion of legality, which confers dynamic character to the sequence. According to this definitional scheme, the criterion of legality can be taken as the defining property of the membership of momentary systems in the legal order:[19] a static system S belongs to a non-momentary system O if and only if:

a. S is the originating system of O; or

b. all new norms in S, comparing its content with the content of the former system S_{-1} that belongs to O, have been promulgated by means of authorized acts according to the norms belonging to S_{-1}, and all norms in S_{-1} that do not belong to S have been derogated by authorized acts according to the norms of S_{-1}.

[16] See Raz 1979: 100.
[17] See Kelsen 1945: 139.
[18] A detailed analysis is offered in Moreso and Navarro 1998: 273–292.
[19] See Caracciolo 1988: 68–69; Bulygin 1991: 262.

3. *Criteria of deducibility.* Rule (5) sets the criterion of deducibility, which incorporates as valid in every momentary system all the logical consequences of legally enacted norms. Therefore, under this reconstruction every momentary system is interpreted as closed under logical consequence.[20]

Once we see that the only satisfactory way to account for the dynamic notion of legal system is in terms of a *sequence* of sets of norms that replace one another over time with each valid normative act of promulgation, amendment, or derogation of norms (the model of membership), it should also be accepted that the role of legality (genetic) and deducibility as criteria of membership cannot be the same: deductibility may operate as a criterion of membership of norms to static systems, but legality is a criterion of membership, not of norms to static systems, but of static systems in the sequence of one and the same dynamic system. Accordingly, *pace* Bulygin, legality does not set conditions of membership of norms in momentary systems, but defines the membership of momentary systems in the dynamic sequence.[21]

Bulygin has replied to this idea that the criterion of legality – expressed in rules (2) and (3) – would serve both functions: defining the membership of momentary systems in the dynamic sequences and (partially) determining the content of each momentary system. Which norms belong to each momentary system would be (partially) determined by rules (1) through (5), which jointly would offer a recursive definition of "valid norm in a system S of legal order O."[22]

But it seems apparent that if these five rules define recursively "valid norm in a system S of the legal order O," what is being defined is the membership of any norm in a certain momentary system that belongs to a given dynamic sequence. The membership of a norm to one static system of the dynamic sequence is a function of its membership in the static system, and the membership of that static system in the dynamic sequence. If norm N is promulgated by an invalid procedure, the resulting system will not be admitted as a new element in the sequence, and thus N will not be part of a momentary system of the sequence. Therefore, it is right to say that rules (1) through (5), through their successive application, make it possible to determine whether a given norm is or is not a member of a certain static system of the dynamic sequence. But from this it does not follow that the criterion of legality is by

---

[20] We discuss this assumption later in this chapter.
[21] See Caracciolo 1988: 67 ff.
[22] See Bulygin 1991: 265.

itself a criterion of membership of norms in momentary systems. Within the five rules specified by Bulygin, we find jointly expressed the criteria of membership of norms to momentary systems, and the criteria of membership of momentary systems to the non-momentary system, but this does not prove that each of these rules simultaneously serve both functions.[23]

As we have already shown, in any static system S there are norms that belong to S in virtue of their relations with other valid norms (*dependent norms*), as well as norms that directly belong to S (*independent norms*) – that is, norms that do not satisfy systematic relations. If both legality and deducibility were criteria of the membership of norms in momentary systems, the class of dependent norms should be subdivided into two subclasses: dependent norms in virtue of deducibility relations and dependent norms in virtue of legality relations. Yet, there is a difference in the conditions of elimination of these two categories of dependent norms. Those norms that are dependent in virtue of the criterion of legality occupy a "privileged position" over the other dependent norms, because if a given norm N has been explicitly enacted by a competent authority, it remains in the system even if the norm that conferred legal power to create N is eliminated.[24]

This "privileged position" of dependent norms in virtue of legality relations is simply a consequence of the fact that legality is not really a criterion of the membership of norms in momentary systems, but a criterion of admission of new momentary systems in the sequence that conforms to the non-momentary legal system. In other words, under this reconstruction of legal dynamics, legality is not a relation between norms, but a qualification of normative acts.

Hence, when a new static system is admitted in the dynamic sequence as a result, for example, of a valid act of promulgation of a norm N by competent authorities, N will be part of this new system. A subsequent derogation of the power-conferring norm N_1 authorizing the creation of N will result in the incorporation of a new momentary system in which N_1 will be absent, but this act by itself has no incidence on the validity of N in the new system, because the validity of N is not grounded in its relation with N_1, but exclusively in the legality of its creation. By contrast, in the case of logically derived norms, the membership of a given norm N in a momentary system depends indeed on the existence of a logical relation between N and at least another norm N_1 of the same momentary system, so that an act of derogation of N_1 produces another system in the sequences in which N will not be derivable. Here, the

---

[23] See Rodríguez 2002: 138.
[24] See Moreso and Navarro 1993: 38.

elimination of N_1 automatically produces the elimination N from the new system.[25]

6.2. PROMULGATION AND DEROGATION OF LEGAL NORMS

Legislation, understood as the deliberate normative activity designed to incorporate and eliminate general legal norms, is the most important technique for bringing about changes in normative systems. For this reason, even if the content of legal systems can change in virtue of customary norms, precedents, or other sources of law, we will limit our analysis here to the promulgation and derogation of legal norms.[26] "Promulgation" and "derogation" are both ambiguous expressions, because each of them refers not only to a certain activity, but also to the specific result of such an activity. As normative actions, the promulgation and derogation of norms are fixed at a certain time t; and although the acts in themselves may last only a brief instant or a long time, the *result* of such acts – the incorporation or elimination of norms in the legal system – is something that always occurs at a certain moment after the performance of those acts.

The analysis of the *act* of promulgation is a topic of classical and contemporary jurisprudence. In general, this type of action has been analyzed by following the framework provided by intentional individual actions, but many controversies stem from discrepancies in the analogy between individual acts and acts attributed to institutions (e.g., the Congress or Parliament), the role played by the intentions of legislators, the connections between legislated texts and ordinary interpretative resources, or the imperative nature of this type of act. By contrast, the analysis of the *results* of these normative acts has been largely neglected in legal theory. Perhaps this lack of interest arises from a widespread idea: promulgation is the incorporation of norms in a legal system, and nothing especially complex or interesting seems to follow from this fact.

Here our focus lies in promulgation as a way of introducing modifications in the content of a legal system; strictly speaking, the generation of a new system in the dynamic sequence. From this point of view, it is necessary to distinguish two notions of promulgation: *material* and *formal* promulgation. In case the enacted norms were *redundant*, in the sense that they merely reproduced other preexistent norms, the normative content of the legal system

---

[25] See Caracciolo 1988: 64–67.

[26] It is not unreasonable to think that the incorporation and elimination of any other legal norm different from legislated norms is analyzable through a sophistication of the simplified framework offered here for legislation.

would not change. The set of relevant legal texts or materials may vary as a consequence of the incorporation of new text, but the *normative system*, understood as the set of norms derivable from such texts or materials, may remain unchanged. We shall say that this act of promulgation is only *formal*, because it only introduces a different presentation of the normative system. For example, let us assume that through a legislative act a new provision is enacted that expresses the norm *Op*, which was already derivable from constitutional provisions. This act produces no modification of the legal system. The idea of formal promulgation can be extended to any normative act of promulgation that effects no changes in the normative system. In that case, the promulgation of an invalid norm can also be regarded as a formal promulgation, for invalid norms do not produce a valid change in the legal system.

By contrast, material promulgation may be defined as any normative act of enactment that produces an alteration in the content of the legal system. A valid act of material promulgation of norms adds a new momentary system in the sequence, where the resulting system will be an *expansion* of the conceptual content of the previous system, at least in the sense that it will include the new norm or set of norms that have been explicitly referred to in the act of promulgation. Now, it could be argued that because norm-applying organs are bound to take into account not only those norms that have been *explicitly* enacted, but the whole set of the logical consequences that follow from them, the expansion operated by an act of material promulgation forces us to consider not only the introduction of explicitly promulgated norms, but also the entire set of all the logical consequences of explicitly enacted norms in the system.[27] Implicitly promulgated norms are *dependent* norms in a given momentary system S, for their validity is justified by the existence of a certain relation to other norms in S (in this case, a logical relation). If an implicitly promulgated norm N_1 is ultimately derivable from only one explicitly enacted norm N_2 that belongs to S,[28] we will say that N_1 has a *simple foundation* in S. However, it may be the case that an implicitly promulgated norm N_1 is derivable, not from any single explicitly enacted norm of S, but from a plurality of such norms, in the sense that all of them are necessary to infer N_1. In such a case we will say that N_1 has a *complex foundation* in S.

An interesting problem of elucidation concerning implicit norms is their place in the hierarchical order of the normative set. Generally speaking, a

---

[27] This assumption is a matter of detailed critical analysis later in this chapter.

[28] An implicitly promulgated norm may be a logical consequence of other logical consequences of explicitly enacted norms. But ultimately, all implicitly promulgated norms are logically derivable from at least one explicitly promulgated norm.

given norm's location in a hierarchical order is determined by the location of the authority that promulgated it – for example, constitutional norms are enacted by constitutional assemblies, which are higher than ordinary legislative assemblies, such as the Congress or Parliament, and thus statutes enacted by the latter organs are deemed of a lower rank in relation to the Constitution. But implicit norms have no canonical formulation, and thus this criterion has no direct application for identifying their hierarchical positions. A possible suggestion regarding implicit norms is that in case they have a simple foundation, their hierarchy is the same as that of the explicitly enacted norm from which it ultimately derives. The same goes for those implicit norms with a complex foundation where the explicitly enacted norms necessary for their derivation are at the same level in the hierarchy. But the problem arises when implicit norms have a complex foundation, and the explicitly enacted norms necessary for their derivation have different levels in the hierarchy. In this case, it seems sound to claim that the level of the implicit norm is the same as that of the lowest ranked explicitly enacted norm necessary for its derivation.

If a given momentary system S were identified with the consequences of a set α of expressly enacted norms, it would be tempting to think that the result of a valid act of material promulgation of a new norm or set of norms β would be a new momentary system containing the sum of the logical consequences of α and the logical consequences of β ($Cn(\alpha) + Cn(\beta)$). However, the incorporation of all logical consequences of enacted norms offers a more complicated picture, for in a case like the former, the new momentary system will be constituted by the consequences of the sum of the logical consequences of α and β ($Cn(\alpha + \beta)$), which may be larger than the set obtained from ($Cn(\alpha) + Cn(\beta)$).[29] For example, let the norm $p{\rightarrow}Or$ be the unique explicitly enacted norm of a certain system S. Although of course the norm $q{\rightarrow}Or$ cannot be inferred from this system, if a legal authority validly promulgates a definition according to which $q{\leftrightarrow}p$, the new momentary system in the sequence will allow the derivation of $q{\rightarrow}Or$ as a consequence of the conjunction of $p{\rightarrow}Or$ and $q{\leftrightarrow}p$, even if this norm is neither a consequence of $p{\rightarrow}Or$ alone, nor of $q{\leftrightarrow}p$ alone.

The valid material promulgation of a new legal norm will always result in another momentary system in the dynamic sequence. The identification of this new system will usually be a complex task, for the logical consequences of the sum of the former set and the new norms can lead to unexpected combinations. Yet, even on these occasions the promulgation of a norm will

[29] See Alchourrón and Bulygin 1991: 398; Alchourrón and Bulygin 1981: 103.

produce a univocal result, because the result of any act of promulgation will always be a unique normative set.[30]

The dynamic nature of law would be unintelligible if legal norms could not be eliminated. To avoid conflicts, the incorporation of a new norm often requires replacing other norms that belong to a certain legal system. Whenever legal authorities realize that a certain norm N, enacted some time ago, has to be replaced, they may consider regulating the same circumstances with an incompatible solution. This decision can be implemented in different ways, but the authorities' aim would be frustrated if N were not eliminated, because the promulgation of the new norm and the persistence of N will result in a normative conflict. Therefore, legislation cannot be exhausted by the introduction of norms in a sequence of momentary legal systems; the explanation of promulgation of legal norms must be supplemented with an adequate analysis of *derogation*.[31]

Just as we saw in the case of promulgation, in certain circumstances, the act of derogation of a certain norm may not yield any change in the normative content of a momentary system, but only affect its presentation. The elimination of redundant norms will thus be called *formal derogation*, in analogy with formal promulgation, because it does not modify the normative consequences of a particular system. Let D, a subset of a normative system $Cn(\alpha)$, be the set of norms explicitly referred to by an act of derogation (henceforth, the *derogated set*). In the case of formal derogation, the system $Cn(\alpha)$ is transformed into another system $Cn(\alpha-D)$, where $Cn(\alpha) = Cn(\alpha-D)$.[32] By contrast, those acts of derogation that yield modifications of the content of legal systems as a result shall be called *material derogations*.

An act of material derogation of a certain norm N from a legal system S paradigmatically results in a new system S_1 in the sequence, where N will no longer be valid. To avoid ambiguities, derogation will be analyzed in two different aspects: (1) the normative act directed towards the elimination of certain norms from a momentary system; and (2) the result of such operation (i.e., the *contraction* of a momentary system).

---

[30] See Alchourrón and Bulygin 1991: 398–399.

[31] Of course, promulgation and derogation are not the only possible normative acts that lead to changes in a legal system. Amendment should at least be added to that list. Nonetheless, amendment will not be analyzed here, as it can be reduced to the more simple acts of promulgation and derogation, as a complex combination of an act of derogation over the norm to be amended, followed by an act of promulgation of the amended norm. See Gärdenfors 1992b: 196–197.

[32] See Alchourrón 1982: 53.

6.2.1. Derogatory Acts

In a certain sense, derogation is a normative act with the opposite aim of promulgation: if the main purpose of promulgation is to introduce a new norm, the main purpose of derogation is to eliminate a norm from a legal system. Derogation can be either explicit or implicit; explicit derogation occurs whenever normative authorities perform a normative act identifying through a derogating provision those normative contents that are intended to be eliminated from a certain momentary systems (the *derogated set* D). By contrast, implicit derogation occurs when the valid promulgation of a new norm produces a conflict with some preexisting norm or set of norms, and we have reasons to prefer the former over the latter (e.g., in virtue of the principle *lex posterior derogat priori*), so that the conflicting preexisting norm or set of norms has to be eliminated to restore consistency.

Under the assumption that momentary systems contain all their logical consequences, derogation can refer either to explicitly enacted norms or to implicit norms. Therefore, prima facie the following four situations may be distinguished:

a. *Explicit derogation of explicitly enacted norms*: A derogating provision explicitly identifies a statue or paragraph of an official text as the one to be eliminated. This is perhaps the paradigmatic case of derogating acts, where the object of derogation is identified by means of certain canonical words.

b. *Explicit derogation of implicit norms*: Legal authorities sometimes add to the promulgation of a new norm a special clause declaring derogated all those norms that are in conflict with the new content that is being promulgated. In this case, an explicitly formulated provision serves to bring about the derogation, but the normative set that has to be eliminated is not expressly identified. To the extent that this normative set can contain implicit norms, this case might be regarded as an example of explicit derogation of implicit norms.[33]

c. *Implicit derogation of implicit norms*: Legal theorists often say that in virtue of the principle *lex posterior derogat priori*, the introduction of a new norm in a legal system "tacitly" derogates preexisting incompatible norms. If these incompatible norms were implicit, this case could be seen as an example of an implicit derogation of implicit norms.

d. *Implicit derogation of explicitly enacted norms*: To remove an implicit norm it is necessary to eliminate its foundation in the corresponding

---

[33] A thorough discussion of this case will be offered in the following section.

momentary system. Consequently, derogation of an implicit norm is also an implicit derogation of certain explicitly enacted norms.

6.2.2. *Contraction of Legal Systems*

The process of derogation encompasses two phases. On the one hand, the identification of the derogated set D in a certain momentary system S and, on the other hand, the identification of all normative subsets in S that entail any norm of the derogated set D. The set of all subsets in a certain momentary system S that entails an element of the derogated set D may be called the *rejected set* (Re). A set C is rejected by a certain derogation D (Re(D)) if and only if some elements of D are consequences of C. This means that the intersection of the set D and the set of the consequences of C is not empty. If we assume that $C \subseteq S$ we may define the set of rejected norms C by D as:

$$C \in Re(D) \text{ if and only if } (Cn(C) \cap D) \neq \phi^{34}$$

According to this, if a derogated set D were entailed by two different normative sets A and B, the elimination of only one of them would not be sufficient for the successful derogation of the set D, because D would still be derivable as a consequence of B. In other words, the result of an act of derogation is a family of rejected sets, and every set of this family must be eliminated to remove all explicitly derogated norms. However, this poses a problem. What does the expression "elimination of a set" mean? In the analysis of non-momentary legal systems, we have stressed that a set changes with any modification of its elements; the addition of a new norm N to a legal system S generates a new system S_1. As we have already seen, to the extent that the identity of S depends on the elements that belong to S, it is a sufficient condition to turn S into another set S_1 that at least one element of S be eliminated. In other words, insofar as no rejected set can be part of the new system, at least one norm of each rejected set must be eliminated. Of course, the removal of the derogated set D is equally obtained when more than a single element of the rejected sets is eliminated. In fact, it is not always possible to remove only one element of the different rejected sets: let us assume that the family of rejected sets is constituted by three rejected sets: $\{N_1, N_2\}$, $\{N_2, N_3\}$, and $\{N_1, N_3\}$. The removal of at least one norm of each rejected set entails that all norms of one of the rejected sets will be eliminated.[35] But in spite of these situations, it is sound to accept the following criterion of adequacy for derogation:

[34] See Alchourrón 1982: 54.
[35] See Alchourrón and Bulygin 1979: 101.

1. No explicitly derogated norm can be part of the new system;
2. No norms other than those actually necessary to satisfy the first condition should be eliminated from the system.[36]

The satisfaction of this criterion of adequacy requires the identification of a set S that selects at least one norm of each rejected set (i.e., S must not intersect vacuously every rejected set), and such a selection must be *minimal*, in the sense that the same result cannot be obtained by the selection of fewer norms.

To illustrate this process, let us introduce a slight adaptation of an example offered by Hilpinen.[37] A father addresses to his son John the following three norms:

N_1: You may watch TV.
N_2: You may play video games only if you eat your lunch.
N_3: You may eat your lunch only if you do your homework.

N_1, N_2, and N_3 provide the basis of the normative system N. As a consequence of both N_2 and N_3 it follows:

N_4: John may play video games only if he does his homework.

Let us assume that John's father cancels this last permission. Thus, the derogated set D is $\{N_4\}$. To remove N_4, it is necessary to eliminate all those sets that entail N_4; these sets are the rejected sets (Re(D)). If a rejected set is included in another set, this second set is also a rejected set, but to satisfy the criterion of adequacy for derogation, it is sufficient to take into account only *minimal rejected sets*. For example, a normative set formed by N_1, N_2, and N_3 is a rejected set, because N_4 can be obtained from these norms. However, N_1 plays no role in the derivation of N_4 and, consequently, it is not a *minimal* rejected set. On the contrary, the set $\{N_2, N_3\}$ is a minimal rejected set, because it is necessary to remove at least one of its norms to eliminate N_4. Moreover, in this example, there are no other minimal rejected sets.

The set of all minimal selections determined by a derogation D (Sel(D)) can be characterized as:

S ∈ Sel(D) if and only if:
  (i) for every R ∈ Re(D), (R ∩ S) ≠ ∅, and
  (ii) for every R ∈ Re(D), there is no C ⊂ S such that (R ∩ C) ≠ ∅.

---

[36] See Alchourrón and Bulygin 1979: 102–103; Alchourrón 1982: 54.
[37] See Hilpinen 1981b: 155–164; also Gärdenfors 1992b: 195.

Consequently, an act of derogation leads to a family of minimal selections.[38] This process assures that no derogated norm will remain in the legal system and, at the same time, it guarantees that no norms will be unnecessarily eliminated.

The logical difficulties of derogation arise in cases in which there is more than one minimal selection. As no minimal selection is included in another minimal selection, the subtraction of more than one minimal selection removes more norms than is strictly necessary to eliminate the derogated set. Alchourrón and Bulygin have claimed that there is a *logical indeterminacy of legal systems*[39] when derogation produces more than one minimal selection. Logical indeterminacies of this kind do not arise if the explicitly rejected norms are independent elements in the set S.[40]

Once the norms that must be eliminated from S as a consequence of an act of derogation have been identified, it is necessary to determine which norms of S will remain after that elimination. Let $S_1 \ldots S_n$ be the minimal selections corresponding to D in S. The process of derogation leads from the normative set S to a family of sets (represented as $(S \perp D)$). Therefore, $(S \perp D) = \{B_1 \ldots B_n\}$, where $B_i = (S - S_i)$. Consequently, the system $Cn(S)$ has been transformed into a family of systems $Cn(B_1) \ldots Cn(B_n)$. Following Alchourrón, it may be said that each set B_i is a *remainder of the derogation*, and the set of all remainders (i.e., $(S \perp D)$) is the result of the process of derogation.[41]

It is important to add that the order of a succession of derogating acts is relevant to determine the outcome of such a complex process. Let us assume that a legal authority derogates a set Y that is included in a legal system S_t. The result of this derogation will be a new system S_{t+1}. Now, suppose that the authority derogates a subset Z from S_{t+1}. This new derogation will result in a new system S_{t+2}, but the content of this new system is not solely determined by the two acts of derogation but also by the order of such operations. According to Alchourrón and Makinson, serial derogation is not the same thing as simultaneous derogation.[42]

---

[38] See Alchourrón 1982: 55.

[39] See Alchourrón and Bulygin 1991: 403; Alchourrón and Bulygin 1979: 107: Alchourrón and Bulygin 1981: 111. See also Lewis 1979: 163–179. According to Alchourrón and Bulygin, this marks an important difference between promulgation and derogation. However, Royyakers has shown that in a legal system with authorities of different hierarchies, promulgation may also lead to indeterminacy. See Royyakers 1998: 162; also Ferrer Beltrán and Rodríguez 2011: 201–202.

[40] See Alchourrón 1982: 55–56.

[41] Let $B \subseteq \alpha$, $B \in (\alpha \perp D)$ if, and only if, there is a $S \in Sel(D)$ and $B = (\alpha - S)$. A non-rejected subset in α is the remainder of a derogation – that is, $B \in (\alpha \perp D)$, if and only if: (1) $B \subseteq \alpha$, (2) $B \notin Re(D)$ and (3) for every C such that $B \subset C$, $C \in Re(D)$. (See Alchourrón 1982: 56.)

[42] See Alchourrón and Makinson 1981: 131.

The following example will shed some light on this idea:

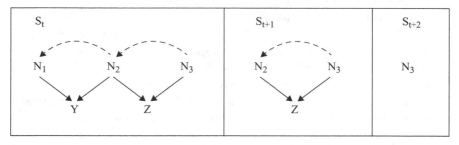

DIAGRAM 6.1

According to Diagram 6.1, the derogated set Y is a logical consequence of two norms N_1 and N_2, and for this reason both norms belong to the rejected set; it is necessary to eliminate at least one of them so as to derogate Y. Let us assume that N_1 is eliminated (e.g., because N_1 is hierarchically at a lower level than N_2). Therefore, the new system S_{t+1} will contain N_2 and N_3. Later, the authority decides to derogate Z; he needs to eliminate N_2 or N_3, but let us assume that N_3 is at a higher hierarchical level. Therefore, the norm to be removed will be N_2. After the derogation of both sets Y and Z, the normative basis of the new system S_{t+2} will be integrated only by N_3.

However, a very different result is obtained if the acts of derogation were performed in a different order.

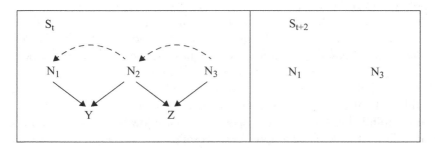

DIAGRAM 6.2

According to Diagram 6.2, if we first perform the derogation of Z, N_2 will be eliminated if we assume again that it is at a lower level in comparison to N_3. But here, the elimination of N_2 also affects the set Y, because Y is a logical consequence of both N_1 and N_2. Therefore, the derogation of Z also removes Y from the new system.

Three consequences are worth stressing regarding this analysis of derogation. First, derogation and elimination are different operations, even though the main objective of any act of material derogation is to begin the process of the elimination of norms. As Diagram 6.2 shows, an element may be eliminated from a normative system even though no derogating act refers directly to it. Second, and in the same line of thought, it seems possible to conceive the idea of derogating a certain norm N that does not belong to a momentary legal system (*derogation in advance*).[43] In such a case, N cannot be eliminated, but the aim of derogation in such a case would be to prevent N from being incorporated as a member of a new momentary system. Finally – and most important from a logical point of view – unlike promulgation, derogation is not a commutative operation. Let us assume that a legal authority is considering the promulgation of two norms, N_1 and N_2. The order in which both norms are promulgated makes no difference from the standpoint of conceptual content of a legal system. However, as the example of derogation of Y and Z shows, the order of derogations is of utmost importance for determining the content of a legal system.

6.3. TWO APPROACHES FOR LEGAL DYNAMICS

The analysis of legal dynamics presented in the previous section follows the line set out by Alchourrón and Bulygin in the late 1970s and the early 1980s. The value of their contribution is unquestionable,[44] so we only remark here on two aspects in which their ideas overcame certain difficulties in previous analyses of legal dynamics. First, Alchourrón and Bulygin provide an adequate solution to the old controversy on the status of *derogating norms*.[45] As we have seen, derogation usually begins with the formulation of a derogating provision, which identifies the explicitly rejected norms. This fact has led some legal philosophers to think that such provisions express a special type of norm: derogatory norms. For example, Kelsen considers that "derogation is the repeal of the validity of an already valid norm by another norm,"[46] and he adds that a derogating norm cannot be obeyed or applied, but rather "once it has fulfilled its function, that is, once the norm to which it relates has lost its validity, the derogating norm loses its validity."[47] However, the existence

---

[43] See Alchourrón and Bulygin 1979: 91–94; Alchourrón and Bulygin 1981: 108. The same idea is found in Raz: "a permission can be granted not only to cancel an existing reason but also to forestall possible reasons by cancelling them in advance" (Raz 1979: 65). Unfortunately, Raz provides only one example and does not offer a detailed analysis.

[44] See, for instance, von Wright 1997: 511.

[45] On the debate concerning derogatory norms, see Aguiló Regla 1995: chapter 4.

[46] Kelsen 1945: 106.

[47] Kelsen 1945: 107.

of this awkward category of ephemeral derogating *norms* is dispensable in as much as the elimination of norms can be explained through an alternative reconstruction, without any loss of explanatory power. In this vein, although Raz agrees with Kelsen that there is no point in regarding repealing norms as existing after the laws it repealed ceased to exist, he adds that it seems better to think that norms are repealed by acts, not by other norms.[48] However, Raz offered no detailed analysis of the derogation of norms.

In their studies, Alchourrón and Bulygin regard derogation as a *normative act*, complementary to that of promulgation. Just as promulgation is conceived of as a normative act incorporating one element in a legal system, derogation would be a normative act eliminating certain elements from a legal system. Under this alternative reading, derogating provisions do not express norms that are incorporated into the system to suppress or repeal the validity of other norms; they express *normative acts* of rejection of other norms, with no substantive difference from the formal clauses used to enact certain norms. For instance, in Spanish Law, the enactment of legal norms is preceded by a formal statement such as "For all the ones that are able to see and understand this, you should know that the General Courts have passed and I (The King of Spain) have come to approve the following law." Such clauses are equally expressive of the performance of a normative act – in this case, of promulgation. It would be completely artificial and surely unnecessary to claim here that when formulating statements such as this, normative authorities have enacted another norm, different from the one that the clause mentions as intended to be enacted, that is, incorporated into the legal system, and whose exclusive aim is exhausted by that very incorporation.[49]

Second, according to the analysis offered by Alchourrón and Bulygin, derogation operates – at least directly – on the validity of legal norms, understood as membership in the legal system, rather than on their applicability. When a norm is derogated, the system, as a set of norms, is substituted by a new system that will not contain the derogated norm. However, derogation does not necessarily affect the applicability of the derogated norm, because it may still be applicable to certain cases even after it has been eliminated. Although it may sound rather counterintuitive, this is tantamount to saying that *non-existent norms* may turn out to be applicable (i.e., judges may have the duty to apply to certain cases norms that do not belong to the corresponding momentary system at the time they make their decisions).[50] In our view, the reasons that

---

[48] See Raz 1970: 58.
[49] See Aguiló Regla 1995: 93.
[50] See Bulygin 1982, with a critical assessment of alternative explanations.

justify distinguishing between the reconstruction of a dynamic legal order and the system of applicable norms to a particular case reinforce the idea of conceiving the processes of promulgation and derogation as having a direct impact on the content of a legal order and not on the applicability of its norms.

In spite of all their virtues, there are certain issues in Alchourrón and Bulygin's reconstruction of legal dynamics that require the introduction of some clarifications.[51] First, the simplified approach presented earlier does not seem to take due notice of the important difference that exists between *derogating acts* (explicit derogation) and *derogation by incompatibility* (implicit of tacit derogation). We have seen that Alchourrón and Bulygin claim that derogation, when it affects a norm that has not been explicitly enacted but is simply a consequence of other enacted norms, is able to produce in certain cases indeterminacies regarding what will be the next momentary system in the dynamic sequence. This thesis is a consequence of the assumption that each set that belongs to the dynamic sequence is closed under logical consequence, because – for reasons to be explained – this assumption places at the same level both explicitly enacted norms and their logical consequences. However, no normative *act* of derogation, performed through the formulation of a canonical clause which identifies a certain text (e.g., article x of the act y) as the object of derogation, can produce such result, because normative authorities only operate on the basis of the system. Derogating acts can only refer directly to one or more explicitly enacted norms, never to those that are only logical consequences of explicitly enacted norms. Therefore, derogating acts (explicit derogation) never produce indeterminacies in legal systems.

In his thorough study on derogation, Josep Aguiló Regla defends the very same point of view.[52] He claims that the only example offered by Alchourrón and Bulygin of a derogating *act* that may cause indeterminacies (explicit derogation of implicit norms) – that is, those general clauses incorporated with the enactment of a statute such as "All legal dispositions that are opposed to the norms of this Law shall be annulled," does not prove what it purports to demonstrate, because such clauses have no normative relevance whatsoever. In fact, if a statute incompatible with preexisting norms containing such a clause is enacted, the principle *lex posterior derogat priori* will either be applicable or inapplicable to the emerging conflicts. In the former case, the new provisions will eventually derogate the preexisting conflicting norms, but exclusively

---

[51] We refer here to the simplified reconstruction offered in their earlier works devoted to the subject, such as Alchourrón and Bulygin 1979 and 1981. The critical observations given in the following are only partially applicable to more sophisticated reconstructions, such as Alchourrón 1982 and Alchourrón and Makinson 1981.

[52] See Aguiló Regla 1995: 56.

as a consequence of the effects of the *lex posterior* principle. In the latter case (e.g., the preexisting norms were issued by a hierarchically higher level authority), the incorporation of a clause such as "All legal dispositions that are opposed to the norms of this Law shall be annulled" in the new statute will have no effect in moving the decision in the direction of the new provisions. Moreover, if a statute incompatible with preexisting norms is enacted but does not contain such a clause, the consequences will be exactly the same: if the principle *lex posterior* is applicable to the conflict, the new provision will prevail for this very reason; if *lex posterior* is not applicable, additional reasons will have to be offered to favor the new provision over the preexisting norms. This shows that the presence or absence of such general derogating clauses is utterly useless, because it is the eventual application of the principle *lex posterior derogat priori* that brings about the derogation of prior incompatible norms.

By contrast, tacit derogation by incompatibility (i.e., when a new norm is incorporated into the system that is incompatible with the consequences of preexisting norms) may indeed lead to indeterminacies. But this is a complex operation, composed of an act of promulgation performed by normative authorities in conjunction with an operation of contraction carried out by theorists or interpreters to restore consistency to the system once a conflict has been introduced.

A possible objection to the idea that no derogating act can produce indeterminacies may be raised through the following counterexample. Suppose norm N has been explicitly enacted in a legal system, but at the same time it is a logical consequence of other enacted norms in the system. Suppose a competent authority decides to derogate N. What will be the result of such an act? There are two alternative interpretations here. First, it may be the case that the authority has merely intended to eliminate a redundancy (i.e., to suppress the explicit formulation of N because it is already derivable as a logical consequence from other explicit norms in the system). In that case, the act of derogation will be what we have called a *formal derogation*, and it will not affect the conceptual content of the system. But, second, it may be the case that the authority's intention is not limited to the suppression of redundancy, but she wants instead to suppress the persistence of N in the system even as a consequence from other enacted norms. This will generate indeterminacy if N is derivable from more than one explicitly enacted norm, and this indeterminacy will be the consequence of an act of explicit derogation.

However, it should be noted that the second alternative, the one in which indeterminacy results, is not solely derivable from the act performed by the normative authority when issuing a derogating clause such as "N shall be revoked." Reference to norm N in such a clause cannot but be understood as relative to a norm formulation, at most to a norm formulation under certain interpretation, but not directly to a consequence of enacted norms. Therefore, from the act of derogation alone the only thing that can be taken as eliminated is the norm formulation. A further understanding that N can no longer be derived as a consequence of other norms in the system requires an activity on the part of the interpreter assigning that effect to the act performed by the authority and, moreover, the identification of some of the various norms that jointly imply N as those to be eliminated to avoid the derivation. In other words, this example does not refute but rather confirms that normative authorities only operate on the basis of the system, and that tacit derogations by incompatibility are the product of interpreters' activities.

A second controversial issue of the reconstruction of legal dynamics offered by Alchourrón and Bulygin stems from the assumption that each momentary system of the dynamic sequence is understood as closed under the notion of logical consequence. Now, if one accepts the importance of distinguishing the membership of a norm in the law of a certain jurisdiction at a certain moment from its applicability to certain cases, it should also be recognized that the logical consequences of the norms enacted by legal authorities, although members of the legal system in the second sense, are not necessarily members of the system understood in the first sense. In particular, from the thesis defended by Legal Positivism that the content of the law depends on certain norm-creating acts identified from contingent social practices, it seems more reasonable to conclude that the norms constituting the law of a certain community are only those that have direct social sources, their logical consequences being *applicable* even if not members of the law. After all, as Marmor rightly claims, from the fact that a norm is entailed by other legal norms it cannot be inferred that it *is* a legal norm just for that reason; only that it *should* be.[53] This, of course, is not meant to deny that the logical consequences of enacted norms have relevance to offer a proper reconstruction of legal dynamics, as shall be shown later.

After the development with Eugenio Bulygin of their basic framework for the analysis of legal dynamics, Carlos Alchourrón contacted David Makinson and told him about his theoretical worries concerning the way of analyzing the process of derogation from a logical point of view, especially the need for a selection in cases of plural remainders. Makinson recalls that his first reaction was to answer that concerning the plurality of results that may be generated

---

[53] See Marmor 2001: 69–70.

by an act of derogation, logical analysis had no place, because, he thought, "the plurality is just an unfortunate fact of life, and logic cannot adjudicate between the different possibilities."[54]

Still, both scholars soon noticed that certain rational conditions of adequacy for the process of derogation could be logically evaluated. In 1981, Alchourrón and Makinson jointly published a paper with a formal framework to examine the problem of how judges should apply a corpus of norms in which derogation with a plurality of remainders comes about.[55] Developing that paper, the authors noticed that the issue under analysis was in fact broader than the one they originally had in mind, because there was no need to restrict the view to a set of norms; the starting point could be any arbitrary set. In fact, philosophical work already existed analyzing the rationality of *belief change* or *belief revision*. Getting in contact with Peter Gärdenfors, who had developed a set of postulates for revision and contraction of beliefs from an epistemological point of view in search of a foundation for the logic of conditionals without ontological commitments with possible worlds, they jointly designed a model for rational changes of beliefs or belief revision that was known since as AGM – the initials of the three authors – in a paper published in 1985, which had an extraordinary impact in different fields, such as philosophy, epistemology, and computational sciences.[56]

Belief revision has been developed in extraordinary ways since then, fundamentally because of the interdisciplinary interest it has generated.[57] Yet, this development has had no comparable impact on the studies of legal dynamics, which has remained substantially untouched, even though it was one of the theoretical areas that triggered the birth of the systematic study of belief revision.

There is one important thing to point out about the evolution of the theory of belief revision for our purposes here. Two different approaches have been followed to examine belief changes, according to two different points of departure: belief *sets* and belief *bases*.[58] In fact, it does not seem quite natural to think of belief changes as operating over entities such as belief *sets*, understood as integrated by the whole set of logical consequences that follow from certain basic beliefs, because those sets would include all kinds of irrelevant statements that have never been considered. As an alternative, one might

---

[54] Makinson 1996: 4.
[55] See Alchourrón and Makinson 1981.
[56] See Alchourrón, Gärdenfors, and Makinson 1985. See also Alchourrón and Makinson 1982; Alchourrón and Makinson 1985; Alchourrón and Makinson 1986.
[57] For an excellent review, see Carnota and Rodríguez 2011.
[58] See Gärdenfors 1990; also Hansson 1999: 24 ff., whom we fundamentally follow here.

represent the belief state of a certain person by means of a limited number of statements, which would correspond to their explicit beliefs. That is why the approach of *belief sets* or *theories* is distinguished from the approach of *belief bases*. According to this distinction, A is a belief base for a theory K if and only if $K = Cn(A)$. In other words, a theory is a set of beliefs that includes all its logical consequences, whereas a belief base is a set not closed under the notion of logical consequence.

In the approach of belief bases, the criterion for determining whether a sentence α is believed by a certain subject is that α is a consequence of the base (i.e., $\alpha \in Cn(A)$). The elements of a belief base will then be *basic beliefs*, and the elements of its logical closure that are not elements of the base itself will merely be *derived beliefs*.

α is a belief if and only if $\alpha \in Cn(A)$
α is a basic belief is and only if $\alpha \in A$
α is a merely derived belief if and only if $\alpha \in Cn(A) \backslash A$

The approach of belief bases was first used in computer science. By contrast, in philosophy, the original approach was to examine belief changes directly on belief sets, but in recent years the interest on belief bases has increased. The model of belief bases is built on the intuition that some of our beliefs have no independent weight, but emerge only as inferences from other more basic beliefs on which they depend entirely. In the analysis of belief sets, on the contrary, all beliefs have the same status, so it is not possible to give greater weight to basic over merely derived beliefs, simply because the difference between basic and merely derived beliefs cannot be represented.

In the approach of belief bases, derived beliefs are modified only as a result of changes in the base. Although we are committed to believe the logical consequences of our basic beliefs, such consequences are only subject to those changes that follow from changes of basic beliefs. The intuition behind this is that it is not worth holding merely derived beliefs in themselves: if one of them loses the support it had in basic beliefs, it must be automatically abandoned. Consider the following example: Giovanni believes that Buenos Aires is the capital of Argentina (α). Moreover, Giovanni believes that in his cellar there are bottles of wine (β). Therefore, by propositional logic he should believe that Buenos Aires is the capital of Argentina if and only if in his cellar there are bottles of wine ($\alpha \leftrightarrow \beta$).[59] Later, he notes that in fact there are no

---

[59] A false proposition implies any other proposition – that is, $(\sim\alpha \rightarrow (\alpha \rightarrow \beta))$ – and a true proposition is implied by any other proposition ($\alpha \rightarrow (\beta \rightarrow \alpha)$). Consequently, if α and β are true, both ($\beta \rightarrow \alpha$) and ($\alpha \rightarrow \beta$) will also be true.

bottles of wine in his cellar, so he should replace his belief in β by the belief in $\sim\beta$. He cannot then, without inconsistency, retain both the belief in α and the belief in $\alpha \leftrightarrow \beta$. In the analysis of belief sets, both α and $\alpha \leftrightarrow \beta$ are elements of the set of beliefs. When Giovanni discovers that there is no wine in his cellar, he should make a choice between retaining α and retaining $\alpha \leftrightarrow \beta$. The rejection of $\alpha \leftrightarrow \beta$ does not follow automatically; it must be warranted through some kind of selection mechanism (as a choice function) that chooses between α and $\alpha \leftrightarrow \beta$. By contrast, in the approach of belief bases, whereas β is a basic belief, $\alpha \leftrightarrow \beta$ is a merely derived belief. The elimination of β automatically produces the elimination of $\alpha \leftrightarrow \beta$. The option of retaining $\alpha \leftrightarrow \beta$ does not even arise, for in this approach, when the elements of the base are removed, all derived beliefs that depended on the removed elements are lost.

This is the first noticeable difference between the two approaches. The second can be presented as follows: for each belief base A there is a belief set $Cn(A)$ that represents the beliefs that are held according to A; however, the same set of beliefs can be represented by different belief bases. Belief bases have more expressive power than belief sets. For example, the belief bases $\{\alpha, \beta\}$ and $\{\alpha, \alpha \leftrightarrow \beta\}$ have the same logical consequences, because $Cn(\{\alpha, \beta\}) = Cn(\{\alpha, \alpha \leftrightarrow \beta\})$. Yet these two belief bases are not identical; they are *statically* equivalent, in the sense that they represent the same beliefs, but this does not mean that they are *dynamically* equivalent, in the sense that they will behave in the same way vis à vis any given belief change. That is the reason why they can be interpreted as different ways of holding the same beliefs. Suppose that one of Giovanni's basic beliefs is that FC Barcelona will win the soccer championship (α) and that FC Barcelona will defeat Real Madrid in the next match (β). Riccardo, in turn, has the basic beliefs that FC Barcelona will defeat Real Madrid in the next match (β) and that FC Barcelona will win the soccer championship if and only if it beats Real Madrid in the next match ($\alpha \leftrightarrow \beta$). Giovanni's and Riccardo's beliefs are then equivalent at the static level, because they have the same consequences. But later, both Giovanni and Riccardo receive the information that β is false (i.e., that FC Barcelona has not defeated Real Madrid), and therefore they both revise their belief states to include the new belief $\sim\beta$. Now, Giovanni has the basic beliefs α and $\sim\beta$, whereas Riccardo has the basic beliefs $\sim\beta$ and $\alpha \leftrightarrow \beta$. As a result of this change, their sets of beliefs are no longer equivalent: Giovanni believes that FC Barcelona will win the soccer championship (α), and Riccardo believes that FC Barcelona will not win the soccer championship ($\sim\alpha$).

A further distinctive characteristic of the approach of belief bases lies in the possibility of giving shape to the idea that two inconsistent belief states are not equivalent. There is only one inconsistent belief set $(K_\perp)$: if K and K' are inconsistent belief sets, then $K = K'$. But this property does not apply to belief bases: The bases $A = \{p, \sim p, q\}$ and $B = \{p, \sim p, \sim q\}$ are both inconsistent, but not identical. They are statically equivalent, because $Cn(A) = Cn(B) = K_\perp$; but they are not dynamically equivalent, because any suitable operator of contraction (represented here as $\div$) should produce $A \div p = \{\sim p, q\}$ and $B \div p = \{\sim p, \sim q\}$, so that $Cn(A \div p) \neq Cn(B \div p)$. This is a valuable property of belief bases, because it should be possible to remove an inconsistency in a belief state while retaining the information that is not affected by the conflict. This result can be achieved if inconsistent belief states are represented by belief bases, but not if they are represented by belief sets. Once we have reached an inconsistent belief set, all distinctions are lost and cannot be easily recovered by operations performed directly over the belief set.[60]

A final difference between both approaches is that within the model of belief bases, besides the usual operations of contraction and revision, there is a third type of belief change that operates over bases and may be called *reorganization*.[61] Reorganization of a belief state is the substitution of a base A of a certain belief set $Cn(A)$ by another base A' of the same belief set – that is, where $Cn(A) = Cn(A')$. In the analysis of belief sets, because A is always equivalent to $Cn(A)$, it is impossible to consider non-trivial reorganizations of belief states.

These few remarks concerning these two alternative trends in the evolution of belief revision studies are sufficient to suggest that two competing approaches should similarly be accepted in the theoretical reconstruction of legal dynamics: one according to which each static momentary system in the dynamic sequence is interpreted as closed under logical consequence – as Alchourrón and Bulygin's analysis assumes – and one according to which each momentary system is exclusively composed of a finite set of enacted norms. The model of finite sets has certain advantages over that of sets closed under logical consequence precisely because bases are finite, which allows computational treatment, and because – as shown previously – finite bases have more expressive power. There is, however, a disadvantage in the case of finite bases applied to the analysis of belief change; it is very difficult to differentiate basic from merely derived beliefs. Nevertheless, this problem does not affect legal systems, because there are conventionally accepted criteria in the law to distinguish explicitly enacted norms from mere logical consequences of enacted norms.

---

[60] See Hansson 1999: 21.
[61] See Hansson 1992: 97.

6.4. LOGICAL CONSEQUENCES AND LEGAL DYNAMICS

Consider the following argument: legal scholars grant that the incorporation of a new norm N in a legal system requires the elimination of all other preexisting norms that are inconsistent with N, as an application of the principle *lex posterior derogat priori*. In fact, this principle is not contingent, but is conceptually linked with the legal powers of authorities to introduce changes in the law.[62] As the new norm may be inconsistent, not directly with any single explicitly enacted norms, but with some of the consequences derivable from them, a proper reconstruction of this kind of change (implicit derogation of implicit norms) would force us to accept that each momentary system in the dynamic sequence includes all the logical consequences of explicitly enacted norms.

Although seemingly compelling, the conclusion of this argument is unwarranted. An appropriate model for legal dynamics need not be committed to the idea that each momentary system is closed under logical consequence, for there is nothing in the preceding argument that rules out the possibility of examining changes in legal systems within a framework of finite bases, such as the one discussed previously. This is so because the case of implicit derogation of implicit norms does not prove the necessary *membership* in momentary legal systems of the logical consequences of enacted norms. Consider the following example:[63]

N_1: Buenos Aires is the capital of Argentina.
N_2: The President of Argentina must reside in the capital of the Republic.

These two norms jointly entail:

N_3: The President of Argentina must reside in Buenos Aires.

Suppose now that, subsequently, normative authorities enact a norm that is incompatible with N_3. For instance:

N_4: The President of Argentina must reside in Mar del Plata.

Although in plain conflict with N_3, N_4 is not inconsistent with N_1, nor with N_2. Assuming for the sake of the argument that all these norms are found at the same hierarchical level, under the principle *lex posterior derogat prior* the enactment of N_4 will force a revision of the system to avoid the possibility

---

[62] See Bulygin 1986: 212–213. As Hart has shown, a normative order immune from deliberate change would not be regarded as a legal system (see Hart 1961: 175–178).
[63] This is an adapted version of an example offered in Hilpinen 1981b.

of deriving N_3 from the enacted norms N_1 and N_2, which is tantamount to saying that the incorporation of N_4 in the system compels us to regard one of these preexisting norms as tacitly derogated. Therefore, as a result of this normative act or promulgation, if consistency is to be preserved by application of the principle *lex posterior derogat priori*, we will have either that (1) the capital of Argentina is Buenos Aires and the President has to reside, not in the capital city, but in Mar del Plata, or that (2) the President has to reside in the capital of Argentina, that is now not Buenos Aires but Mar del Plata. Which of these two alternatives is regarded as the most appropriate outcome of the revision operated into the system to eliminate the conflict generated by the incorporation of N_4 will depend on interpretative or evaluative considerations.

Under the assumption that each momentary system includes all the logical consequences of enacted norms, we should say in this example that the original system S_1 is constituted by N_1 and N_2 plus all their logical consequences, N_3 among them. Suppose further that there are reasons to prefer N_1 over N_2 if we have to choose which of them should be preserved in the system. The enactment of N_4 should lead to a new system integrated by the logical consequences of N_1 and N_4. Strictly speaking, from a formal point of view there are two ways to achieve this goal. The first involves replacing S_1 by a new system S_2 that has been adequately "purified" for the subsequent incorporation of N_4. In other words, we need to contract S_1, eliminating possible conflicts with the new norm to be incorporated, which in our case will lead to a new system S_2 integrated by the logical consequences of N_1. Now, N_4 can be incorporated through an expansion of the system without generating any conflict, producing a new system S_3:

S_1: S_2: S_3:

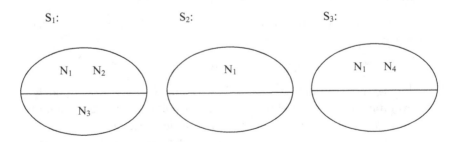

The second alternative is to expand S_1 to include N_4, generating an inconsistent system, and then contracting this system to eliminate the generated conflict:

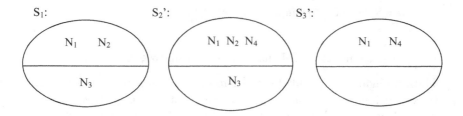

The relevance of this second alternative (not strictly equivalent to the first) rests in its allowing us to take the possibility that N_4 does not survive the conflict, because this new element is first incorporated into the system, and then the evaluation proceeds to determine which of the elements in conflict will be eliminated. This seems to be a particularly well-suited way to account for the operation of revision when the elements of the system have different hierarchies. More specifically, when applied to the analysis of legal systems, it seems very important for two reasons: first, because it looks rather counterintuitive to reconstruct the operation of derogation by application of the principle *lex posterior* as a sequence where the first step is the "purification" of the system to avoid future inconsistencies, and the second step is the incorporation of the new norm. Second, because the only way to explain the operation of the principle *lex superior derogat inferior* is by not assuming that the new norm will necessarily be preferred over those preexisting norms in conflict with it.

Considering what has been said up to this point, we may specify formally these two alternatives as follows:

Revision$_1$:

$$S_1^{*1}\alpha = (S_1 \div \sim\alpha) + \alpha$$

Revision$_2$:

$$S_1^{*2}\alpha = (S_1 + \alpha) \div \perp$$

The symbols + and ÷ represent, respectively, the operations of expansion and contraction. The first of these operations can be defined as follows:

$$S_1 + \alpha = Cn(S_1 \cup \{\alpha\})$$

As for the operation of contraction, although its characterization is rather difficult, considering what was stated in Section 6.2, it may be regarded as some form of selection within the set of maximal subsets of S_1 that do not contain the element to be eliminated ($S_1 \perp \alpha$), where:

$S_1 \perp \alpha = S_2/S_2 \in (S_1 \perp \alpha)$ iff:
  1. $S_2 \subseteq S_1$
  2. $\alpha \notin S_2$
  3. There is no set S_2' such that $S_2 \subset S_2' \subseteq S_1$ and $\alpha \notin S_2'$

Thus, it might be concluded that the result legal theorists intuitively assign to certain implicit derogations in application of the principle *lex posterior derogat priori* can only be properly reconstructed on the assumption that legal systems are closed under logical consequence. Were this argument sound, it would have the peculiarity of justifying the membership in legal systems of *all* – not just some – logical consequences of explicitly enacted norms, because any of them could be potentially relevant for the identification of the new system in the dynamic sequence as a result of a normative change.

However, this argument is unable to justify such a conclusion without assuming what it purports to prove. Suppose that we now analyze exactly the same process, but without the assumption that each legal system is closed under logical consequence. Our original system S_1 will now be S_1', exclusively integrated by N_1 and N_2. The question arises: Which will be the result produced by the enactment of N_4, assuming – as before – that N_4 is compatible with N_1 and with N_2, individually considered, but incompatible with N_3, a logical consequence of the conjunction of N_1 and N_2? In this case, N_3 is not a member of S_1', but this does not mean that N_3 should not be taken into account in a proper evaluation of the results of this revision. Instead, what we are supposed to be modeling is precisely the *safe* incorporation of N_4 (i.e., a way to incorporate this new norm in the system avoiding the possibility of inconsistent consequences). Thus, the two previously analyzed alternative views on revision might be reproduced here. On the one hand, we may first contract S_1' to prevent the derivation of incompatible consequences with N_4 (e.g., through the elimination of N_2; assuming, as before, that N_1 is higher-ranked), and thus the undesired consequence N_3 will no longer be derivable from the resulting system. Now it will be possible to expand the system by N_4 without generating any conflict:

S_1': S_2'': S_3'':

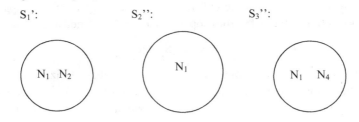

Alternatively, we could first expand S_1' with the incorporation of N_4, thus creating a system with inconsistent consequences, and then proceed to contract the resulting system to remove inconsistent consequences:

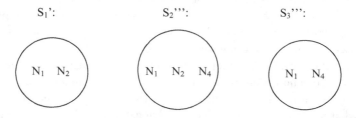

S_1': S_2''': S_3''':

N_1 N_2 N_1 N_2 N_4 N_1 N_4

From a formal point of view, these alternatives may be defined exactly as before:

Revision$_1$:

$$S_1^{*1}\alpha = (S_1 \div \sim\alpha) + \alpha$$

Revision$_2$:

$$S_1^{*2}\alpha = (S_1 + \alpha) \div \bot$$

But here the expansion of the system (represented by +) should be read:

Expansion:

$$S_1 + \alpha = S_1 \cup \{\alpha\}$$

And contraction, in its turn, will refer here to a selection within the set of maximal subsets of S_1 that do not entail the element to be removed $(S_1 \bot \alpha)$, but where:

$S_1 \bot \alpha = S_2/S_2 \in (S_1 \bot \alpha)$ iff : iff:
  1. $S_2 \subseteq S_1$
  2. $\alpha \notin Cn(S_2)$
  3. There is no set S_2' such that $S_2 \subset S_2' \subseteq S_1$ and $\alpha \notin Cn(S_2')$

The difference with the former reconstruction is that here conditions 2 and 3 refer to the logical consequences of a set rather than simply to a set. Previously we worked on the assumption that each system was closed under logical consequence, and so it was valid that $S = Cn(S)$. Therefore, conditions 2 and 3 could be formulated indicating merely that the element to be eliminated should not be part of the system. But this characterization of the operation of contraction is only appropriate under the assumption of closure under logical consequence. If the operation of contraction (or derogation, in the case of legal systems) is not simply to remove an item from a set, but to avoid its possible derivation from the set – that is, the way in which derogation is understood in both reconstructions – a satisfactory explanation of this operation need only be clearly expressed, and there is no need to assume that each set includes all its logical consequences, a conclusion whose apparent plausibility is simply a disguised way of presupposing what was to be proved.[64]

To put it briefly, the argument under consideration may be summarized as follows. Derogation is ordinarily understood as the elimination of a norm or set of norms from a legal system; however, legal scholars frequently consider that what has to be removed by certain derogations is a logical consequence of enacted norms. This may suggest that momentary systems should include all their logical consequences, because otherwise there would be no possible explanation of this intuition. We have tried to demonstrate that this line of reasoning is incorrect because it is perfectly possible to make sense of this intuition, conceding that logical consequences should be taken into account for a proper reconstruction of legal dynamics, but without accepting their necessary membership in legal systems. In that sense, it is possible to grant that derogation involves avoiding certain consequences to be derivable from a set of enacted norms (i.e., that the basic condition derogation must satisfy is that the element to be derogated should not be a member, not of the new set, but of the logical consequences of the new set). Derogation of explicitly enacted norms may be seen as a special case of such characterization, because any explicitly enacted norm is a consequence of itself and, therefore, also integrates the set of consequences that follow from these enacted norms. This is not to redefine the operation of derogation; in fact, under the reconstruction of momentary systems as closed under logical consequence derogation is characterized in similar terms, but this is masked by the fact that within this approach each system S is equivalent to $Cn(S)$. Hence, to claim that logical consequences "should be taken into account," or that they "are relevant" for an adequate reconstruction of legal dynamics, does not mean that one must accept their

---

[64] In Alchourrón and Makinson 1981, a distinction is made between *derogation* and *abrogation* in the following terms. *Derogation*: If A is a set of norms and α is a norm implied by A, and a legislator wants to prevent α from being logically derivable from A, then she must reject implicitly what in A implies α, retaining the remainder: $A \bot \alpha = B/B \in A \bot \alpha$ iff: 1. $B \subseteq A$; 2. $\alpha \notin Cn(B)$; 3. There is no set B' such that $B \subset B' \subseteq A$ y $\alpha \notin Cn(B')$. *Abrogation*: $A \bot \alpha$ will have only one element iff $\alpha \in A$. When a subset D of A is abrogated, it is simply excluded from the set, leaving $A - D$ intact even if it implies some norm in D. Derogation coincides with abrogation only in the case that no element of the rejected set D is implied by the complement $A - D$. In that case, $Cn(A - D) \cap D = \phi$ (see Alchourrón and Makinson, 1981: 130).

membership in each momentary system. The argument cannot prove, without begging the question, that every legal system must be interpreted as closed under logical consequence.

Additionally, it should be noted that logical closure of momentary systems is not only unnecessary, but it also may lead to undesirable results. In other words, there is at least one reason to favor a reconstruction of legal dynamics in terms of finite bases of enacted norms: on the assumption that momentary systems are closed under logical consequence, two different normative bases with the same consequences are indistinguishable and yet they may react differently at the dynamic level.[65]

There may be a plurality of different bases for the same deductive system. Regarding legal systems, if they are interpreted as closed under the notion of consequence, different axiomatic bases can be constructed for the same system (i.e., it is possible to reformulate the normative base while preserving the same logical consequences). Two independent axiomatic bases, in the sense that they do not contain regulations that are logical consequences of other regulations of the system under consideration, may nevertheless be different, and this difference may only be noticeable when attention is centered on the way they both react to the same normative act of amendment.[66] As we have seen, in some cases, the consistent incorporation of a new norm can lead to logical indeterminacies regarding which will be the new momentary system in the dynamic sequence. So it may occur that the same normative act produces, as a result, a logical indeterminacy over one axiomatic base but not over another with identical logical consequences. Consider this slight variation in our previous example.[67] Suppose normative authorities have enacted two formulations, one of which admits two possible interpretations:

NF$_1$: "Buenos Aires is the capital of Argentina."
NF$_2$: "The President of Argentina must reside in the place indicated in the previous norm."

NF$_2$ is ambiguous, because the clause "the place indicated in the previous norm" can be read as a reference to the capital of Argentina or to the city of Buenos Aires, what leads to these two different normative bases:

---

[65] See Ferrer Beltrán and Rodríguez 2011: 121–133.
[66] See Bulygin 1986: 201–203.
[67] The issue is discussed in Hilpinen 1981b and Bulygin 1986.

NS_1:

N_1: Buenos Aires is the capital of Argentina.

N_2: The President of Argentina must reside in the capital of the Republic.

NS_2:

N_1: Buenos Aires is the capital of Argentina.

N_2': The President of Argentina must reside in Buenos Aires.

These two interpretations are logically equivalent because they have the same consequences. However, they are not identical, because the enactment of a new norm such as:

N_4: The President of Argentina must reside in Mar del Plata,

will lead to indeterminacy regarding which is the new system in the sequence if we take into account the first set of norms but not the second, because in the latter (NS_2), N_4 clearly will result in the derogation of N_2' by application of the principle *lex posterior* (assuming all norms are at the same level in the hierarchy). As both sets of norms react differently to the same normative act, there has to be some difference between them. Nevertheless, this difference is not *extensional*, because the logical consequences of both sets are equivalent, but *intensional*.

On the interpretation that each momentary system is closed under logical consequence, all bases with the same logical consequences become equivalent, in the sense that any reformulation of the normative base with the same logical consequences should be accepted. In our case, if NS_1 and NS_2 are two normative bases that have identical consequences, because $Cn(NS_1) = Cn(NS_2)$, they should be considered as two different presentations of the same system, and the law at time t will be equally constituted by either of them. But then the difference the example exposes will remain unexplained.

Moreover, it is important to stress that all the distinctive characteristics of the analysis in terms of finite bases seem particularly suitable when applied to legal dynamics. Recall, first, that from the approach of finite bases it is possible to give due account of the idea that two inconsistent sets may not be equivalent. Take the following two sets of explicitly enacted norms: $A = \{Op; O\sim p; Oq\}$ and $B = \{Op; O\sim p; O\sim q\}$. The consequences of both sets are equivalent – that is, $Cn(A) = Cn(B)$. Therefore, assuming that each momentary system is closed under logical consequence, we would have a unique momentary system. But although bases A and B are both inconsistent and thus statically equivalent, in the dynamic level they may react differently. For instance, derogation of Op

over each base should obviously lead to:

$$A \div Op = \{O{\sim}p;\ Oq\}$$
$$B \div Op = \{O{\sim}p;\ O{\sim}q\}$$

And now the consequences of each of these two new bases will not be equivalent – that is, $Cn(A \div Op) \neq Cn(B \div Op)$. Consequently, operating under finite bases has the advantage of allowing us to deal with inconsistencies while preserving those parts of the system that are not affected by the contradiction, a possibility that is not available in case momentary systems are interpreted as closed under logical consequence.

Finally, within the approach of finite bases, it is possible to represent, besides the operations of promulgation and derogation of norms, a third type of normative change that can affect normative bases. In *Normative Systems* Alchourrón and Bulygin make explicit reference to what they call *reformulations of the basis of a legal system*, an operation performed by legal scholars that consists of a modification of the normative base that preserves all its logical consequences to obtain a more economic and ordered base for the same system. This process corresponds exactly to the operation Hansson calls *reorganization* of a belief state (i.e., changing a given base A of a certain set of beliefs $Cn(A)$ by another base A' of the same set of beliefs – that is, where $Cn(A) = Cn(A')$). As Hansson rightly observes, from the point of view of the approach of beliefs sets or theories, because A is equivalent to $Cn(A)$, there is no possibility of accounting for non-trivial reorganizations of belief states; therefore, there is no conceptual possibility of offering an adequate explanation of this kind of operation.[68]

The idea that the reconstruction of legal dynamics need not assume logical closure of each momentary system of the sequence, whereas logical consequences are necessarily part of the system of relevant or applicable norms to solve a case, is reinforced by the following argument. As we said, in *Normative Systems* Alchourrón and Bulygin characterize the law as a system. But at the same time, they recognize that one of the main activities of legal scholars is that of *systematization*, understood as the derivation of the logical consequences from the normative basis, and the reformulation of that basis to present the system in a more general and economic, but logically equivalent, way.[69] Now, if the law *is* a system, the activity of systematization as a task of legal scholars

---

[68] See Hansson 1992.
[69] Alchourrón and Bulygin 1971: 78–79.

does not seem to make sense.[70] However, the problem disappears when we notice that in each case there comes into play a different idea of a legal system – when holding that the law *is* a system, the notion of legal system as a dynamic legal order is being assumed; when claiming that legal scholars *systematize* the law, the notion of legal system as the set of applicable norms to solve a case is being assumed.

6.5. LOGICAL CONSEQUENCES AND SOCIAL SOURCES

Do legal systems contain all the logical consequences of enacted norms? Are our legal rights and duties only determined by explicit authoritative decisions or by the whole set of their logical consequences? Linguistic reasons may be offered to justify the incorporation of the logical consequences of enacted norms into legal systems. First, it is certainly common to speak of "implicit law," or "the implicit content of law." Although these expressions have not been exclusively coined to make reference to logical consequences of enacted norms, this seems to be their most obvious reference. Second, logical consequences of legal norms are often explicitly mentioned as grounds for our critical attitudes in the evaluation of human behavior. For example, if the enactment of a statute requires a majority of votes in the Parliament, we accept the validity of a statute approved by unanimity because "unanimity" and "majority" are logically connected. Third, law-applying organs often justify their decisions by appealing to the logical consequences of explicitly formulated norms and, on the contrary, their decisions are regarded as arbitrary if they cannot be reconstructed as logically valid arguments. Finally, as we have seen in the preceding section, on some occasions our legal rights and duties do not stem from a single legal norm, but from the logical consequences of a *plurality* of legal norms. Thus, a true description of our legal rights and duties is not exhausted by a description of every single norm of a legal system.

However, none of these arguments is able to demonstrate the truth of the general statement "legal systems include all the logical consequences of enacted legal norms," fundamentally because the truth of that statement depends, on the one hand, on controversial ontological and methodological issues of legal theory – that will not be dealt with here as they are far beyond the scope of this book – and, on the other hand, on the very concept of "legal system" we have in mind. From this latter point of view, it has been shown that applicable sets of norms, in as much as they are conceived as

---

[70] See Caracciolo 1996.

normative *systems*, should be considered closed under logical consequence, given that the purpose of systematization in this case is precisely to explore the consequences that follow from applicable norms to certain cases. However, if our attention is focused on legal dynamics, the static sets of norms (momentary systems) that successively integrate the same sequence (non-momentary legal system) can alternatively be reconstructed with or without logical closure. And although we have presented at least one argument in favor of the latter reconstruction, this very argument shows the relevance of taking into account (all) the logical consequences that follow from enacted legal norms to identify the elements of each set in the dynamic sequence. Therefore, the general claim that all legal systems include the logical consequences of enacted legal norms should be abandoned, at least for not being very illuminating. But this must not obscure the relevance of logical consequences for a proper evaluation of the various aspects of the theory of normative systems in their different senses.

Now, a number of theorists have argued in defense of the opposite general thesis (i.e., that legal systems *do not include* the logical consequences of enacted legal norms). To conclude these pages, we want to offer some remarks regarding an idea frequently used to ground this claim, centered on the tension between the incorporation of logical consequences of enacted norms into legal systems and the social sources thesis advanced by Legal Positivism. Insofar as logical consequences are neither social facts nor conventions – which are the most common explanations of the positive nature of legal norms and systems[71] – it might be claimed that there is a genuine conflict between the social nature of law and the incorporation of logical consequences of enacted norms into legal systems. Logical consequences of enacted norms extend our duties and rights beyond explicit decisions and conventions, so one can wonder whether the identification of law is actually exhausted by social facts or conventions. Arguments in defense of an affirmative answer to this question have been offered by Raz and Marmor.[72]

---

[71] Admittedly, this is a crude statement of the problem, but we hope that a more sophisticated presentation of the social sources thesis will not be necessary to examine the incorporation of logical consequences. Neither do we take sides on the debate concerning the relations between positivism and conventionalism. See, for example, Raz 1979: 37–52; Postema 1982; Coleman 2001: 65–148; Shapiro 1998. However, the precise nature of legal conventions is a highly controversial issue in contemporary legal positivism. See, for example, Coleman 2001: 114–121; Marmor 2001: 1–48; 2009. Moreover, conventionalism is far from being a unanimously accepted approach to law or legal theory. See, for example, Green 1999: 35–52; Dworkin 1986: 114–150.

[72] See Raz 1994: 210–214; Marmor 2001: 69–70.

Raz explicitly rejects what he calls the *incorporation thesis* (i.e., that law includes all logical products[73] of source-based law),[74] but his objections may assume at least two interpretations depending on the notion of entailment Raz has in mind.[75] Under the first interpretation, if norms N_1 and N_2 belong to a certain legal system S, and they logically entail another norm N_3, then N_3 also belongs to S (N_3 is *logically derived* from N_1 and N_2). Under the alternative version, if norms N_1 and N_2 belong to a certain legal system S, and they exemplify a general normative principle P that justifies both norms, and P entails another norm N_3, then N_3 also belongs to S (N_3 is *evaluatively derived* from N_1 and N_2). This second interpretation is the more interesting version of incorporationism, but Raz rejects it, too.[76] Despite this rejection of the incorporation of logical consequences of enacted norms, Raz is not a skeptic about deontic logic; his arguments against the incorporation thesis are related neither to the nature of logic nor to the possibility of deontic logic. Instead, his main argument is directed to the *authoritative nature of law*.

However, a general argument in favor of the relevance of logical consequences of enacted legal norms is that they reveal the implicit conceptual content of explicit norms. The distinction between explicit and implicit law is actually presupposed by a communication model of law (i.e., the idea that law is paradigmatically produced by deliberate actions, and that legal norms are mainly expressed by means of language).[77] In fact, in his analysis of legal rights, Raz argues that a legal system can be regarded as a system of practical reason, in the sense that legal norms are nested in hierarchical chains, where some of them provide justification to others, and that this is compatible with the idea that law is a normative system.[78] In his view, in certain cases legal norms provide content-dependent justifications of other legal norms. To exemplify this, he proposes to consider the following two statements:

(1) Everyone has a legal right to his good name.
(2) Jimmy has a legal right to his good name.

And wonders whether the fact that (2) is legally justified by (1) is the only way in which its truth can be established. In Raz's view, Kelsen would deny

---

[73] It should be noted that the set of propositions entailed by any finite set of propositions is an infinite set.

[74] See Raz 1994: 213.

[75] This distinction is borrowed from Marmor 2001: 69.

[76] He writes that "the incorporation thesis receives no sustenance from the institutional complexity of the law, since it insists that the law includes all the logical consequences of source-based law" (Raz 1994: 213–214).

[77] Raz seems to recognize this in Raz 1986: 1106–1107.

[78] See Raz 1994: 263–266.

this, for he did not admit that a content-dependent justification could ever establish the truth of the justified legal statement. The opposite view would be that all successful legal justifications establish the truth of the justified statement – possibly attributable to Dworkin. By contrast, Raz claims that both approaches have to be rejected. On the one hand, Dworkin does not provide a proper account of the connection between authority and justification, and, for this reason, his theory is not able to explain the nature of law. On the other hand, Kelsen does not provide a sound reconstruction of practical reasoning. In particular, the Kelsen of the last period endorses a view on justification that leads him to conclude that practical reasoning is impossible. Thus, only a "mad logic" can demand that specific normative acts justify each and every legal obligation.[79]

Raz thinks that incorporationism has to be rejected if law necessarily claims authority.[80] His thesis is based on two main arguments: the nature of a content-dependent justification and the mediating role of legal authorities. Raz clearly distinguishes between moral arguments and legal justifications, and thinks that a successful content-dependent legal justification can establish the truth of the justified statement only if it does not involve moral premises. Raz believes that, in its strongest version, the social sources thesis not only claims that the existence and content of law can be determined without recourse to moral justifications, but that, in more general terms, it would also determine the truth of all (pure or applied) legal statements.

However, this reconstruction of legal justification is still compatible with the incorporation of logical consequences into the law, for there would be no problem in accepting that content-dependent legal justifications determine the validity of logically derived norms, insofar as this does not require appealing to moral premises. For this reason, it seems that Raz's argument is not directed against the validity of *logically derived* norms, but against other modes of derivation, related to the incorporation of moral principles into the law.

It is clear that Raz does not grant that legal systems include *all* logical consequences of valid norms, but this rejection still leaves room for the admission of *some* of the logical consequences of source-based norms into legal system. Raz believes that the incorporation of *all* logical consequences is not compatible with the mediating role that defines legal authority. What Raz calls the *normal justification thesis* states that if the law claims to have legitimate authority, its addressees should be better placed to act in each case according to the result of the balance of reasons applicable to the case following the prescriptions of the

---

[79] See Raz 1976: 503.
[80] See Raz 1994: 229.

law than calculating by themselves what the result of that balance comes to. If this idea is to be accepted, it should be possible to identify the law without any evaluation of those underlying reasons. Hence, this mediating role of law involves, in Raz's view, that its authoritative directives be confined to what legal authorities can be said to have held. From this perspective, and based on his conception of legitimate authority, Raz restricts the set of admissible logical consequences of enacted norms to those that can be justifiably attributed to the authority. The identification of these consequences would not go beyond the limits of the attribution of beliefs.[81]

It would be tempting to say that Raz only shows that *his conception of legal authority* (i.e., *the service conception*), and not the social sources thesis, requires a restriction of the set of admissible logical consequences. However, Raz stresses that the kernel of his thesis can be derived from other assumptions that are weaker than those made by the service conception. Be that as it may, Raz's ideas can be challenged through an independent argument constructed following the lines of Schauer's analysis of the role of language in rule-based decision-making.[82] According to Schauer, rules can be regarded as linguistic expressions that are entrenched in relation to the reasons that justify their formulations. The linguistic expression of any general rule will necessarily have recalcitrant cases of under- and over-inclusion facing its background justification. If in every recalcitrant case, the option favored is the solution dictated by the reasons justifying the rule, the decision to be taken will not be grounded on the rule but on those other reasons. This means that a rule can only be used as a ground for a decision if it is treated as not completely transparent regarding its underlying justification. From this idea it follows – concerning general norms deliberately formulated in a certain language – that the authority must be assigned to the text and not to its author, to the law and not to the legislator, on pain of completely ignoring the role that rules play in decision-making environments.

Following this idea, it is possible to elaborate a serious challenge to the thesis that only those consequences of enacted norms that can justifiably be attributed to the legislator may be incorporated as members of legal systems. We do not intend to develop such an argument here in its full extension, but its basic lines would be as follows. Authority should be assigned to the verbal formulations expressed by legal authorities. In fact, this is not an unusual assumption. As Marmor shows, it is not accidental for democratic procedures to result in

---

[81] See Raz 1994: 228.
[82] See Schauer 1991: 47–52.

authoritative texts – that is, in statutes.[83] One of the reasons parliamentary debates culminate in a vote on an authoritative text is to "generate a record of just what there was sufficient agreement on to gain majority consent."[84] The fact that a given legal authority has foreseen, admitted, or wished certain logical consequences of the norms she enacted is completely irrelevant to determining whether those consequences have to be taken as a part of the law. Whether logical consequences of enacted norms have any relevance in the identification or application of the law depends on the logical connection to those other norms from which they are derived, not on the fact that someone (even the legislator) performs the concrete act of inferring them. This latter idea seems to rest in a quite common and widespread confusion between logic and psychology.[85]

Logical consequences can be regarded as legally relevant not because they were intended by legal authorities, but because we cannot make sense of what an authority actually attempts to decide without taking into account the logical consequences of the norms she enacts. It is clear that our practices of interpretation can restrict the relevance of the logical consequences of legal norms. Moreover, it could be the case that the attribution of intentions to legal authorities plays a prominent role both in legal adjudication and interpretation. But it does not follow from these facts that logical consequences can be accepted in a legal system only inasmuch as they can be attributed to the intentions of legal authorities.

Marmor also devotes a couple of pages to the problem of conventionalism and the logical consequences of enacted norms.[86] Like Raz, he claims that logical consequences are not valid members of a legal system, but unlike Raz, his arguments are not grounded on the authority of law:

> [S]uppose a legal system, say, Si contains the norms Ni . . . n. Suppose further, that norms Ni . . . n entail the truth of a further norm, say, Nx. May we not conclude, then that Nx is also legally valid in Si? But what would it mean to say that Nx is entailed by Ni . . . n? There are several possibilities here. On the most restricted notion of entailment, one would think of it only in terms of logical entailment. (Coupled, I presume, with certain truths about facts). On the least restricted notion, one could also think of

---

[83] See Marmor 1992: 175.
[84] See Ely 1980: 17.
[85] See Alchourrón 1995: 11–48; Weinberger 1995: 261–270.
[86] He hesitates recognizing the incorporation of logically derived norms as a genuine version of incorporationism, and conjectures that this type of incorporationism was invented (and repudiated) by Raz. However, as we have stressed in this book, there is an old tradition in Legal Positivism that assumes the validity of derived norms.

it as moral-evaluative entailment.... Despite the considerable differences
between these two views of entailments and perhaps other possible views in
between these two extremes, they share a crucial assumption: namely that
the law is necessarily coherent.[87]

Apart from his problematic reference to the "truth" of norms, after emphasizing
that he is not referring to coherence as a value in legal interpretation, Marmor
remarks that the validity of logical consequences of enacted norms presupposes
that the law itself is necessarily coherent. For this reason, he writes:

> Therefore, the only question we should ask now is whether it makes any
> sense to assume that the law is necessarily coherent, logically or otherwise. A
> negative answer is hardly deniable.[88]

Once these premises have been accepted, it is not very surprising that Marmor
concludes that there is no reason to assume that logical consequences of
enacted norms are valid law simply in virtue of entailment relations.[89]

Marmor's argument has two crucial premises: (1) that the legal validity of
logical consequences of enacted norms presupposes coherence as a necessary
property of legal systems; and (2) that law is not necessarily coherent. We have
no objections to the latter claim; in fact, in the previous chapter we have raised
serious doubts about the thesis that law is necessarily consistent. Therefore,
at least if coherence is equated with logical consistency, we would subscribe
to Marmor's second premise. The problem, in our view, rests with his first
premise.

An initial difficulty in Marmor's argument is that, after distinguishing various
possible conceptions of entailment, he rejects the validity of those norms
entailed by enacted norms with the argument that under any of those views
of entailment, the incorporation thesis would assume that law is necessarily
coherent. Now, it seems obvious that under different notions of entailment,
"coherence" will mean different things. Consequently, despite the use of the
same expression, there cannot be a unique argument for the rejection of all
kinds of entailed norms.

Now, restricting our attention to logical entailment, it is very simple to show
that Marmor's first premise is false. Imagine we group into the same set two
incompatible norms N_1 and N_2 and their logical consequences. Of course,
there is no conceptual impossibility in the selection of this collection. But
such a normative system would be incoherent in spite of containing all logical
consequences entailed by N_1 and N_2. Thus, contrary to what Marmor seems

---

[87] Marmor 2001: 69.
[88] Marmor 2001: 69.
[89] See Marmor 2001: 70.

to think, the incorporation of logical consequences in a normative set does not presuppose its coherence. Moreover, coherence and incoherence under the current reading are logical properties of normative systems, and thus, only analyzable on the assumption that there are logical relations between norms. And although this is not equivalent to saying that all logical consequences of a normative set also belong to it for this very reason, the only way to identify possible inconsistencies in a normative system is through the analysis of the logical consequences of enacted norms. Consequently, contrary to Marmor's suggestions, the identification of logical consequences of enacted norms is an unavoidable step to evaluate a legal system as coherent or incoherent.

Our discussion of Raz's and Marmor's ideas seems to show that there is no conclusive argument to show that the incorporation of logical consequences of enacted legal norms is incompatible with the social sources thesis. Undoubtedly, the fact that the main premise of Legal Positivism is not incompatible with the incorporation into legal systems of the logical consequences of enacted norms is not by itself a sufficient reason to justify their membership in legal systems. In other words, from a positivistic conception, law can be reconstructed as a normative set integrated by all norms identifiable by their social sources plus all their logical consequences, or as solely composed by the former. A defense of the social sources thesis does not by itself force us to set aside either of these two possible alternatives. But even if the option favors the more restrictive reconstruction, excluding logical consequences of enacted norms as part of the law, it should be noted that whoever accepts certain norms as grounds for decision-making is rationally bound to accept the logical consequences that follow from them as well. Consequently, the idea that only those norms that have an appropriate social source are part of the law is feasible when we are dealing with the problem of the identification of norms that are part of each momentary system of a dynamic sequence. By contrast, when we are dealing with the identification of those norms that judges are bound to apply to legal cases (applicable systems), the set that has to be taken into consideration is not restricted to the norms that have the appropriate social source, but encompasses all their logical consequences.

Hence, the concluding remarks of these final chapters may be summarized briefly as follows:

1. The social sources thesis in itself – that is, without the assumption of controversial arguments like those used by Raz to justify it – is compatible both with the admission and the rejection as members in legal systems of the logical consequences of those norms that directly originate in social sources.

2. However, a proper reconstruction of the static concept of applicable system, as well as the dynamic concept of legal order, has to take into account all logical consequences of norms with a direct social source.

3. Assigning relevance to the logical consequences of norms identifiable by their social origin does not necessarily imply that every static set of norms integrating the same sequence that constitutes a legal order has to be reconstructed as closed under logical consequence.

4. The choice between (a) interpreting the static sets of a dynamic legal order as closed under logical consequence, and (b) interpreting them as finite bases only integrated by norms identifiable by their social sources, but preserving the relevance of logical consequences for an adequate analysis of legal dynamics, is not trivial, for both reconstructions differ in interesting ways that are well worth exploring.

Epilogue

Throughout this book, we have attempted to show some of the possibilities that logical analysis offers for the study of legal systems. To do so, we have presented an introduction to the basic aspects of deontic logic and contrasted the attitudes of optimism and skepticism about the possibility of accepting logical relationships among norms. In the first chapters, we briefly reviewed the connections between propositional logic, predicate calculus, alethic modal logic, and deontic logic, and then offered a schematic outline of the different systems of deontic logic that constitute the conceptual basis that has generated the most important technical developments in deontic logic. Unlike philosophers who regard norms as a special type of propositions, we have emphasized the pragmatic aspects that characterize directive discourse, and defended the idea that the most promising way to justify the existence of a logic of norms is on the basis of an abstract notion of logical consequence, which allows the development of a genuine logic of norms without making the controversial assumption that norms have truth-values.

The plurality of systems of deontic logic may be taken as a symptom of the fact that there are no logical laws in normative discourse. However, although it is true that there is a considerable variety of deontic logics and none of them can claim to be the only correct one, this still leaves room for the possibility that certain laws are valid in all or at least most of those deontic systems. The central disagreements over the laws of deontic logic arise from the relations of those formulas, which result in certain paradoxes of deontic logic. The analysis of these paradoxes is valuable for investigating the differences between deontic logic and alethic modal logic and examining the difficulties in the representation of conditional norms; and it has generated a vast literature on normative conflicts and the defeasible character of conditional norms.

More specifically, the attempts to elude some of the most famous of these paradoxes have led to distinguishing two ways of representing conditional norms, identified as the *insular conception* ($O(p{\rightarrow}q)$) and the *bridge conception* ($p \rightarrow Oq$). Unlike what some philosophers have suggested, we have tried to demonstrate that each of these reconstructions corresponds to different kinds of conditional norms, which should be duly integrated into a general theory of the formal aspects of normative discourse. The analysis of these two conceptions of conditional norms is also important in accounting for the various ways in which norms regulate the cases to which they apply: whereas the bridge conception is intuitively appropriate for representing the connection between actions and states of affairs (cases) that are not under the control of the agent, the insular conception is apt for representing the normative consequences that follow from situations that the agent can produce or avoid.

Although we have rejected the view that norms have a propositional nature, there is hardly any doubt that descriptive propositions can be formulated *about* norms (norm-propositions). The study of the logic of norm-propositions is a necessary starting point for clarifying the logical aspects of deontic discourse. In the particular domain of law, legal statements may be reconstructed as norm-propositions relative to the validity of norms in the legal system. These propositions are clearly descriptive and their truth-value is dependent only on certain social facts (the so-called legal sources).

In the second part of the book, we have discussed in what sense deontic logic and the logic of norm-propositions are useful for a proper understanding of the systematic structure of law. Law is a normative system that paradigmatically exhibits specific characteristics, such as its coercive character and its institutional nature. We have emphasized, however, the need to distinguish two fundamental notions of legal system, one dynamic (the *legal order*), understood as a series of sets of norms related to the changes in the content of the law as a result of the introduction and elimination of norms, and the other static (the *applicable system*), that has been defined as the set of logical consequences that follow from the norms that are relevant to the solution of a given problem, a concept linked to the justification of institutional decisions. The analysis of the formal connections between these two notions of legal system is of great importance, because it is impossible to understand the way in which the law regulates human conduct without a consistent integration of its static and dynamic aspects. In this regard, we have attempted to show how the study of the logical consequences of enacted legal norms can serve as a link to articulate both perspectives.

Municipal legal systems are paradigmatic examples of *open* normative systems, in the sense that they contain norms to the effect that certain cases should be solved by application of other norms, even if those other norms are not members of the same system. For that reason, we have tried to differentiate the membership of norms in a municipal legal system, their *internal applicability* (the scope of cases they regulate), and their *external applicability* (the duty to apply them to certain cases imposed by other legal norms). These differences are particularly relevant when examining institutional normative systems (such as the law) in which specific bodies or persons are entitled to justify their resolution of cases using internally applicable norms.

For the logical analysis of applicable systems, it is especially important to examine three traditional and very controversial themes in legal theory: the completeness of legal systems, the possibility of normative conflicts, and the defeasibility of legal norms. We have given reasons to conclude that completeness, consistency, and the defeasible character of their norms are three contingent characteristics of applicable systems, and that an evaluation of such properties must be carefully distinguished from the problem of judicial discretion. This is so because judicial discretion may occur not only when legal systems have gaps, normative conflicts or their norms are subject to implicit exceptions, but also when legal norms confer upon judges the power to modify legal outcomes. Moreover, in the cases the law leaves unregulated or regulates inconsistently, judicial discretion is not always necessary, as the system itself may prescribe specific answers for those situations.

A rational reconstruction of the outcome of acts of enactment and derogation of legal norms requires taking into account not merely sets of norms, but sequences of sets of norms (the *legal order*). Thus, whereas the elements of the applicable systems are norms, the elements of the legal order are normative systems; and whereas the structure of applicable systems is *deductive*, the structure of the legal order is *genetic*. The logical analysis of legal dynamics is relevant to highlight the peculiarities of the changes in the content of the law, especially those produced by the operation of derogation. We have tried to show that although it is not necessary to assume that momentary systems include all the logical consequences of enacted legal norms, the identification of the successive momentary systems of the dynamic sequence requires taking into account the logical consequences of explicitly enacted rules.

Finally, with these distinctions, it is possible to dissolve a controversy that has arisen regarding the compatibility between the incorporation of logical consequences of valid legal norms and the authoritative nature of law. A strong version of Legal Positivism (so-called *exclusive positivism*) claims that accepting the validity of the logical consequences of enacted norms is incompatible with a satisfactory explanation of the authoritative nature of law. We have shown, however, that a legal positivist approach is neutral on this issue, and that although legal dynamics may be reconstructed without interpreting each momentary system of the dynamic sequence as closed under the notion of deductive consequence, the logical consequences of enacted norms play a central role in the explanation of the structure of applicable systems as well as in any adequate account of the dynamic character of the legal order.

Bibliography

Aguiló Regla, Josep 1995: *Sobre la derogación* (México D.F.: Fontamara).

Alchourrón, Carlos 1969: "Logic of Norm and Logic of Normative Propositions," *Logique et Analyse* 12, 47: 242–268.

    1982: "Normative Order and Derogation," in Martino, A. (ed.), *Deontic Logic, Computational Linguistics and Legal Information Systems*, Vol. II (Dordrecht: North Holland Publishing Company, 51–60).

    1986: "Conditionality and the Representation of Legal Norms," in Martino, A. et al. (eds.), *Automated Analysis of Legal Texts* (North-Holland: Elsevier, 175–186).

    1991: "Conflicts of Norms and the Revision of Normative Systems," *Law and Philosophy* 10(4): 413–425.

    1993: "Philosophical Foundations of Deontic Logic and the Logic of Defeasible Conditionals," in Meyer and Wieringa 1993: 43–84.

    1995: "Concepciones de la lógica," in Alchourrón, C. et al. (eds.), *Lógica. Enciclopedia Iberoamericana de Filosofía*, 7 (Madrid: Trotta, 11–48).

    1996: "Detachment and Defeasibility in Deontic Logic," *Studia Logica* 57: 5–18.

Alchourrón, Carlos and Eugenio Bulygin 1971: *Normative Systems* (Wein, New York: Springer Verlag).

    1979: *Sobre la existencia de las normas jurídicas* (Venezuela: Universidad de Carabobo).

    1981: "The Expressive Conception of Norms," in Hilpinen 1981a: 95–124.

    1984: "Pragmatic Foundations for a Logic of Norms," *Rechtstheorie* 15: 453–464.

    1988: "Perils of Level Confusion in Normative Discourse," *Rechtstheorie* 19: 230–237.

    1989: "Von Wright on Deontic Logic and the Philosophy of Law," in Schilpp, P. et al. (eds.), *The Philosophy of Georg Henrik von Wright* (Illinois: Open Court, 665–693).

    1991: *Análisis lógico y derecho* (Madrid: Centro de Estudios Constitucionales).

Alchourrón, Carlos, Peter Gärdenfors, and David Makinson 1985: "On the Logic of Theory Change: Partial Meet Contraction and Revision Functions," *The Journal of Symbolic Logic* 50: 510–530.

Alchourrón, Carlos and David Makinson 1981: "Hierarchies of Regulations and their Logic," in Hilpinen 1981a: 125–148.

1982: "On the Logic of Theory Change: Contraction Functions and Their Associated Revision Functions," *Theoria* 48(1): 14–37.

1985: "On the Logic of Theory Change: Safe Contraction," *Studia Logica* 44: 405–422.

1986: "Maps between Some Different Kinds of Contraction Function: The Finite Case," *Studia Logica* 45: 187–198.

Alchourrón, Carlos and Antonio Martino 1990: "Logic without Truth," *Ratio Iuris* 3(1): 46–67.

Alexander, Larry and Emily Sherwin 2008: *Demystifying Legal Reasoning* (Cambridge: Cambridge University Press).

Alexy, Robert 1986: *Theorie der Grundrechte* (Suhrkamp-Verlag).

Anderson, Alan Ross 1956: "The Formal Analysis of Normative Systems," in Rescher, N. (ed.), *The Logic of Decision and Action* (Pittsburgh: University of Pittsburgh Press, 147–213).

1958: "A Reduction of Deontic Logic to Alethic Modal logic," *Mind* 67, 265: 100–103.

Anscombe, Gertrude Elizabeth Margaret 1957: *Intention* (Oxford: Basil Blackwell).

Åqvist, Lennart 1967: "Good Samaritans, contrary-to-duty imperatives and epistemic obligations," *Nôus* 1: 361–379.

1984: "Deontic Logic," in Gabbay, D. and Guethner, F. (eds.), *Handbook of Philosophical Logic. Volume II: Extentions of Classical Logic* (Dordrecht: Reidel, 605–714), citations are to the 2002 second edition, volume 8 (The Netherlands: Kluwer, 147–264).

1987: *Introduction to Deontic Logic and the Theory of Normative Systems* (Napoli; Bibliopolis).

Atienza, Manuel and Juan Ruiz Manero 1998: *A Theory of Legal Sentences* (Dordrecht: Kluwer).

Atria, Fernando 2001: *On Law and Legal Reasoning* (Oxford: Hart Publishing).

Baker, G. P. and P. M. S. Hacker 1984: *Scepticism, Rules & Language* (Oxford: Blackwell).

Bayón, Juan Carlos 1991: *La normatividad del derecho. Deber jurídico y razones para la acción* (Madrid: Centro de Estudios Constitucionales).

Beirlaen, Mathieu and Christian Straßer 2013: "Two Adaptive Logics of Norm-propositions," *Journal of Applied Logic* 11(2): 147–168.

Belnap, D. N. 1962: "Tonk, Plonk, and Plink," *Analysis* 22 (6): 130–134.

Belzer, Marvin and Barry Loewer 1997: "Deontic Logics of Defeasibility," in Nute 1997: 45–58.

Bentham, Jeremy 1872: *Of Laws in General*, citations are to the 1970 edition by Hart, H. L. A. (London: Athlone Press).

Bix, Brian 1993: *Law, Language and Legal Determinacy* (Oxford: Oxford University Press).

Blackburn, Simon 1984: *Spreading the Word* (Oxford: Clarendon Press).

Brandom, Robert 1994: *Making it Explicit, Reasoning, Representing and Discursive Commitment* (Cambridge, MA, London: Harvard University Press).

Bulygin, Eugenio 1982: "Time and Validity," in Martino, A. (ed.), *Deontic Logic, Computational Linguistics and Legal Information Systems* (Amsterdam, New York: North Holland Publishing Company, 51–63).

1985: "Norms and Logic," *Law and Philosophy* 4 (2): 145–163.

1986: "Legal Dogmatics and the Systematization of Law," in Torstein Eckhoff et al. (eds.), *Vernunft und Erfahrung im Rechtsdenken der Gegenwart, Rechtstheorie* 10: 193–210.

1991: "Algunas consideraciones sobre los sistemas jurídicos," *Doxa* 9: 257–279.

1994: "Lógica y normas," *Isonomía* 1: 28–36.

1995: "Lógica deóntica," in Alchourrón, C. et al. (eds.), *Lógica. Enciclopedia Iberoamericana de Filosofía*, volumen 7 (Madrid: Trotta, 129–142).

2003: "On Legal Gaps," *Analisi e Diritto*: 21–28.

Canale, Damiano and Giovanni Tuzet 2007: "On Legal Inferentialism. Toward a Pragmatics of Semantic Content in Legal Interpretation?", *Ratio Juris* 20, N° 1: 32–44.

Caracciolo, Ricardo 1988: *El sistema jurídico. Problemas actuales* (Madrid: Centro de Estudios Constitucionales).

1996: "Sistema jurídico," in Garzón Valdés, E. and Laporta, F. (eds.), *El derecho y la justicia* (Madrid: Trotta, 161–176).

Carmo, José and Jones, Andrew J.I. 2002: "Deontic Logic and Contrary-to-Duties," in Gabbay, Dov M. and Guenthner, F. (eds.), *Handbook of Philosophical Logic*, 8, 2nd edition (Netherlands: Kluwer, 265–343).

Carnota, Raúl and Ricardo Rodríguez 2011: "AGM Theory and Artificial Intelligence," in Olsson, E. et al. (eds.), *Belief Revision Meets Philosophy of Science* (Dordrecht: Springer, 1–42).

Castañeda, Héctor Neri 1981: "The Paradoxes of Deontic Logic: The Simplest Solution to All of Them in one Fell Swoop," in Hilpinen 1981a: 37–85.

1986: "Obligations, Aspectual Actions and Circumstances," *Philosophical Papers* 15: 155–170.

Celano, Bruno 1999: *La teoria del diritto di Hans Kelsen. Una introduzione critica* (Bologna: Il Mulino).

Chellas, Brian F. 1980: *Modal Logic. An Introduction* (Cambridge: Cambridge University Press).

Chisholm, Roderick 1963: "Contrary-to-Duty Imperatives and Deontic Logic," *Analysis* 34, 2: 33–36.

Church, Alonzo 1956: *Introduction to Mathematical Logic* (Princeton, NJ: Princeton University Press).

1965: "The History of the Question of Existential Import for Categorical Propositions," in Y. Bar-Hillel (ed.), *Logic, Methodology and Philosophy of Sciences. Proceedings of the 1964 International Congress* (Amsterdam: North-Holland, 417–424).

Coleman, Jules 2000: "Constraints on the Criteria of Legality," *Legal Theory* 6(2): 171–183.

2001: *The Practice of Principle* (Oxford: Oxford University Press).

Coleman, Jules and Brian Leiter 1993: "Determinacy, Objectivity and Authority," *University of Pennsylvania Law Review* 142(2): 549–637.

Duarte d'Almeida, Luís 2011: "Legal Statements and Normative Language," *Law and Philosophy* 30: 167–199.

Dummett, Michael 1973: *Frege. Philosphy of Language* (Cambridge, MA: Harvard University Press), citations are to the 1981 second edition.

1991: *The Logical Basis of Metaphysics* (Cambridge, MA: Harvard University Press).

Dworkin, Ronald 1977: *Taking Rights Seriously* (Cambridge, MA: Harvard University Press).

1985: *A Matter of Principle* (Cambridge, MA: Harvard University Press).

1986: *Law's Empire* (Cambridge, MA: Harvard University Press).

2006: *Justice in Robes* (Cambridge, MA: Harvard University Press).

Ely, John Hart 1980: *Democracy and Distrust* (Cambridge, MA: Harvard University Press).

Endicott, Timothy 2000: *Vagueness in Law* (Oxford: Oxford University Press).

2003: "Raz on Gaps: the Surprising Part," in Paulson, S. L. et al. (eds.), *Rights, Culture, and the Law* (Oxford: Oxford University Press, 99–118).

Engel, Pascal 1989: *La norme du vrai* (Paris: Gallimard), citations are to the 1991 English edition, *The Norm of Truth* (New York, London: Harvester Wheatsheaf).

Ferrer Beltrán, Jordi and Jorge Rodríguez 2011: *Jerarquías normativas y dinámica de los sistemas jurídicos* (Madrid-Barcelona, Buenos Aires: Marcial Pons).

Feys, Richard 1937: "Les Logiques Nouvelles des Modalités," *Revue Néoscolastique de Philosophie* 40: 517–553.

Fletcher, George P. 1996: *Basic Concepts of Legal Thought* (New York: Oxford University Press).

Føllesdal, Dagfinn and Risto Hilpinen 1971: "Deontic Logic: An Introduction," in Hilpinen 1971: 1–35.

Forrester, James William 1984: "Gentle Murder, or the Adverbial Samaritan," *The Journal of Philosophy* 81, Num 4: 193–197.

Frege, Friedrich Ludwig Gotlob 1919: "Die Verneinung. Eine Logische Untersuchung," Beiträge zur Philosophie des deutschen Idealismus, I: 143–157, citations are to the 1977 English translation by Geach, P. and Stoothoff, R., "Negation," in *Logical Investigations* (Oxford: Blackwell).

Gamut, L. T. F. 1991: *Logic, Language, and Meaning. Volume 1: Introduction to Logic* (Chicago: University of Chicago Press).

Gärdenfors, Peter 1990: "The Dynamics of Belief Systems: Foundations vs. Coherence Theories," *Revue Internationale de Philosophie* 1: 24–46.

1992a: (ed.) *Belief Revision* (Cambridge: Cambridge University Press).

1992b: "The Dynamics of Normative Systems," in Martino, A. (ed.), *Expert Systems in Law* (North Holland: Elsevier Science Publishers, 293–299).

Gardner, John 2004: "The Legality of Law," *Ratio Juris* 17(2): 168–181.

Geach, Peter T. 1965: "Assertion," *Philosophical Review* 74: 449–465.

Gentzen, Gerhard 1934: "Untersuchungen über das Logische Schliessen," *Mathematische Zeitschrift* 39: 176–210.

Gianformaggio, Leticia 1991: (ed.) *Sistemi Normativi Statici e Dinamici. Analisi di una Tipologia Kelseniana* (Torino: Giapichelli).

Gibbard, Allan 2003: *Thinking How to Live* (Cambridge, MA, London: Harvard University Press).

Golding, Martin 1961: "Kelsen and the Concept of 'Legal System,'" *Archiv für Rechts und Sozialphilosophie* 47: 355–364.

Grayling, A. C. 1997: *An Introduction to Philosophical Logic*, 3rd edition (Oxford: Blackwell).

Green, Leslie 1999: "Positivism and Conventionalism," *Canadian Journal of Law and Jurisprudence* 12: 35–52.

Greenspan, Patricia 1975: "Conditional Oughts and Hypothetical Imperatives," *Journal of Philosophy* 72: 259–276.

Guastini, Riccardo 1995: "Normas Supremas," *Doxa* 17–18: 257–270.

Haack, Susan 1978: *Philosophy of Logics* (Cambridge: Cambridge University Press).

Hansson, Bengt 1969: "An Analysis of Some Deontic Logics," *Nous* 3: 373–398; reprinted in Hilpinen 1971: 121–147.

Hansson, Sven Ove 1988: "Deontic Logic without Misleading Alethic Analogies," *Logique et Analyse* 31: 337–370.

1992: "A Dyadic Representation of Belief," in Gärdenfors, 1992a: 89–121.

1999: *A Textbook of Belief Dynamics. Theory Change and Database Updating* (Dordrecht: Kluwer Academic Publishers).

2001: *The Structure of Values and Norms* (Cambridge: Cambridge University Press).

2004: "A New Representation Theorem for Contranegative Deontic Logic," *Studia Logica* 77: 1–7.

2006, "Ideal Worlds – Wishful Thinking in Deontic Logic," *Studia Logica* 82: 329–336.

Hansson, Sven Ove and David Makinson 1997: "Applying Normative Rules with Restraint," in Dalla Chiara, M. et al. (eds.) *Logic and Scientific Method* (Dordrecht: Kluwer, 313–332).

Harris, J. W. 1979: *Law and Legal Science* (Oxford: Oxford University Press).

Hart, H. L. A. 1948: "The Ascription of Responsibility and Rights," *Proceedings of the Aristotelian Society* 49, reprinted in Flew, A. G. N. (ed.), *Logic and Language* (First Series, Oxford: Blackwell, 145–166).

1961: *The Concept of Law* (Oxford: Oxford University Press), citations are to the 1994 2nd edition, Raz, J. and Bullock, P (eds.) (Oxford: Oxford University Press).

1962: "Kelsen Visited," *UCLA Law Review* 10: 709–728.

1982: *Essays on Bentham* (Oxford: Oxford University Press).

1983: *Essays in Jurisprudence and Philosophy* (Oxford: Oxford University Press).

Hartney, Michael 1991: "Introduction. The Final Form of the Pure Theory of Law," in Kelsen, H., *General Theory of Norms* (Oxford: Oxford University Press, ix–liii).

Hedenius, Ingmar 1941: *Om rätt och moral* (Stockholm: Wahlström & Widstrand).

Hilpinen, Risto 1971: (ed.) *Deontic Logic: Introductory and Systematic Readings* (Dordrecht, Boston, London: Reidel).

1981a: (ed.) *New Studies in Deontic Logic* (Dordrecht, Boston, London: Reidel).

1981b: "On Normative Change," in Morscher, E. et al. (eds.), *Ethics: Foundations, Problems and Applications* (Wein: Hölder-Pichier-Tempsky, 155–164).

1987: "Conflict and Change in Norm Systems," in Frändberg, A. et al. (eds.), *The Structure of Law* (Uppsala: Iustus Forlag, 37–49).

2001: "Deontic Logic," in Globe, Lou (ed.), *The Blackwell Guide to Philosophical Logic* (Oxford: Blackwell, 159–182).

Hintikka, Jaakko 1957: "Quantifiers in Deontic Logic," *Societas Scientiarum Fennica, Commentationes Humanarum Literarum* XXIII, 4: 1–23.

1971: "Some Main Problems in Deontic Logic," in Hilpinen 1971: 59–104.

Hofstadter, Albert and J. C. C. McKinsey 1939: "On the Logic of Imperatives," *Philosophy of Science* 6, Num. 4: 446–357.

Holmes, Oliver Wendell 1881: *The Common Law* (Boston: Little, Brown & Co), citations are to the 2005 edition (New Brunswick, NJ: Transaction Publishers).

Hughes, George Edward and Maxwell John Cresswell 1996: *A New Introduction to Modal Logic* (London, New York: Routledge).

Hurley, Susan 1989: *Natural Reasons* (Oxford: Oxford University Press).

Jakson, Frank 1985: "On the Semantics and Logic of Obligation," *Mind* 94: 177–195.

Jakson, Frank and Robert Pargetter 1986: "Oughts, Options, and Actualism," *Philosophical Review* 95: 233–255.

Jørgensen, Jørgen 1937–1938: "Imperatives and Logic," *Erkenntnis* 7: 288–296.

Kalinowski, George 1967: *Le probleme de la vérité en morale et en droit* (Lyon: Emmanuel Vitte).

Kanger, Stig 1957: *New Foundations for Ethical Theory* (Stockholm: Almqvist & Wiksell), reprinted in Hilpinen 1971: 36–58.

Kant, Immanuel 1781: "Preface to the Second Edition" to *The Critique of Pure Reason* (Riga: Johann Friedrich Hartknoch), citations are to *The Cambridge Edition of the Works of Immanuel Kant*, translated and edited in 1998 by Guyer, P. and Wood, A. (Cambridge: Cambridge University Press).

Kelsen, Hans 1945: *General Theory of Law and State* (Cambridge, MA: Harvard University Press).

    1960: *Pure Theory of Law*, 2nd edition, citations are to the 1989 English version (Gloucester, MA: Peter Smith).

    1979: *Allgemeine Theorie der Normen* (Wien: Manzsche Verlags und Universitätsbuchhandlung) citations are to the 1991 English edition *General Theory of Norms* (Oxford: Oxford University Press).

Kelsen, Hans and Ulrich Klug 1981: *Rechtsnormen und logische Analyse* (Wien: Verlag Franz Deuticke).

Kripke, Saul 1959: "A Completeness Theorem in Modal Logic," *Journal of Symbolic Logic* 24(1): 1–14.

    1963: "Semantical Analysis of Modal Logic I: Normal Propositional Calculi," *Zeitschrift für Mathematische Logik und Grundlagen der Mathematik* 9: 67–96.

    1982: *Wittgenstein on Rules and Private Language* (Oxford: Basil Blackwell).

Leibniz, G. W. 1672: *Elementa iuris naturalis*, citations are to the 1930 edition (Darmstadt: Otto Reichl Verlag).

Lewis, David 1973: *Counterfactuals* (Oxford: Basil Blackwell).

    1974: "Semantical Analysis for Dyadic Deontic Logic," in Stanlund, S. (ed.), *Logical Theory and Semantic Analysis*, Synthese Library, (Dordrecht, Boston: Reidel, 1–14).

    1979: "A Problem about Permission," in Saarinen, E. et al. (eds.), *Essays in Honour of Jaakko Hintikka* (Dordrecht: Reidel, 163–175).

    1986: *On the Plurality of Worlds* (Oxford: Blackwell).

Lindahl, Lars 1992: "Conflicts in Systems of Legal Norms: A Logical Point of View," in Brouwer, P. et al. (eds.), *Coherence and Conflict in Law* (Dordrecht: Kluwer, 39–64).

Llewellyn, Karl N. 1930: *The Bramble Bush: On Our Law and Its Study* (Oceana: New York).

MacCallum, Gerald 1993: *Legislative Intent and Other Essays on Law, Politics, and Morality* (Wisconsin: The University of Wisconsin Press).

MacCormick, Neil 1978: *Legal Reasoning and Legal Theory* (Oxford: Clarendon Press), citations are to the 1994 new edition with revised foreword (Oxford: Oxford University Press).

  1995: "Defeasibility in Law and Logic," in Bankowski, Z. et al. (eds.), *Informatics and the Foundation of Legal Reasoning* (Dordrecht: Kluwer, 99–117).

Makinson, David 1993: "Five Faces of Minimality," *Studia Logica* 52: 339–379.

  1996: "In Memoriam Carlos Eduardo Alchourrón," *Nordic Journal of Philosophical Logic* 1(1): 3–10.

  1999: "On a Fundamental Problem of Deontic Logic," in McNamara and Prakken 1999: 29–54.

  2005: *Bridges from Classical to Non-monotonic Logic* (London: King's College Publications).

  2008: *Sets, Logic and Maths for Computing* (London: Springer).

Makinson, David and Leendert van der Torre 2000: "Input-output Logics," *Journal of Philosophical Logic* 29: 383–408.

  2001: "Constraints for Input-output Logics," *Journal of Philosophical Logic* 30 (2): 155–185.

  2003: "Permission from an Input-output Perspective," *Journal of Philosophical Logic* 32: 391–416.

Marmor, Andrei 1992: *Interpretation and Legal Theory* (Oxford: Oxford University Press).

  2001: *Positive Law and Objective Values* (Oxford: Oxford University Press).

  2009: *Social Conventions: From Language to Law* (Princeton, NJ: Princeton University Press).

McLaughlin, R. N. 1955: "Further Problems of Derived Obligations," *Mind* 64: 400–402.

McNamara, Paul 2006: "Deontic Logic," in Gabbay, D. et al. (eds.), *Handbook of the History of Logic*, vol. 7 (The Neatherlands: Elsevier).

McNamara, Paul and Henry Prakken 1999: (eds.) *Norms, Logics and Information Systems* (Amsterdan; Berlin; Oxford; Tokyo; Washington, DC: IOS Press).

Meyer, John Jules Charles and Roel Wieringa 1993: (eds.) *Deontic Logic in Computer Science: Normative System Specification* (Chichester, New York, Brisbane, Toronto, Singapore: Wiley & Sons).

Montague, Richard 1960: "Logical Necessity, Physical Necessity, Ethics, and Quantifiers," *Inquiry: An Interdisciplinary Journal of Philosphy*, vol. 3: 259–269.

Moore, G. E. 1903: *Principia Ethica* (Cambridge: Cambridge University Press).

Moreso, José Juan 1998: *Legal Indeterminacy and Constitutional Interpretation* (Dordrecht: Kluwer).

Moreso, José Juan and Pablo Navarro 1993: *Orden jurídico y sistema jurídico. Una investigación sobre la identidad y la dinámica de los sistemas jurídicos* (Madrid: Centro de Estudios Constitucionales).

  1997: "Applicability and Effectiveness of Legal Norms," *Law and Philosophy* 16(2): 201–219.

1998: "The Reception of Norms and Open Legal Systems," in Paulson, S. L. and Litschewesky, B. (eds.), *Normativity and Norms. Critical perspectives on Kelsenian Themes* (Oxford: Oxford University Press, 273–291).

Moreso, José Juan, Pablo Navarro and María Cristina Redondo 2001: "Sobre la lógica de las lagunas en el derecho," *Crítica* 33(99): 47–73.

Munzer, Stephen 1973: "Validity and Legal Conflicts," *The Yale Law Journal*, 82: 1140–1174.

Navarro, Pablo, Claudina Orunesu, Jorge Rodríguez, and Germán Sucar 2004: "Applicability of Legal Norms," *Canadian Journal of Law and Jurisprudence* XVII (2): 337–359.

Nino, Carlos 1984: *Introducción al análisis del derecho* (Buenos Aires: Astrea).

Nute, Donald 1997: (ed.) *Defeasible Deontic Logic* (Dordrecht, Boston, London: Kluwer Academic Publishers).

Nute, Donald and Xiaochang Yu 1997: "Introduction," in Nute 1997: 1–16.

Paulson, Stanley L. 1992: "Kelsen's Legal Theory: The Final Round," *Oxford Journal of Legal Studies* 12: 265–274.

Postema, Gerald 1982: "Coordination and Convention at the Foundations of Law," *Journal of Legal Studies* 11(1): 165–203.

Prakken, Henry and Marek Sergot 1996: "Contrary-to-duty Obligations," *Studia Logica* 57, 1: 91–115.

Prior, Arthur N. 1954: "The Paradoxes of Derived Obligation," *Mind* 63: 64–65.

1955: *Formal Logic* (Oxford: Clarendon Press).

1958: "Escapism: The Logical Basis of Ethics," in Melden, A. (ed.), *Essays in Moral Philosphy* (Seattle: University of Washington Press, 135–146).

Quine, Willard Van Orman 1950: *Methods of Logic* (New York: Holt), citations are to the 1982 fourth edition (Cambridge, MA: Harvard University Press).

1953: "On What There Is," in *From a Logical Point of View* (Cambridge, MA: Harvard University Press), citations are to the fourteenth printing, 2003 (Cambridge, MA: Harvard University Press).

1970: *Philosophy of Logic* (New Jersey: Prentice Hall).

1990: *Pursuit of Truth* (Cambridge, MA: Harvard University Press).

Ratti, Giovanni Battista 2008: *Sistema giuridico e sistemazione del diritto* (Torino: Giappichelli).

Rawls, John 1971: *A Theory of Justice* (Cambridge, MA: Harvard University Press), citations are to the 1999 revised edition.

Raz, Joseph 1970: *The Concept of a Legal System. An Introduction to the Theory of Legal System* (Oxford: Clarendon Press), citations are to the 1980 2nd edition (Oxford: Oxford University Press).

1972: "Legal Principles and the Limits of Law," *The Yale Law Journal*, 81(5): 823–854.

1975: *Practical Reason and Norms* (London: Hutchinson), citations are to the 1990 second edition (Princeton, NJ: Princeton University Press).

1976: "Kelsen's General Theory of Norms. Critical Study," *Philosophia* 6: 495–504.

1979: *The Authority of Law* (Oxford: Oxford University Press).

1986: *The Morality of Freedom* (Oxford: Clarendon Press).

1994: *Ethics in the Public Domain* (Oxford: Oxford University Press).

2009: *Between Authority and Interpretation* (Oxford: Oxford University Press).

Rescher, Nicholas 1966: *The Logic of Commands* (London: Routledge & Kegan Paul).

Rodríguez, Jorge 2002: *Lógica de los sistemas normativos* (Madrid: Centro de Estudios Constitucionales).

2003: "Naturaleza y lógica de las proposiciones normativas. Contribución en homenaje a G. H. von Wright," *Doxa* 26: 87–108.

2013: "Norms, Truth, and Legal Statements," in Jordi Ferrer Beltrán, José Juan Moreso y Diego Papayanis (eds.), *Neutrality and Theory of Law* (The Netherlands, Springer, 127–146).

Rodríguez, Jorge and Germán Sucar 1998: "Las trampas de la derrotabilidad. Niveles de análisis de la indeterminación del derecho," *Analisi e Diritto. Ricerche di Giurisprudenza Analítica*: 277–305.

Rönnedal, Daniel 2010: *An Introduction to Deontic Logic* (Stockholm: CreateSpace).

Ross, Alf 1941, "Imperatives and Logic," *Theoria* 7: 53–71.

1958: *On Law and Justice* (London: Stevens & Sons Ltd.).

1962: "Review: H. L. A. Hart, The Concept of Law," *The Yale Law Journal* 71: 1185–1190.

1968: *Directives and Norms* (London: Routledge and Keang Paul).

1998: "Validity and the Conflict between Legal Positivism and Natural Law," in Paulson, S. L. and Litschewski, B. (eds.), *Norms and Normativity* (Oxford: Oxford University Press, 147–164).

Ross, David 1930: *The Right and the Good* (Oxford: Oxford University Press).

Royyakers, L. M. M. 1998: *Extending Deontic Logic for the Formalisation of Legal Rules* (Dordrecht, Boston, London: Kluwer Academic Publishers).

Russell, Bertrand 1905: "On Denoting," *Mind* XIV (4): 479–493.

Russell, Bertrand and Alfred North Whitehead 1910: *Principia Mathematica* (Cambridge: Cambridge University Press), citations are to the 1999 edition (Cambridge: Cambridge University Press).

Sainsbury, R. M. 1987: *Paradoxes* (Cambridge: Cambridge University Press), citations are to the 1995 second edition.

Schauer, Frederick 1991: *Playing by the Rules. A Philosophical Examination of Rule-Based Decision-Making in Law and in Life* (Oxford: Clarendon Press).

1998: "On the Supposed Defeasibility of Legal Rules," in Freeman, M. D. A. (ed.), *Current Legal Problems* 51 (1): 223–240.

Schreiber, Rupert 1962: *Logik des Rechts* (Berlin, Göttingen, Heilderberg: Springer Verlag).

Schroeder, Mark 2004: "The Scope of Instrumental Reason," *Philosophical Perspectives* 18(1): 337–64.

Shapiro, Scott J. 1998: "The Difference that Rules Make," in Bix, B. (ed.), *Analyzing Law. New Essays in Legal Theory* (Oxford: Oxford University Press, 33–62).

Shiner, Roger 1992: *Norm and Nature* (Oxford: Oxford University Press).

Sinnott-Armstrong, Walter 1985: "A Solution to Forrester's Paradox of Gentle Murder," *The Journal of Philosophy* 82 (3): 162–168.

Soeteman, Arend 1989: *Logic in Law* (Dordrecht: Kluwer Academic Publishers).

1997: "On Legal Gaps," in Garzón Valdés, E. et al. (eds.), *Normative Systems in Legal and Moral Theory. Festschrift for Carlos E. Alchourrón and Eugenio Bulygin*, (Berlin: Duncker & Humblot, 323–332).

Stalnaker, Robert C. 2003: *Ways a World Might Be. Metaphysical and Antimetaphysical Essays* (Oxford: Clarendon Press).

Stenius, Erik 1963: "The Principles of a Logic of Normative Systems," *Acta Philosophica Fennica* 16: 247–260.

Suppes, Patrick 1957: *Introduction to Logic* (New York: Van Nostrand Reinhold), citations are to the 1999 edition (New York: Dover).

Tarski, Alfred 1931: "The Concept of Truth in Formalized Languages," citations are to the 1956 version included in Tarski 1956: 152–278.

    1956: *Logic, Semantics, Metamathematics* (Oxford: Oxford University Press).

Van Fraassen, Bass C. 1972: "The Logic of Conditional Obligation," *Journal of Philosphical Logic* 1: 417–438.

Vernengo, Roberto 1986: "Sobre algunos criterios de verdad normativa," *Doxa – Cuadernos de Filosofía del Derecho* 3: 233–242.

Von Wright, Georg Henrik 1951a: "Deontic Logic," *Mind* 60: 1–15.

    1951b: *An Essay in Modal Logic* (Amsterdam: North-Holland).

    1956: "A Note on Deontic Logic and Derived Obligation," *Mind* 65: 507–9.

    1957: *Logical Studies* (London: Routledge & Kegan Paul).

    1963a: *Norm and Action. A Logical Inquiry* (London: Routledge & Kegan Paul).

    1963b: *The Logic of Preference: an Essay* (Edinburgh: Edinburg University Press).

    1964: "A New System of Deontic Logic," *Danish Yearbook of Philosophy* 1: 173–182.

    1965: "A Correction to a New System of Deontic Logic," *Danish Yearbook of Philosophy* 2: 103–107.

    1967: "The Logic of Action – A Sketch," in Rescher, N. (ed.), *The Logic of Decision and Action* (Pittsburgh, PA: University of Pittsburgh Press, 121–136).

    1968: *An Essay in Deontic Logic and the General Theory of Action* (Amsterdam: North Holland Publishing Company).

    1969: "On the Logic and Ontology of Norms," in Davis, J. W. (ed.), *Philosophical logic* (Dordrecht: Reidel, 89–107).

    1971: "Deontic Logic and the Theory of Conditions," in Hilpinen 1971: 159–177.

    1980: "Problems and Prospects of Deontic Logic," in Agazzi, E. (ed.), *Modern Logic – A Survey* (Dordrecht: Reidel, 399–423).

    1983: *Practical Reason. Philosophical Papers*, vol. I (Oxford: Basil Blackwell).

    1984: *Truth, Knowledge and Modality* (Oxford: Blackwell).

    1985: "Is and Ought," in Bulygin, E. et al. (eds.), *Man, Law and Modern Forms of Life* (Dordrecht: Reidel, 31–48).

    1989: "Intellectual Autobiography," in Schilpp, P. et al. (eds.), *The Philosophy of Georg Henrik von Wright* (Illinois: Open Court, 1–55).

    1993: *The Tree of Knowledge and Other Essays* (New York: E. J. Brill).

    1996: *Six Essays in Philosophical Logic. Acta Philosophica Fennica*, vol. 60 (Helsinki: North-Holland Publishers).

    1997: "Epilogue, " in Garzón Valdés, E. et al. (eds.), *Normative Systems in Legal and Moral Theory. Festschrift for Carlos E. Alchourrón and Eugenio Bulygin* (Berlin: Duncker & Humblot).

    1999: "Deontic Logic – As I See It," in McNamara and Prakken 1999: 15–25.

2000: "On Norms and Norm-Propositions. A Sketch," in Krawietz, W. et al. (eds.), *The Reasonable as Rational? On Legal Argumentation and Justification. Festschrift for Aulis Aarnio* (Berlin: Duncker & Humblot, 173–178).

Waluchow, Wilfrid J. 1994: *Inclusive Legal Positivism* (Oxford: Oxford University Press).

Wedberg, Anders 1951: "Some Problems in the Logical Analysis of Legal Science," *Theoria* 17: 246–275.

Weinberger, Ota 1981: *Normentheorie als Grudlage der Jurisprudenz und Ethik* (Berlin: Duncker & Humblot).

1984: "On the Meaning of Norm Sentences, Normative Inconsistency, and Normative Entailment," *Rechtstheorie* 15: 465–475.

1985: "The Expressive Conception of Norms – An Impasse for the Logic of Norms," *Law and Philosophy* 4(2): 165–198.

1986: "Logic and the Pure Theory of Law," in Tur, R. and Twining, W. (eds.), *Essays on Kelsen* (Oxford: Clarendon Press).

1991: *Law, Institutions and Legal Politics* (Dordrecht: Kluwer).

1995: "Normological Inferences and the Generation of Legal Norms," *Ratio Iuris* 8(3): 261–270.

2001: "A Philosophical Approach to Norm Logic," *Ratio Iuris* 14(1): 130–141.

Wittgenstein, Ludwig 1921: "Tractatus Logico-Philosophicus," first published as "Logisch-Philosophische Abhandlung," in *Annalen der Naturphilosophische* XIV (3/4), citations are to the 1922 English version (London: Routledge & Kegal Paul).

1953: *Philosophical Investigations* (Oxford: Basil Blackwell).

Woleński, Jan 1990: "Deontic Logic and Possible Worlds Semantics: A Historical Sketch," *Studia Logica* 49 (2): 273–282.

Zimmerman, Michael 1996: *The Concept of Moral Obligation* (Cambridge: Cambridge University Press).

Zuleta, Hugo 2008: *Normas y justificación* (Madrid, Barcelona, Buenos Aires: Marcial Pons).

Index